THE ELYSIAN FIELDS OF THE EGYPTIANS ACCORDING TO THE PAPYRUS OF ANI.

1. Ani adoring the gods of Sekhet-Aaru.
2. Ani reaping in the Other World.
3. Ani ploughing in the Other World.
4. The abode of the perfect spirits, and the magical boats.

An Introduction to
Ancient Egyptian Literature

E. A. Wallis Budge

DOVER PUBLICATIONS, INC.
Mineola, New York

Published in Canada by General Publishing Company, Ltd., 30 Lesmill Road, Don Mills, Toronto, Ontario.

Published in the United Kingdom by Constable and Company, Ltd., 3 The Lanchesters, 162–164 Fulham Palace Road, London W6 9ER.

Bibliographical Note

This Dover edition, first published in 1997, is an unabridged republication of *The Literature of the Ancient Egyptians*, originally published by J. M. Dent & Sons Limited, London, 1914.

Library of Congress Cataloging-in-Publication Data

Budge, E. A. Wallis (Ernest Alfred Wallis), Sir, 1857–1934.
    [Literature of the ancient Egyptians]
    An introduction to ancient Egyptian literature / E. A. Wallis Budge.
        p.   cm.
    Originally published: The literature of the ancient Egyptians. London : J. M. Dent & Sons, 1914.
    Includes bibliographical references and index.
    ISBN 0-486-29502-8 (pbk.)
    1. Egyptian literature—History and criticism. 2. Egyptian literature—Translations into English. I. Title.
PJ1482.B8   1997
893'.1—dc20   96-43172
                                                                      CIP

Manufactured in the United States of America
Dover Publications, Inc., 31 East 2nd Street, Mineola, N.Y. 11501

PREFACE

THIS little book is intended to serve as an elementary introduction to the study of Egyptian Literature. Its object is to present a short series of specimens of Egyptian compositions, which represent all the great periods of literary activity in Egypt under the Pharaohs, to all who are interested in the study of the mental development of ancient nations. It is not addressed to the Egyptological specialist, to whom, as a matter of course, its contents are well known, and therefore its pages are not loaded with elaborate notes and copious references. It represents, I believe, the first attempt made to place before the public a summary of the principal contents of Egyptian Literature in a handy and popular form.

The specimens of native Egyptian Literature printed herein are taken from tombs, papyri, stelæ, and other monuments, and, with few exceptions, each specimen is complete in itself. Translations of most of the texts have appeared in learned works written by Egyptologists in English, French, German, and Italian, but some appear in English for the first time. In every case I have collated my own translations with the texts, and, thanks to the accurate editions of texts which have appeared in recent years, it has been found possible to make many hitherto difficult passages clear. The translations are as literal as the difference between the Egyptian and English idioms will permit, but it has been necessary to insert particles and often to invert the order of the words in the original works in order to produce a connected meaning in English. The result of this has been in many cases to break up the short abrupt sentences in which the Egyptian author delighted, and which he used frequently with dramatic effect. Extraordinarily concise phrases have been paraphrased, but the meanings given to several unknown words often represent guess-work.

In selecting the texts for translation in this book an attempt has been made to include compositions that are not only the best of their kind, but that also illustrate the most important branches of Egyptian Literature. Among these religious, mythological, and moral works bulk largely, and in many respects these represent the peculiar bias of the mind of the ancient Egyptian better than compositions of a purely historical character. No man was more alive to his own material interests, but no man has ever valued the things of this world less in comparison with the salvation of his soul and the preservation of his physical body. The immediate result of this was a perpetual demand on his part for information concerning the Other World, and for guidance during his life in this world. The priests attempted to satisfy his craving for information by composing the Books of the Dead and the other funerary works with which we are acquainted, and the popularity of these works seems to show that they succeeded. From the earliest times the Egyptians regarded a life of moral excellence upon earth as a necessary introduction to the life which he hoped to live with the blessed in heaven. And even in pyramid times he conceived the idea of the existence of a God Who judged rightly, and Who set " right in the place of wrong." This fact accounts for the reverence in which he held the Precepts of Ptah-hetep, Kaqemna, Herutataf, Amenemhāt I, Ani, Tuauf, Amen-hetep, and other sages. To him, as to all Africans, the Other World was a very real thing, and death and the Last Judgment were common subjects of his daily thoughts. The great antiquity of this characteristic of the Egyptian is proved by a passage in a Book of Precepts, which was written by a king of the ninth or tenth dynasty for his son, who reigned under the name of Merikarā. The royal writer in it reminds his son that the Chiefs [of Osiris]

who judge sinners perform their duty with merciless justice
on the Day of Judgment.   It is useless to assume that length
of years will be accepted by them as a plea of justification.
With them the lifetime of a man is only regarded as a
moment.   After death these Chiefs must be faced, and the
only things that they will consider will be his works.   Life
in the Other World is for ever, and only the reckless fool
forgets this fact.   The man who has led a life free from lies
and deceit shall live after death like a god.

The reader who wishes to continue his studies of Egyptian
Literature will find abundant material in the list of works
given on pp. 256–8.

E. A. WALLIS BUDGE.

British Museum,
April 17, 1914.

CONTENTS

CHAP.   PAGE
I. THOTH, THE AUTHOR OF EGYPTIAN LITERATURE.
   WRITING MATERIALS, PAPYRUS, INK AND INK-
   POT, PALETTE, &c.   1
II. THE PYRAMID TEXTS: 9
    The Book of Opening the Mouth   .   .   .   13
    The Liturgy of Funerary Offerings .   .   .   16
    Hymns to the Sky-goddess and Sun-god .   .   18
    The King in Heaven   20
    The Hunting and Slaughter of the Gods by
       the King   21
III. STORIES OF MAGICIANS WHO LIVED UNDER THE
     ANCIENT EMPIRE: 25
     Ubaaner and the Wax Crocodile   .   .   .   25
     The Magician Tchatchamānkh and the Gold
        Ornament   27
     Teta, who restored Life to Dead Animals, &c. .   29
     Rut-tetet and the Three Sons of Rā   .   .   33
IV. THE BOOK OF THE DEAD: 37
    Summary of Chapters   42
    Hymns, Litany, and Extracts from the Book
       of the Dead   44
    The Great Judgment   51
V. BOOKS OF THE DEAD OF THE GRÆCO-ROMAN
   PERIOD: 59
   Book of Breathings   59
   Book of Traversing Eternity   61
   The Lamentations of Isis and Nephthys .   .   62
   The Festival Songs of Isis and Nephthys .   .   64
   The Book of Making Splendid the Spirit of Osiris   64

ix

CHAP. PAGE

VI. The Egyptian Story of the Creation . . 67

VII. Legends of the Gods : 71

The Destruction of Mankind 71

The Legend of Rā and Isis 74

The Legend of Horus of Behutet . . . 77

The Legend of Khnemu and the Seven Years'
Famine 83

The Legend of the Wanderings of Isis . . 87

The Legend of the Princess of Bekhten . . 92

VIII. Historical Literature : 98

Extract from the Palermo Stone . . . 100

Edict against the Blacks 101

Inscription of Usertsen III at Semnah . . 101

Campaign of Thothmes II in the Sūdān . . 102

Capture of Megiddo by Thothmes III . . 103

The Conquests of Thothmes III summarised by
Amen-Rā 106

Summary of the Reign of Rameses III . . 110

The Invasion and Conquest of Egypt by
Piānkhi 116

IX. Autobiographical Literature : 126

The Autobiography of Una 127

The Autobiography of Herkhuf . . . 131

The Autobiography of Ameni Amenemhāt . 135

The Autobiography of Thetha 137

The Autobiography of Amasis, the Naval
Officer 140

The Autobiography of Amasis, surnamed Pen-
Nekheb 143

The Autobiography of Tehuti, the Erpā . . 145

The Autobiography of Thaiemhetep . . 149

X. Tales of Travel and Adventure : . . . 155

The Story of Sanehat 155

The Story of the Educated Peasant Khuenanpu 169

The Journey of the Priest Unu-Amen into Syria 185

CHAP.		PAGE
XI. FAIRY TALES :		196
The Tale of the Two Brothers . . .		196
The Story of the Shipwrecked Traveller .		207
XII. EGYPTIAN HYMNS TO THE GODS : . .		214
Hymn to Amen-Rā		214
Hymn to Amen		219
Hymn to the Sun-god		220
Hymn to Osiris		221
Hymn to Shu		222
XIII. MORAL AND PHILOSOPHICAL LITERATURE : .		224
The Precepts of Ptah-hetep . . .		225
The Maxims of Ani		228
The Talk of a Man who was tired of Life with His Soul		231
The Lament of Khakhepersenb, surnamed Ankhu		235
The Lament of Apuur		236
XIV. EGYPTIAN POETICAL COMPOSITIONS : . .		241
The Poem in the Tomb of Antuf . .		242
XV. MISCELLANEOUS LITERATURE : . . .		244
The Book of Two Ways		244
The Book "Am Tuat"		244
The Book of Gates		246
The Ritual of Embalmment . . .		247
The Ritual of the Divine Cult . . .		248
The Book " May My Name Flourish " .		250
The Book of Āapep		250
The Instructions of Tuauf . . .		250
Medical Papyri		252
Magical Papyri		252
Legal Documents		253
Historical Romances		254
Mathematical Papyri		254
EDITIONS OF EGYPTIAN TEXTS, TRANSLATIONS, &C.		256
INDEX		259

ILLUSTRATIONS

PAGE

THE ELYSIAN FIELDS OF THE EGYPTIANS . . *Frontispiece*

THOTH, THE SCRIBE OF THE GODS 3

THOTH AND AMEN-RĀ SUCCOURING ISIS . . . 5

EGYPTIAN WRITING PALETTES . . . *To face* 6

VIGNETTE FROM THE BOOK OF THE DEAD (Chapter XCII)

To face 42

HER-HERU AND QUEEN NETCHEMET RECITING A HYMN

To face 44

HER-HERU AND QUEEN NETCHEMET STANDING IN THE

HALL OF OSIRIS . . . . . *To face* 52

STELE RELATING THE STORY OF THE HEALING OF

BENTRESHT 94

STELE ON WHICH IS CUT THE SPEECH OF AMEN-RĀ . 107

A PAGE FROM THE GREAT HARRIS PAPYRUS *To face* 110

STELE ON WHICH IS CUT THE AUTOBIOGRAPHY OF THAIEM-

HETEP 150

A PAGE OF THE TALE OF THE TWO BROTHERS *To face* 196

THE LITERATURE OF THE ANCIENT EGYPTIANS

CHAPTER I

THOTH, THE AUTHOR OF EGYPTIAN LITERATURE. WRITING MATERIALS, ETC.

THE Literature of ancient Egypt is the product of a period of about four thousand years, and it was written in three kinds of writing, which are called hieroglyphic, hieratic, and demotic. In the first of these the characters were pictures of objects, in the second the forms of the characters were made as simple as possible so that they might be written quickly, and in the third many of them lost their picture form altogether and became mere symbols. Egyptian writing was believed to have been invented by the god Tehuti, or Thoth, and as this god was thought to be a form of the mind and intellect and wisdom of the God who created the heavens and the earth, the picture characters, or hieroglyphs as they are called, were held to be holy, or divine, or sacred. Certain religious texts were thought to possess special virtue when written in hieroglyphs, and the chapters and sections of books that were considered to have been composed by Thoth himself were believed to possess very great power, and to be of the utmost benefit to the dead when they were written out for them in hieroglyphs, and buried with them in their coffins. Thoth also invented the science of numbers, and as he fixed the courses of the sun, moon, and stars, and ordered the seasons, he was thought to be the first astronomer. He was the lord of wisdom, and the possessor of all knowledge, both heavenly and earthly, divine and human ; and he was the author of every attempt made by man to draw, paint, and carve. As the lord and maker of books, and as the skilled scribe, he was the clerk of the gods, and kept the registers wherein the deeds of men were written down. The deep knowledge of Thoth enabled him to find out the truth at all times, and this ability caused the Egyptians to assign to him the position of Chief Judge of the dead. A very ancient legend states that Thoth acted in this capacity in the great trial that took place in heaven when Osiris was accused of certain crimes by his twin-brother Set, the god of evil. Thoth examined the evidence, and proved to the gods that the charges made by Set were untrue, and that Osiris had spoken the truth and that Set was a liar. For this reason every Egyptian prayed that Thoth might act for him as he did for Osiris, and that on the day of the Great Judgment Thoth might preside over the weighing of his heart in the Balance. All the important religious works in all periods were believed to have been composed either by himself, or by holy scribes who were inspired by him. They were believed to be sources of the deepest wisdom, the like of which existed in no other books in the world. And it is probably to these books that Egypt owed her fame for learning and wisdom, which spread throughout all the civilised world. The " Books of Thoth," which late popular tradition in Egypt declared to be as many as 36,525 in number, were revered by both natives and foreigners in a way which it is difficult for us in these days to realise. The scribes who studied and copied these books were also specially honoured, for it was believed that the spirit of Thoth, the twice-great and thrice-great god, dwelt in them. The profession of the scribe was considered to be most honourable, and its rewards were great, for no rank and no dignity were too high for the educated scribe. Thoth appears in the papyri and on the monuments as an ibis-headed man, and his companion is usually a dog-headed ape called " Asten." In the Hall of the Great Judgment he is seen holding in one hand a reed with which he is writing on a palette the result of the weighing of the heart of the dead man in the Balance. The gods accepted the report of Thoth without question, and

Thoth, the Scribe of the Gods.

rewarded the good soul and punished the bad according to his statement. From the beginning to the end of the history

of Egypt the position of Thoth as the "righteous judge,"
and framer of the laws by which heaven and earth, and
men and gods were governed, remained unchanged.

The substances used by the Egyptians for writing upon
were very numerous, but the commonest were stone of
various kinds, wood, skin, and papyrus. The earliest writings were probably traced upon these substances with some
fluid, coloured black or red, which served as ink. When
the Egyptians became acquainted with the use of the metals
they began to cut their writings in stone. The text of one
of the oldest chapters of the Book òf the Dead (LXIV) is
said in the Rubric to the chapter to have been "found"
cut upon a block of "alabaster of the south" during the
reign of Menkaurā, a king of the fourth dynasty, about
3700 B.C. As time went on and men wanted to write long
texts or inscriptions, they made great use of wood as a
writing material, partly on account of the labour and expense
of cutting in stone. In the British Museum many wooden
coffins may be seen with their insides covered with religious
texts, which were written with ink as on paper. Sheepskin,
or goatskin, was used as a writing material, but its use was
never general ; ancient Egyptian documents written on skin
or, as we should say, on parchment, are very few. At a
very early period the Egyptians learned how to make a sort
of paper, which is now universally known by the name of
"papyrus." When they made this discovery cannot be
said, but the hieroglyphic inscriptions of the early dynasties
contain the picture of a roll of papyrus, and the antiquity
of the use of papyrus must therefore be very great. Among
the oldest dated examples of inscribed papyrus may be
noted some accounts which were written in the reign of King
Assa (fourth dynasty, 3400 B.C.), and which were found at
Sakkārah, about 20 miles to the south of Cairo.

Papyrus was made from the papyrus plant that grew and
flourished in the swamps and marshes of Lower Egypt,
and in the shallow pools that were formed by the annual
Nile flood. It no longer grows in Egypt, but it is found in
the swamps of the Egyptian Sūdān, where it grows some-

times to a height of 25 feet. The roots and the stem, which is often thicker than a man's arm, are used as fuel, and the head, which is large and rounded, is in some districts boiled and eaten as a vegetable. The Egyptian variety of the papyrus plant was smaller than that found in the Sūdān, and the Egyptians made their paper from it by cutting the inner part of the stem into thin strips, the width of which

Thoth and Amen-Rā Succouring Isis in the Papyrus Swamps.

depended upon the thickness of the stem; the length of these varied, of course, with the length of the stem. To make a sheet of papyrus several of these strips were laid side by side lengthwise, and several others were laid over them crosswise. Thus each sheet of papyrus contained two layers, which were joined together by means of glue and water or gum. Pliny, a Roman writer, states (Bohn's edition, vol. iii. p. 189) that Nile water, which, when in a muddy state, has the peculiar qualities of glue, was used in fastening the two layers of strips together, but traces of gum have actually been found on papyri. The sheets were next pressed and then dried in the sun, and when rubbed with a hard polisher in order to remove roughnesses, were ready for use.[1] By adding sheet to sheet, rolls of papyrus of almost any length could be made. The longest roll in the British Museum is 133 feet long by 16½ inches high (Harris Papyrus, No. 1), and the second in length is a copy of the Book of the Dead, which is 123 feet long and 18½ inches high; the latter contains 2666 lines of writing arranged in 172 columns. The rolls on which ordinary compositions were written were much shorter and not so high, for they are rarely more than 20 feet long, and are only from 8 to 10 inches in height.

The scribe mixed on his palette the paints which he used. This palette usually consisted of a piece of alabaster, wood, ivory, or slate, from 8 to 16 inches in length and from 2 to 3½ inches in width; all four corners were square. At one end of the palette a number of oval or circular hollows were sunk to hold ink or paint. Down the middle was cut a groove, square at one end and sloping at the other, in which the writing reeds were placed. These were kept in position by a piece of wood glued across the middle of the palette, or by a sliding cover, which also served to protect the reeds from injury. On the sides of this groove are often found inscriptions that give the name of the owner of the palette, and that contain prayers to the gods for funerary offerings, or invocations to Thoth, the inventor of the art of writing. The black ink used by the scribes was made of lamp-black or of finely-powdered charcoal mixed with water, to which a very small quantity of gum was probably added. Red and yellow paint were made from mineral earths or ochres,

---

[1] In some parts of Mesopotamia where scribes at the present day use rough paper made in Russia, each sheet before being written upon is laid upon a board and polished by means of a glass bottle.

Wooden Palette of Rāmeri,
an Official of Thothmes IV.
1470 B.C.

Wooden Palette of Aāhmes I,
King of Egypt 1600 B.C.

blue paint was made from lapis-lazuli powder, green paint from sulphate of copper, and white paint from lime-white. Sometimes the ink was placed in small wide-mouthed pots made of Egyptian porcelain or alabaster. The scribe rubbed down his colours on a stone slab with a small stone muller. The writing reed, which served as a pen, was from 8 to 10 inches long, and from one-sixteenth to one-eighth of an inch in diameter ; the end used in writing was bruised and not cut. In late times a very much thicker reed was used, and then the end was cut like a quill or steel pen. Writing reeds of this kind were carried in boxes of wood and metal specially made for the purpose. Many specimens of all kinds of Egyptian writing materials are to be seen in the Egyptian Rooms of the British Museum.

As papyrus was expensive the pupils in the schools attached to the great temples of Egypt wrote their exercises and copies of standard literary compositions on slices of white limestone of fine texture, or upon boards, in the shape of modern slates used in schools, whitened with lime. The " copies " from which they worked were written by the teacher on limestone slabs of somewhat larger size. Copies of the texts that masons cut upon the walls of temples and other monuments were also written on slabs of this kind, and when figures of kings or gods were to be sculptured on the walls their proportions were indicated by perpendicular and horizontal lines drawn to scale. Portions of broken earthenware pots were also used for practising writing upon, and in the Ptolemaic and Roman Periods lists of goods, and business letters, and the receipts given by the tax-gatherers, were written upon potsherds. In still later times, when skin or parchment was as expensive as papyrus, the Copts, or Egyptian Christians, used slices of limestone and potsherds for drafts of portions of the Scriptures and letters in much the same way as did their ancestors.

A roll of papyrus when not in use was kept in shape by a string or piece of papyrus cord, which was tied in a bow ; sometimes, especially in the case of legal documents, a clay seal bearing the owner's name was stamped on the cord.

Valuable rolls were kept in wooden cases or " book boxes," which were deposited in a chamber or " house " set apart for the purpose, which was commonly called the " house of books," *i.e.* the library. Having now described the principal writing materials used by the ancient Egyptians, we may pass on to consider briefly the various classes of Egyptian Literature that have come down to us.

CHAPTER II

" PYRAMID Texts " is the name now commonly given to the long hieroglyphic inscriptions that are cut upon the walls of the chambers and corridors of five pyramids at Sakkārah. The oldest of them was built for Unas, a king of the fifth dynasty, and the four others were built for Teta, Pepi I, Merenrā, and Pepi II, kings of the sixth dynasty. According to the calculation of Dr. Brugsch, they were all built between 3300 and 3150 B.C., but more recent theories assign them to a period about 700 years later. These Texts represent the oldest religious literature known to us, for they contain beliefs, dogmas, and ideas that must be thousands of years older than the period of the sixth dynasty when the bulk of them was drafted for the use of the masons who cut them inside the pyramids. It is probable that certain sections of them were composed by the priests for the benefit of the dead in very primitive times in Egypt, when the art of writing was unknown, and that they were repeated each time a king died. They were first learned by heart by the funerary priests, and then handed on from mouth to mouth, generation after generation, and at length after the Egyptians had learned to write, and there was danger of their being forgotten, they were committed to writing. And just as these certain sections were absorbed into the great body of Pyramid Texts of the sixth dynasty, so portions of the Texts of the sixth dynasty were incorporated into the great Theban Book of the Dead, and they appear in papyri that were written more than 2000 years later. The Pyramid Texts supply us with much information concerning the religious beliefs of the primitive

9

Egyptians, and also with many isolated facts of history that are to be found nowhere else, but of the meaning of a very large number of passages we must always remain ignorant, because they describe states of civilisation, and conditions of life and climate, of which no modern person can form any true conception. Besides this the meanings of many words are unknown, the spelling is strange and often inexplicable, the construction of the sentence is frequently unlike anything known in later texts, and the ideas that they express are wholly foreign to the minds of students of to-day, who are in every way aliens to the primitive Egyptian African whose beliefs these words represent. The pyramids at Sakkārah in which the Pyramid Texts are found were discovered by the Frenchman, Mariette, in 1880. Paper casts of the inscriptions, which are deeply cut in the walls and painted green, were made for Professor Maspero, the Director of the Service of Antiquities in Egypt, and from these he printed an edition in hieroglyphic type of all five texts, and added a French translation of the greater part of them. Professor Maspero correctly recognised the true character of these old-world documents, and his translation displayed an unrivalled insight into the true meaning of many sections of them. The discovery and study of other texts and the labours of recent workers have cleared up passages that offered difficulties to him, but his work will remain for a very long time the base of all investigations.

The Pyramid Texts, and the older texts quoted or embodied in them, were written, like every religious funerary work in Egypt, for the benefit of the king, that is to say, to effect his glorious resurrection and to secure for him happiness in the Other World, and life everlasting. They were intended to make him become a king in the Other World as he had been a king upon earth; in other words, he was to reign over the gods, and to have control of all the powers of heaven, and to have the power to command the spirits and souls of the righteous, as his ancestors the kings of Egypt had ruled their bodies when they lived on earth. The Egyptians found that their king, who was an incarnation of the "Great God," died like other men, and they feared that, even if they succeeded in effecting his resurrection by means of the Pyramid Texts, he might die a second time in the Other World. They spared no effort and left no means untried to make him not only a "living soul" in the Tuat, or Other World, but to keep him alive there. The object of every prayer, every spell, every hymn, and every incantation contained in these Texts, was to preserve the king's life. This might be done in many ways. In the first place it was necessary to provide a daily supply of offerings, which were offered up in the funerary temple that was attached to every pyramid. The carefully selected and duly appointed priest offered these one by one, and as he presented each to the spirit of the king he uttered a formula that was believed to convert the material food into a substance possessing a spiritual character and fit to form the food of the *ka*, or "double," or "vital power," of the dead king. The offerings assisted in renewing his life, and any failure to perform this service was counted a sin against the dead king's spirit. It was also necessary to perform another set of ceremonies, the object of which was to "open the mouth" of the dead king, *i.e.* to restore to him the power to breathe, think, speak, taste, smell, and walk. At the performance of these ceremonies it was all-important to present articles of food, wearing apparel, scents and unguents, and, in short, every object that the king was likely to require in the Other World. The spirits of all these objects passed into the Other World ready for use by the spirit of the king. It follows as a matter of course that the king in the Other World needed a retinue, and a bodyguard, and a host of servants, just as he needed slaves upon earth. In primitive times a large number of slaves, both male and female, were slain when a king died, and their bodies were buried in his tomb, whilst their spirits passed into the Other World to serve the spirit of the king, just as their bodies had served his body upon earth. As the king had enemies in this world, so it was thought he would have enemies in the Other World, and men feared that he would be attacked or molested by evilly-disposed gods and spirits, and by deadly animals and serpents, and other noxious reptiles.   To ward off the attacks of these from his tomb, and his mummified body, and his spirit, the priest composed spells of various kinds, and the utterance of such, in a proper manner, was believed to render him immune from the attacks of foes of all kinds.   Very often such spells took the form of prayers.   Many of the spells were exceedingly ancient, even in the Pyramid Period ; they were, in fact, so old that they were unintelligible to the scribes of the day. They date from the time when the Egyptians believed more in magic than religion ; it is possible that when they were composed, religion, in our sense of the word, was still undeveloped among the Egyptians.

When the Pyramid Texts were written men believed that the welfare of souls and spirits in the Other World could be secured by the prayers of the living.   Hence we find in them numerous prayers for the dead, and hymns addressed to the gods on their behalf, and extracts from many kinds of ancient religious books.   When these were recited, and offerings made both to the gods and to the dead, it was confidently believed that the souls of the dead received special consideration and help from the gods, and from all the good spirits who formed their train.   These prayers are very important from many points of view, but specially so from the fact that they prove that the Egyptians who lived under the sixth dynasty attached more importance to them than to magical spells and incantations.   In other words, the Egyptians had begun to reject their belief in the efficacy of magic, and to develop a belief of a more spiritual character. There were many reasons for this development, but the most important was the extraordinary growth of the influence of the religion of Osiris, which had before the close of the period of the sixth dynasty spread all over Egypt.   This religion promised to all who followed it, high or low, rich or poor, a life in the world beyond the grave, after a resurrection that was made certain to them through the sufferings, death, and resurrection of Osiris, who was the incarnation of the great primeval god who created the heavens and the earth. A few extracts illustrating the general contents of the Pyramid Texts may now be given.

I. Mention has already been made of the " opening of the mouth " of the dead king : under the earliest dynasties this ceremony was performed on a statue of the king. Water was sprinkled before it, and incense was burnt, and the statue was anointed with seven kinds of unguents, and its eyes smeared with eye paint. After the statue had been washed and dressed a meal of sepulchral offerings was set before it. The essential ceremony consisted in applying to the lips of the statue a curiously shaped instrument called the PESH KEF, with which the bandages that covered the mouth of the dead king in his tomb were supposed to be cut and the mouth set free to open. In later times the Liturgy of Opening the Mouth was greatly enlarged and was called the Book of Opening the Mouth. The ceremonies were performed by the Kher-heb priest, the son of the deceased, and the priests and ministrants called Sameref, Sem, Smer, Am-as, Am-khent, and the assistants called Mesentiu. First of all incense was burnt, and the priest said, " Thou art pure," four times. Water was then sprinkled over the statue and the priest said, " Thou art pure. Thou art pure. Thy purifications are the purifications of Horus,[1] and the purifications of Horus are thy purifications." This formula was repeated three times, once with the name of Set,[2] once with the name of Thoth,[3] and once with the name of Sep. The priest then said, " Thou hast received thy head, and thy bones have been brought unto thee before Keb." [4] During the performance of the next five ceremonies, in which incense of various kinds was offered, the priest said : " Thou art pure (four times). That which is in the two eyes of Horus hath been presented unto thee with the two vases of Thoth, and they purify thee so that there may not exist

---

[1] A form of the Sun-god.
[2] Originally a benevolent god : later the great god of evil.
[3] The scribe of the gods, lord of wisdom : see pp. 1, 2.   [4] The Earth-god.

in thee the power of destruction that belongeth unto thee. Thou art pure. Thou art pure. Pure is the *seman* incense that openeth thy mouth. Taste the taste thereof in the divine dwelling. *Seman* incense is the emission of Horus ; it stablisheth the heart of Horus-Set, it purifieth the gods who are in the following of Horus. Thou art censed with natron. Thou art established among the gods thy brethren. Thy mouth is like that of a sucking calf on the day of its birth. Thou art censed. Thou art censed. Thou art pure. Thou art pure. Thou art established among thy brethren the gods. Thy head is censed. Thy mouth is censed. Thy bones are purified. [Decay] that is inherent in thee shall not touch thee. I have given thee the Eye of Horus,[1] and thy face is filled therewith. Thou art shrouded in incense (say twice)."[2]

The next ceremony, the ninth, represented the re-birth of the king, who was personified by a priest. The priest, wrapped in the skin of a bull, lay on a small bed and feigned death. When the chief priest had said, " O my father," four times, the priest representing the king came forth from the bull's skin, and sat up ; this act symbolized the resurrection of the king in the form of a spirit-body (*sāhu*). The chief priest then asserted that the king was alive, and that he should never be removed, and that he was similar in every way to Horus. The priest personifying the king then put on a special garment, and taking a staff or sceptre in his hand, said, " I love my father and his transformation. I have made my father, I have made a statue of him, a large statue. Horus loveth those who love him." He then pressed the lips of the statue, and said, " I have come to embrace thee. I am thy son. I am Horus. I have pressed for thee thy mouth. . . . I am thy beloved son." The words then said by the chief priest, " I have delivered this mine eye from his mouth, I have cut off his leg," mean that the king was delivered from the jaws of death, and that a grievous wound had been inflicted on the god of death, *i.e.* Set.

---

[1] Horus gave his eye to Osiris, and thereby restored life to him.
[2] Repetitions are omitted.

Whilst these ceremonies were being performed the animals brought to be sacrificed were slain. Chief of these were two bulls, gazelle, geese, &c., and their slaughter typified the conquest and death of the enemies of the dead king. The heart and a fore-leg of each bull were presented to the statue of the king, and the priest said : " Hail, Osiris ! I have come to embrace thee. I am Horus. I have pressed for thee thy mouth. I am thy beloved Son. I have opened thy mouth. Thy mouth hath been made firm. I have made thy mouth and thy teeth to be in their proper places. Hail, Osiris ! [1] I have opened thy mouth with the Eye of Horus." Then taking two instruments made of metal the priest went through the motion of cutting open the mouth and eyes of the statue, and said : " I have opened thy mouth. I have opened thy two eyes. I have opened thy mouth with the instrument of Anpu.[2] I have opened thy mouth with the Meskha instrument wherewith the mouth of the gods was opened. Horus openeth the mouth and eyes of the Osiris. Horus openeth the mouth of the Osiris even as he opened the mouth of his father. As he opened the mouth of the god Osiris so shall he open the mouth of my father with the iron that cometh forth from Set, with the Meskha instrument of iron wherewith he opened the mouth of the gods shall the mouth of the Osiris be opened. And the Osiris shall walk and shall talk, and his body shall be with the Great Company of the Gods who dwell in the Great House of the Aged One (*i.e.* the Sun-god) who dwelleth in Anu.[3] And he shall take possession of the Urrt Crown therein before Horus, the Lord of mankind. Hail, Osiris ! Horus hath opened thy mouth and thine eyes with the instruments Sebur and An, wherewith the mouths of the gods of the South were opened. . . . All the gods bring

---

[1] It was assumed that the king after death became a being with the nature of Osiris, and he was therefore addressed as "Osiris."

[2] Or Anubis, a very ancient god who presided over embalming ; he appears in the form of a man with the head of a dog or jackal.

[3] The On of the Bible, the Heliopolis of the Greeks. This city lay a few miles to the east of the modern city of Cairo.

words of power. They recite them for thee. They make
thee to live by them. Thou becomest the possessor of twofold strength. Thou makest the passes that give thee the
fluid of life, and their life fluid is about thee. Thou art
protected, and thou shalt not die. Thou shalt change thy
form [at pleasure] among the Doubles[1] of the gods. Thou
shalt rise up as a king of the South. Thou shalt rise up as
a king of the North. Thou art endowed with strength like
all the gods and their Doubles. Shu[2] hath equipped thee.
He hath exalted thee to the height of heaven. He hath
made thee to be a wonder. He hath endowed thee with
strength.''

The ceremonies that followed concerned the dressing of
the statue of the king and his food. Various kinds of
bandlets and a collar were presented, and the gift of each
endowed the king in the Other World with special qualities.
The words recited by the priest as he offered these and
other gifts were highly symbolic, and were believed to
possess great power, for they brought the Double of the
king back to this earth to live in the statue, and each time
they were repeated they renewed the life of the king in the
Other World.

II. The *Liturgy of Funerary Offerings* was another all-
important work. The oldest form of it, which is found in
the Pyramid Texts, proves that even under the earliest
dynasties the belief in the efficacy of sacrifices and offerings
was an essential of the Egyptian religion. The opening
ceremonies had for their object the purification of the
deceased by means of sprinkling with water in which salt,
natron, and other cleansing substances had been dissolved,
and burning of incense. Then followed the presentation
of about one hundred and fifty offerings of food of all kinds,
fruit, flowers, vegetables, various kinds of wine, seven kinds
of precious ointments, wearing apparel of the kind suitable

---

[1] Every living thing possessed a KA or " double," which was the vital power
of the heart and could live after the death of the body.

[2] The Air-god, the son of Keb and Nut.

for a king, &c. As each object was presented to the spirit of the king, which was present in his statue in the Tuat Chamber of the tomb, the priest recited a form of words, which had the effect of transmuting the substance of the object into something which, when used or absorbed by the king's spirit, renewed the king's life and maintained his existence in the Other World. Every object was called the " Eye of Horus," in allusion to its life-giving qualities. The following extracts illustrate the Liturgy of Funerary Offerings :

32. This libation is for thee, Osiris, this libation is for thee, Unas.[1] (*Here offer cold water of the North.*) It cometh forth before thy son, cometh forth before Horus. I have come, I have brought unto thee the Eye of Horus, that thy heart may be refreshed thereby. I have brought it and have set it under thy sandals, and I present unto thee that which flowed forth from thee. There shall be no stoppage to thy heart whilst it is with thee, and the offerings that appear at the command[2] shall appear at thy word of command. (*Recite four times.*)

37. Thou hast taken possession of the two Eyes of Horus, the White and the Black, and when they are in thy face they illumine it. (*Here offer two jugs of wine, one white, one black.*)

38. Day hath made an offering unto thee in the sky. The South and the North have given offerings unto thee. Night hath made an offering unto thee. The South and the North have made an offering unto thee. An offering is brought unto thee, look upon it ; an offering, hear it. There is an offering before thee, there is an offering behind thee, there is an offering with thee. (*Here offer a cake for the journey.*)

41. Osiris Unas, the white teeth of Horus are presented unto thee so that they may fill thy mouth. (*Here offer five bunches of onions.*)

[1] The king who is identified with Osiris.
[2] The deceased who possessed the words of power uttered in the tomb the names of the offerings he required, and the offerings appeared forthwith.

47. O Rā, the worship that is paid to thee, the worship of every kind, shall be paid [also] to Unas. Everything that is offered to thy body shall be offered to the Double of Unas also, and everything that is offered to his body shall be thine. (*Here offer the table of holy offerings.*)

61. O ye oils, ye oils, which are on the forehead of Horus, set ye yourselves on the forehead of Unas, and make him to smell sweet through you. (*Here offer oil of cedar of the finest quality.*)

62. Make ye him to be a spirit-soul (*khu*) through possession of you, and grant ye him to have the mastery over his body, let his eyes be opened, and let all the spirit-souls see him, and let them hear his name. Behold, Osiris Unas, the Eye of Horus hath been brought unto thee, for it hath been seized for thee that it may be before thee. (*Here offer the finest Thehenu oil.*)

III. As specimens of the hymns in the Pyramid Texts may be quoted the following : the first is a hymn to Nut, the Sky-goddess, and the second is a hymn to Rā, the Sun-god.

[O] Nut, thou hast extended thyself over thy son the Osiris Pepi,
Thou hast snatched him out of the hand of Set ; join him to thy-
    self, Nut.
Thou comest, snatch thy son ; behold, thou comest, form this great
    one [like] unto thyself.
[O] Nut, cast thyself upon thy son the Osiris Pepi.
[O] Nut, cast thyself upon thy son the Osiris Pepi.
Form thou him, O Great Fashioner ; this great one is among thy
    children.
Form thou him, O Great Fashioner ; this great one is among thy
    children.
Keb [was to] Nut. Thou didst become a spirit.
Thou wast a mighty goddess in the womb of thy mother Tefnut
    when thou wast not born.
Form thou Pepi with life and well-being ; he shall not die.
Strong was thy heart,
Thou didst leap in the womb of thy mother in thy name of " Nut."
[O] perfect daughter, mighty one in thy mother, who art crowned
    like a king of the North,

Make this Pepi a spirit-soul in thee, let him not die.

[O] Great Lady, who didst come into being in the sky, who art mighty.

Who dost make happy, and dost fill every place (or being), with thy beauty,

The whole earth is under thee, thou hast taken possession of it.

Thou hast encompassed the earth, everything is in thy two hands,

Grant thou that this Pepi may be in thee like an imperishable star.

Thou hast associated with Keb in thy name of " Pet " (*i.e.* Sky).

Thou hast united the earth in every place.

[O] mistress over the earth, thou art above thy father Shu, thou hast the mastery over him.

He hath loved thee so much that he setteth himself under thee in everything.

Thou hast taken possession of every god for thyself with his boat (?).

Thou hast made them shine like lamps,

Assuredly they shall not cease from thee like the stars.

Let not this Pepi depart from thee in thy name of " Hert " (ll. 61–64).

The Hymn to the Sun-god is as follows :

Hail to thee, Tem !   Hail to thee, Kheprer, who created himself.

Thou art the High, in this thy name of " Height."

Thou camest into being in this thy name of " Kheprer."

Hail to thee, Eye of Horus,[1] which he furnisheth with his hands completely.

He permitteth not thee to be obedient to those of the West ;

He permitteth not thee to be obedient to those of the East ;

He permitteth not thee to be obedient to those of the South ;

He permitteth not thee to be obedient to those of the North ;

He permitteth not thee to be obedient to those who are in the earth ;

[For] thou art obedient to Horus.

He it is who hath furnished thee, he it is who hath builded thee, he it is who hath made thee to be dwelt in.

Thou doest for him whatsoever he saith unto thee, in every place whither he goeth.

Thou liftest up to him the water-fowl that are in thee.

Thou liftest up to him the water-fowl that are about to be in thee.

Thou liftest up to him every tree that is in thee.

Thou liftest up to him every tree that is about to be in thee.

Thou liftest up to him the cakes and ale that are in thee.

Thou liftest up to him the cakes and ale that are about to be in thee.

---

[1] Here a name of Egypt,

Thou liftest up to him the gifts that are in thee.
Thou liftest up to him the gifts that are about to be in thee.
Thou liftest up to him everything that is in thee.
Thou liftest up to him everything that is about to be in thee.
Thou takest them to him in every place wherein it pleaseth him
    to be.
The doors upon thee stand fast [shut] like the god Anmutef,[1]
They open not to those who are in the West ;
They open not to those who are in the East ;
They open not to those who are in the North ;
They open not to those who are in the South ;
They open not to those who are in the middle of the earth ;
But they open to Horus.

He it was who made them, he it was who made them stand [firm],
he it was who delivered them from every evil attack which the god
Set made upon them. He it was who made thee to be a settled
country in this thy name of " Kerkut." He it was who passed
bowing after thee in thy name of " Nut." He it was who delivered
thee from every evil attack which Set made upon thee. (Pepi II,
ll. 767–774.)

IV. The following passages describe the power of the king
in heaven, and his felicity there :

" The sky hath withdrawn the life of the star Septet
(Sothis, the Dog-star) ; behold Unas a living being, the
son of Septet. The Eighteen Gods have purified him in
Meskha (the Great Bear), [he is] an imperishable star. The
house of Unas perisheth not in the sky, the throne of Unas
perisheth not on the earth. Men make supplication [there],
the gods fly [thither]. Septet hath made Unas fly to heaven
to be with his brethren the gods. Nut,[2] the Great Lady,
hath unfolded her arms to Unas. She hath made them
into two divine souls at the head of the Souls of Anu, under
the head of Rā. She made them two weeping women when
thou wast on thy bier (?). The throne of Unas is by thee,
Rā, he yieldeth it not up to anyone else. Unas cometh
forth into heaven by thee, Rā. The face of Unas is like the
[faces of the] Hawks. The wings of Unas are like [those of]
geese. The nails of Unas are like the claws of the god Tuf.

---

[1] The god who was " the pillar of his mother."   [2] The Sky-goddess.

There is no [evil] word concerning Unas on earth among men. There is no hostile speech about him with the gods. Unas hath destroyed his word, he hath ascended to heaven. Upuatu hath made Unas fly up to heaven among his brethren the gods. Unas hath drawn together his arms like the Smen goose, he striketh his wings like a falcon, flying, flying. O men, Unas flieth up into heaven.

" O ye gods of the West, O ye gods of the East, O ye gods of the South, O ye gods of the North, ye four groups who embrace the holy lands, devote ye yourselves to Osiris when he appeareth in heaven. He shall sail into the Sky, with his son Horus by his fingers. He shall announce him, he shall make him rise up like the Great God in the Sky. They shall cry out concerning Unas : Behold Horus, the son of Osiris ! Behold Unas, the firstborn son of Hathor ! Behold the seed of Keb ! Osiris hath commanded that Unas shall rise as a second Horus, and these Four Spirit-souls in Anu have written an edict to the two great gods in the Sky. Rā set up the Ladder [1] in front of Osiris, Horus set up the Ladder in front of his father Osiris when he went to his spirit, one on this side [and] one on the other side ; Unas is between them. Behold, he is the god of the pure seats coming forth from the bath (?). Unas standeth up, lo Horus ; Unas sitteth down, lo Set. Rā graspeth his hand, spirit to heaven, body to earth."

The power of the king in heaven was almost as absolute as it was upon earth, and in a very remarkable passage in the text of Unas, which is repeated in the text of Teta, we have a graphic description of the king as a mighty hunter, who chases the gods and lassoes them, and then kills and eats them in order that he may absorb their strength and wisdom, and all their divine attributes, and their power of living eternally. The passage reads :

" The skies lower, the Star-gods tremble, the Archers [2] quake, the bones of the Akeru [2] gods tremble, and those who

---

[1] The Ladder by which souls ascended to heaven. A picture of the Ladder is given in the Papyrus of Ani, Plate XXII.

[2] These are names of groups of stars.

are with them are struck dumb when they see Unas rising up
as a soul, in the form of the god who liveth upon his fathers,
and who turneth his mothers into his food. Unas is the
lord of wisdom, and his mother knoweth not his name. The
adoration of Unas is in heaven, he hath become mighty in
the horizon like Temu, the father that gave him birth, and
after Temu had given him birth Unas became stronger than
his father. The Doubles (*i.e.* vital strength) of Unas are
behind him, the soles of his feet are beneath his feet, his gods
are over him, his serpents are [seated] upon his brow, the
serpent-guides of Unas are in front of him, and the spirit of
the flame looketh upon [his] soul. The powers of Unas protect him. Unas is a bull in heaven. He directeth his steps
where he willeth. He liveth upon the form which each god
taketh upon himself, and he eateth the flesh of those who
come to fill their bellies with the magical charms in the Lake
of Fire. Unas is equipped with power against the spirit-
souls thereof, and he riseth in the form of the mighty one,
the lord of those who dwell in power (?). Unas hath taken
his seat with his back turned towards Keb (the Earth-god).
Unas hath weighed his words [1] with the hidden god (?) who
hath no name, on the day of hacking in pieces the firstborn.
Unas is the lord of offerings, the untier of the knot, and he
himself maketh abundant the offerings of meat and drink.
Unas devoureth men, and liveth upon the gods, he is the
lord of envoys whom he sendeth forth on his missions. ' He
who cutteth off hairy scalps,' who dwelleth in the fields,
tieth the gods with ropes. Tcheser-tep shepherdeth them for
Unas and driveth them unto him ; and the Cord-master
hath bound them for slaughter. Khensu, the slayer of the
wicked, cutteth their throats, and draweth out their intestines, for it is he whom Unas sendeth to slaughter [them],
and Shesmu [2] cutteth them in pieces, and boileth their
members in his blazing caldrons of the night. Unas eateth
their magical powers, and he swalloweth their spirit-souls.
The great ones among them serve for his meal at daybreak,

---

[1] *i.e.* entered into judgment.   [2] The executioner of Osiris.

the lesser serve for his meal at eventide, and the least among them serve for his meal in the night. The old gods and the old goddesses become fuel for his furnace. The mighty ones in heaven light the fire under the caldrons wherein are heaped up the thighs of the firstborn ; and he who maketh those who live in heaven to go about for Unas lighteth the fire under the caldrons with the thighs of their women ; he goeth about the Two Heavens in their entirety, and he goeth round about the two banks of the Celestial Nile. Unas is the Great Power, the Power of Powers, and Unas is the Chief of the gods in visible forms. Whatsoever he findeth upon his path he eateth forthwith, and the magical might of Unas is before that of all the spirit-bodies who dwell in the horizon. Unas is the firstborn of the firstborn gods. Unas is surrounded by thousands, and oblations are made unto him by hundreds ; he is made manifest as the Great Power by Saah (Orion), the father of the gods. Unas repeateth his rising in heaven, and he is crowned lord of the horizon. He hath reckoned up the bandlets and the arm-rings [of his captives], he hath taken possession of the hearts of the gods. Unas hath eaten the Red Crown, and he hath swallowed the White Crown ; the food of Unas is the intestines, and his meat is hearts and their words of power. Behold, Unas eateth of that which the Red Crown sendeth forth, he increaseth, and the words of power of the gods are in his belly ; his attributes are not removed from him. Unas hath eaten the whole of the knowledge of every god, and the period of his life is eternity, and the duration of his existence is everlastingness. He is in the form of one who doeth what he wisheth, and who doth not do what he hateth, and he abideth on the horizon for ever and ever and ever. The Soul of the gods is in Unas, their spirit-souls are with Unas, and the offerings made unto him are more than those that are made unto the gods. The fire of Unas is in their bones, for their soul is in Unas, and their shades are with those who belong unto them. Unas hath been with the two hidden (?) Kha (?) gods, . . . ; the seat of the heart of Unas is among those who live upon this earth for ever and ever and ever."

The following extract is from one of the later Pyramid Texts :

" Pepi was brought forth by the god Nu, when there was no heaven, when there was no earth, when nothing had been established, when there was no fighting, and when the fear of the Eye of Horus did not exist. This Pepi is one of the Great Offspring who were brought forth in Anu (Heliopolis), who have never been conquered by a king or ruled by chiefs, who are irresistible, whose words cannot be gainsaid. Therefore this Pepi is irresistible ; he can neither be conquered by a king nor ruled by chiefs. The enemies of Pepi cannot triumph. Pepi lacketh nothing. His nails do not grow long [for want of prey]. No debt is reckoned against Pepi. If Pepi falleth into the water Osiris will lift him out, and the Two Companies of the Gods will bear him up on their shoulders, and Rā, wheresoever he may be, will give him his hand. If Pepi falleth on the earth the Earth-god (Keb) will lift him up, and the Two Companies of the Gods will bear him up on their shoulders, and Rā, wheresoever he may be, will give him his hand. . . . Pepi appeareth in heaven among the imperishable stars. His sister the star Sothis (the Dog-star), his guide the Morning Star (Venus) lead him by the hand to the Field of Offerings. He taketh his seat on the crystal throne, which hath faces of fierce lions and feet in the form of the hoofs of the Bull Sma-ur. He standeth up in his place between the Two Great Gods, and his sceptre and staff are in his hands. He lifteth up his hand to the Henmemet spirits, and the gods come to him with bowings. The Two Great Gods look on in their places, and they find Pepi acting as judge of the gods. The word of every spirit-soul is in him, and they make offerings to him among the Two Companies of the Gods.

CHAPTER III

STORIES OF MAGICIANS WHO LIVED UNDER THE
ANCIENT EMPIRE

THE short stories of the wonderful deeds of ancient
Egyptian magicians here given are found in the Westcar
Papyrus, which is preserved in the Royal Museum in Berlin,
where it is numbered P. 3033. This papyrus was the property of Miss Westcar of Whitchurch, who gave it to the
eminent German Egyptologist, Richard Lepsius, in 1839 ;
it was written probably at some period between the twelfth
and eighteenth dynasties. The texts were first edited and
translated by Professor Erman.

THE MAGICIAN UBAANER AND THE WAX CROCODILE

The first story describes an event which happened in the
reign of Nebka, a king of the third dynasty. It was told
by Prince Khāfrā to King Khufu (Cheops). The magician
was called Ubaaner,[1] and he was the chief Kher-heb in the
temple of Ptah of Memphis, and a very learned man. He
was a married man, but his wife loved a young man who
worked in the fields, and she sent him by the hands of one
of her maids a box containing a supply of very fine clothes.
Soon after receiving this gift the young man proposed to the
magician's wife that they should meet and talk in a certain
booth or lodge in her garden, and she instructed the steward
to have the lodge made ready for her to receive her friend
in it. When this was done, she went to the lodge, and she

---

[1] This name means "splitter of stones." It will be remembered that the
late Sir H. M. Stanley was called the " stone-splitter," because of his great
strength of deed and word.

sat there with the young man and drank beer with him until the evening, when he went his way. The steward, knowing what had happened, made up his mind to report the matter to his master, and as soon as the morning had come, he went to Ubaaner and informed him that his wife had spent the previous day drinking beer with such and such a young man. Ubaaner then told the steward to fetch him his casket made of ebony and silver-gold, which contained materials and instruments used in working magic, and when it was brought him, he took out some wax, and fashioned a figure of a crocodile seven spans long. He then recited certain magical words over the crocodile, and said to it, "When the young man comes to bathe in my lake thou shalt seize him." Then giving the wax crocodile to the steward, Ubaaner said to him, "When the young man goes down to the lake to bathe according to his daily habit, thou shalt throw the crocodile into the water after him." Having taken the crocodile from his master the steward departed.

Then the wife of Ubaaner told the steward to set the little lodge in the garden in order, because she was going to spend some time there. When the steward had furnished the lodge, she went there, and the young peasant paid her a visit. After leaving the lodge he went and bathed in the lake, and the steward followed him and threw the wax crocodile into the water; it immediately turned into a large crocodile 7 cubits (about 11 feet) long and seized the young man and swallowed him up. When this took place the magician Ubaaner was with the king, and he remained in attendance upon him for seven days, during which time the young man was in the lake, with no air to breathe. When the seven days were ended King Nebka proposed to take a walk with the magician. Whilst they were going along Ubaaner asked the king if he would care to see a wonderful thing that had happened to a young peasant, and the king said he would, and forthwith walked to the place to which the magician led him. When they arrived at the lake Ubaaner uttered a spell over the crocodile, and commanded it to come up out of the water bringing the young man with him ; and the crocodile did so. When the king saw the beast he exclaimed at its hideousness, and seemed to be afraid of it, but the magician stooped down fearlessly, and took the crocodile up in his hand, and lo, the living crocodile had disappeared, and only a crocodile of wax remained in its place. Then Ubaaner told King Nebka the story of how the young man had spent days in the lodge in the garden talking and drinking beer with his wife, and His Majesty said to the wax crocodile, " Get thee gone, and take what is thine with thee." And the wax crocodile leaped out of the magician's hand into the lake, and once more became a large, living crocodile. And it swam away with the young man, and no one ever knew what became of it afterwards. Then the king made his servants seize Ubaaner's wife, and they carried her off to the ground on the north side of the royal palace, and there they burned her, and they scattered her ashes in the river. When King Khufu had heard the story he ordered many offerings to be made in the tomb of his predecessor Nebka, and gifts to be presented to the magician Ubaaner.

THE MAGICIAN TCHATCHAMĀNKH AND THE GOLD ORNAMENT

The Prince Baiufrā stood up and offered to relate to King Khufu (Cheops) a story of a magician called Tchatchamānkh, who flourished in the reign of Seneferu, the king's father. The offer having been accepted, Baiufrā proceeded to relate the following : On one occasion it happened that Seneferu was in a perplexed and gloomy state of mind, and he wandered distractedly about the rooms and courts of his palace seeking to find something wherewith to amuse himself, but he failed to do so. Then he bethought himself of the court magician Tchatchamānkh, and he ordered his servants to summon him to the presence. When the great Kher-heb and scribe arrived, he addressed him as " my brother," and told him that he had been wandering about in his palace seeking for amusement, and had failed to find it. The magician promptly suggested to the king that he should have a boat got ready, decorated with pretty things that would give pleasure, and should go for a row on the lake. The motions of the rowers as they rowed the boat about would interest him, and the sight of the depths of the waters, and the pretty fields and gardens round about the lake, would give him great pleasure. " Let me," said the magician, " arrange the matter. Give me twenty ebony paddles inlaid with gold and silver, and twenty pretty maidens with flowing hair, and twenty network garments wherein to dress them." The king gave orders for all these things to be provided, and when the boat was ready, and the maidens who were to row had taken their places, he entered the boat and sat in his little pavilion and was rowed about on the lake. The magician's views proved to be correct, for the king enjoyed himself, and was greatly amused in watching the maidens row. Presently the handle of the paddle of one of the maidens caught in her long hair, and in trying to free it a malachite ornament which she was wearing in her hair fell into the water and disappeared. The maiden was much troubled over her loss, and stopped rowing, and as her stopping threw out of order the strokes of the maidens who were sitting on the same seat as she was, they also stopped rowing. Thereupon the king asked why the rowing had ceased, and one of the maidens told him what had happened ; and when he promised that the ornament should be recovered, the maiden said words which seem to mean that she had no doubt that she should recover it. On this Seneferu caused Tchatchamānkh to be summoned into the presence, and when he came the king told him all that had happened. Then the magician began to recite certain spells, the effect of which was to cause the water of the lake first to divide into two parts, and then the water on one side to rise up and place itself on the water on the other side. The boat, presumably, sank down gently on the ground of the lake, for the malachite ornament was seen lying there, and the magician fetched it, and returned it to its owner. The depth of the water in the middle of the lake where the ornament dropped was 12 cubits (between 18 and 19 feet), and when the water from one side was piled up on that on the other, the total depth of the two sections taken together was, we are told, 24 cubits. As soon as the ornament was restored to the maiden, the magician recited further spells, and the water lowered itself, and spread over the ground of the lake, and so regained its normal level. His Majesty, King Seneferu, assembled his nobles, and having discussed the matter with them, made a handsome gift to his clever magician. When King Khufu had heard the story he ordered a large supply of funerary offerings to be sent to the tomb of Seneferu, and bread, beer, flesh, and incense to the tomb of Tchatchamānkh.

THE MAGICIAN TETA WHO RESTORED LIFE TO DEAD ANIMALS, ETC.

When Baiufrā had finished the story given above, Prince Herutataf, the son of King Khufu, and a very wise man, with whose name Egyptian tradition associated the discovery of certain chapters of the Book of the Dead, stood up before his father to speak, and said to him, " Up to the present thou hast only heard tales about the wisdom of magicians who are dead and gone, concerning which it is quite impossible to know whether they be true or not. Now, I want Thy Majesty to see a certain sage who is actually alive during thy lifetime, whom thou knowest not." His Majesty Khufu said, " Who is it, Herutataf ? " And Prince Herutataf replied, " He is a certain peasant who is called Teta, and he lives in Tet-Seneferu. He is one hundred and ten years old, and up to this very day he eats five hundred bread-cakes (*sic*), and a leg of beef, and drinks one hundred pots of beer. He knows how to reunite to its body a head which has been cut off, he knows how to make a lion follow him whilst the rope with which he is tied drags behind him on the ground, and he knows the numbers of the Apet chambers (?) of the shrine (?) of Thoth." Now His Majesty had been seeking for a long time past for the number of the

Apet chambers (?) of Thoth, for he had wished to make
something like it for his "horizon."[1]   And King Khufu
said to his son Herutataf, "My son, thou thyself shalt go
and bring the sage to me"; thereupon a boat was made
ready for Prince Herutataf, who forthwith set out on his
journey to Tet-Seneferu, the home of the sage.   When the
prince came to the spot on the river bank that was nearest
to the village of Teta, he had the boat tied up, and he continued his journey overland seated in a sort of sedan chair
made of ebony, which was carried or slung on bearing poles
made of costly *sesentchem* wood inlaid or decorated with
gold.   When Herutataf arrived at the village, the chair was
set down on the ground, and he got out of it and stood up
ready to greet the old man, whom he found lying upon a
bed, with the door of his house lying on the ground.   One
servant stood by the bed holding the sage's head and fanning
him, and another was engaged in rubbing his feet.   Herutataf addressed a highly poetical speech to Teta, the gist of
which was that the old man seemed to be able to defy the
usual effects of old age, and to be like one who had obtained
the secret of everlasting youth, and then expressed the hope
that he was well.   Having paid these compliments, which
were couched in dignified and archaic language, Herutataf
went on to say that he had come with a message from his
father Khufu, who hereby summoned Teta to his presence.
"I have come," he said, "a long way to invite thee, so
that thou mayest eat the food, and enjoy the good things
which the king bestows on those who follow him, and so
that he may conduct thee after a happy life to thy fathers
who rest in the grave."   The sage replied, "Welcome, Prince
Herutataf, welcome, O thou who lovest thy father.   Thy
father shall reward thee with gifts, and he shall promote
thee to the rank of the senior officials of his court.   Thy
Ka[2] shall fight successfully against thine enemy, thy soul
knows the ways of the Other World, and thou shalt arrive

---

[1] These were probably books and instruments which the magicians of the
day used in making astrological calculations, or in working magic.

[2] The "double," or the vital force.

at the door of those who are apparelled in . . . I salute thee, O Prince Herutataf."

Herutataf then held out his hands to the sage and helped him to rise from the bed, and he went with him to the river bank, Teta leaning on his arm. When they arrived there Teta asked for a boat wherein his children and his books might be placed, and the prince put at his disposal two boats, with crews complete ; Teta himself, however, was accommodated in the prince's boat and sailed with him. When they came to the palace, Prince Herutataf went into the presence of the king to announce their arrival, and said to him, " O king my lord, I have brought Teta " ; and His Majesty replied, " Bring him in quickly." Then the king went out into the large hall of his palace, and Teta was led into the presence. His Majesty said, " How is it, Teta, that I have never seen thee ? " And Teta answered, " Only the man who is summoned to the presence comes ; so soon as the king summoned me I came." His Majesty asked him, saying, " Is it indeed true, as is asserted, that thou knowest how to rejoin to its body the head which hath been cut off ? " Teta answered, " Most assuredly do I know how to do this, O king my lord." His Majesty said, " Let them bring in from the prison a prisoner, so that his death-sentence may be carried out." Then Teta said, " Let them not bring a man, O king my lord. Perhaps it may be ordered that the head shall be cut off some other living creature." So a goose was brought to him, and he cut off its head, and laid the body of the goose on the west side of the hall, and its head on the east side. Then Teta recited certain magical spells, and the goose stood up and waddled towards its head, and its head moved towards its body. When the body and the head came close together, the head leaped on to the body, and the goose stood up on its legs and cackled.

Then a goose of another kind called *khetâa* was brought to Teta, and he did with it as he had done with the other goose. His Majesty next caused an ox to be taken to Teta, and when he had cut off its head, and recited magical spells over the head and the body, the head rejoined itself to the body, and the ox stood up on its feet. A lion was next brought to Teta, and when he had recited spells over it, the lion went behind him, and followed him [like a dog], and the rope with which he had been tied up trailed on the ground behind the animal.

King Khufu then said to Teta, " Is it true what they say that thou knowest the numbers of the Apet chambers (?) of the shrine (?) of Thoth ? " Teta replied, " No. I do not know their number, O king my lord, but I do know the place where they are to be found." His Majesty asked, " Where is that ? " Teta replied, " There is a box made of flint in a house called Sapti in Heliopolis." The king asked, " Who will bring me this box ? " Teta replied, " Behold, O king my lord, I shall not bring the box to thee." His Majesty asked, " Who then shall bring it to me ? " Teta answered, " The oldest of the three children of Rut-tetet shall bring it unto thee." His Majesty said, " It is my will that thou shalt tell me who this Rut-tetet is." Teta answered, " This Rut-tetet is the wife of a priest of Rā of Sakhabu,[1] who is about to give birth to three children of Rā. He told her that these children should attain to the highest dignities in the whole country, and that the oldest of them should become high priest[2] of Heliopolis." On hearing these words the heart of the king became sad ; and Teta said, " Wherefore art thou so sad, O king my lord? Is it because of the three children ? I say unto thee, Verily thy son, verily his son, verily one of them." His Majesty asked, " When will these three children be born ? " Teta answered, " Rut-tetet will give them birth on the fifteenth day of the first month of Pert."[3] The king then made a remark the exact meaning of which it is difficult to follow, but from one part of it is clear that he expressed his determination to go and visit the temple of Rā of Sakhabu, which seems to have been situated on or near the great canal of

[1] A town which seems to have been situated in the second nome or " county " of Lower Egypt ; the Greeks called the nome Letopolites.

[2] His official title was " Ur-mau."

[3] The season Pert = November 15–March 15.

the Letopolite nome. In reply Teta declared that he would take care that the water in the canal should be 4 cubits (about 6 feet) deep, *i.e.* that the water should be deep enough for the royal barge to sail on the canal without difficulty. The king then returned to his palace and gave orders that Teta should have lodgings given him in the house of Prince Herutataf, that he should live with him, and that he should be provided with one thousand bread-cakes, one hundred pots of beer, one ox, and one hundred bundles of vegetables. And all that the king commanded concerning Teta was done.

THE STORY OF RUT-TETET AND THE THREE SONS OF RĀ

The last section of the Westcar Papyrus deals with the birth of the three sons of Rā, who have been mentioned above. When the day drew nigh in which the three sons were to be born, Rā, the Sun-god, ordered the four god-desses, Isis, Nephthys,[1] Meskhenet,[2] and Heqet,[3] and the god Khnemu,[4] to go and superintend the birth of the three children, so that when they grew up, and were exercising the functions of rule throughout all Egypt, they should build temples to them, and furnish the altars in them with offerings of meat and drink in abundance. Then the four goddesses changed themselves into the forms of dancing women, and went to the house wherein the lady Rut-tetet lay ill, and finding her husband, the priest of Rā, who was called Rāuser, outside, they clashed their cymbals together, and rattled their sistra, and tried to make him merry. When Rāuser objected to this and told them that his wife lay ill inside the house, they replied, " Let us see her, for we know

---

[1] Isis and Nephthys were the daughters of Keb and Nut, and sisters of Osiris and Set ; the former was the mother of Horus, and the latter of Anubis.

[2] A goddess who presided over the birth of children.

[3] A very ancient Frog-goddess, who was associated with generation and birth.

[4] A god who assisted at the creation of the world, and who fashioned the bodies of men and women.

how to help her " ; so he said to them and to Khnemu who
was with them, " Enter in," and they did so, and they went
to the room wherein Rut-tetet lay. Isis, Nephthys, and
Heqet assisted in bringing the three boys into the world.
Meskhenet prophesied for each of them sovereignty over
the land, and Khnemu bestowed health upon their bodies.
After the birth of the three boys, the four goddesses and
Khnemu went outside the house, and told Rāuser to rejoice
because his wife Rut-tetet had given him three children.
Rāuser said, " My Ladies, what can I do for you in return
for this ? " Having apparently nothing else to give them,
he begged them to have barley brought from his granary,
so that they might take it away as a gift to their own
granaries ; they agreed, and the god Khnemu brought the
barley. So the goddesses set out to go to the place whence
they had come.

When they had arrived there Isis said to her companions :
" How is it that we who went to Rut-tetet [by the command
of Rā] have worked no wonder for the children which we
could have announced to their father, who allowed us to
depart [without begging a boon] ? " So they made divine
crowns such as belonged to the Lord (*i.e.* King), life, strength,
health [be to him !], and they hid them in the barley. Then
they sent rain and storm through the heavens, and they
went back to the house of Rāuser, apparently carrying the
barley with them, and said to him, " Let the barley abide
in a sealed room until we dance our way back to the north."
So they put the barley in a sealed room. After Rut-tetet
had kept herself secluded for fourteen days, she said to one
of her handmaidens, " Is the house all ready ? " and the
handmaiden told her that it was provided with everything
except jars of barley drink, which had not been brought.
Rut-tetet then asked why they had not been brought, and
the handmaiden replied in words that seem to mean that
there was no barley in the house except that which belonged
to the dancing goddesses, and that that was in a chamber
which had been sealed with their seal. Rut-tetet then told
her to go and fetch some of the barley, for she was quite

certain that when her husband Rāuser returned he would make good what she took. Thereupon the handmaiden went to the chamber, and broke it open, and she heard in it loud cries and shouts, and the sounds of music and singing and dancing, and all the noises which men make in honour of the birth of a king, and she went back and told Rut-tetet what she had heard. Then Rut-tetet herself went through the room, and could not find the place where the noises came from, but when she laid her temple against a box, she perceived that the noises were inside it. She then took this box, which cannot have been of any great size, and put it in another box, which in turn she put in another box, which she sealed, and then wrapping this in a leather covering, she laid it in a chamber containing her jar of barley beer or barley wine, and sealed the door. When Rāuser returned from the fields, Rut-tetet related to him everything that had happened, and his heart was exceedingly glad, and he and his wife sat down and enjoyed themselves.

A few days after these events Rut-tetet had a quarrel with her handmaiden, and she slapped her well. The handmaiden was very angry, and in the presence of the household she said words to this effect : Dost thou dare to treat me in this way ? I who can destroy thee ? She has given birth to three kings, and I will go and tell the Majesty of King Khufu of this fact. The handmaiden thought that, if Khufu knew of the views of Rāuser and Rut-tetet about the future of their three sons, and the prophecies of the goddesses, he would kill the children and perhaps their parents also. With the object in her mind of telling the king the handmaiden went to her maternal uncle, whom she found weaving flax on the walk, and told him what had happened, and said she was going to tell the king about the three children. From her uncle she obtained neither support nor sympathy ; on the contrary, gathering together several strands of flax into a thick rope he gave her a good beating with the same. A little later the handmaiden went to the river or canal to fetch some water, and whilst she was filling her pot a crocodile seized her and carried her away and,

presumably, ate her. Then the uncle went to the house
of Rut-tetet to tell her what had happened, and he found
her sitting down, with her head bowed over her breast, and
exceedingly sad and miserable. He asked her, saying, " O
Lady, wherefore art thou so sad ? " And she told him
that the cause of her sorrow was the handmaiden, who had
been born in the house and had grown up in it, and who
had just left it, threatening that she would go and tell the
king about the birth of the three kings. The uncle of the
handmaiden nodded his head in a consoling manner, and
told Rut-tetet how she had come to him and informed him
what she was going to do, and how he had given her a good
beating with a rope of flax, and how she had gone to the
river to fetch some water, and how a crocodile had carried
her off.

There is reason to think that the three sons of Rut-tetet
became the three kings of the fifth dynasty who were known
by the names of Khāfrā, Menkaurā, and Userkaf. The
stories given above are valuable because they contain elements
of history, for it is now well known that the immediate suc-
cessors of the fourth dynasty, of which Khufu, Khāfrā, and
Menkaurā, the builders of the three great pyramids at
Gīzah, were the most important kings, were kings who
delighted to call themselves sons of Rā, and who spared
no effort to make the form of worship of the Sun-god that
was practised at Anu, or Heliopolis, universal in Egypt.
It is probable that the three magicians, Ubaaner, Tchatchamānkh, and Teta were historical personages, whose abilities
and skill in working magic appealed to the imagination of
the Egyptians under all dynasties, and caused their names
to be venerated to a remote posterity.

CHAPTER IV

THE BOOK OF THE DEAD

" Book of the Dead " is the name that is now generally given to the large collection of " Chapters," or compositions, both short and long, which the ancient Egyptians cut upon the walls of the corridors and chambers in pyramids and rock-hewn tombs, and cut or painted upon the insides and outsides of coffins and sarcophagi, and wrote upon papyri, etc., which were buried with the dead in their tombs. The first modern scholar to study these Chapters was the eminent Frenchman, J. François Champollion ; he rightly concluded that all of them were of a religious character, but he was wrong in calling the collection as a whole " Funerary Ritual." The name " Book of the Dead " is a translation of the title " Todtenbuch," given by Dr. R. Lepsius to his edition of a papyrus at Turin, containing a very long selection of the Chapters,[1] which he published in 1842. " Book of the Dead " is on the whole a very satisfactory general description of these Chapters, for they deal almost entirely with the dead, and they were written entirely for the dead. They have nothing to do with the worship of the gods by those who live on the earth, and such prayers and hymns as are incorporated with them were supposed to be said and sung by the dead for their own benefit. The author of the Chapters of the Book of the Dead was the god Thoth, whose greatness has already been described in Chapter I of this book. Thus they were considered to be of divine origin, and were held in the greatest reverence by the Egyptians at all periods of their long history. They do not all belong to the same period, for many of them allude to the dismemberment and

---

[1] The actual number of Chapters in this papyrus is 165.

burning of the dead, customs that, though common enough in very primitive times, were abandoned soon after royal dynasties became established in Egypt.

It is probable that in one form or another many of the Chapters were in existence in the predynastic period,[1] but no copies of such primitive versions, if they ever existed, have come down to us. One Egyptian tradition, which is at least as old as the early part of the eighteenth dynasty (1600 B.C.), states that Chapters XXXB and LXIV were "discovered" during the reign of Semti, a king of the first dynasty, and another tradition assigns their discovery to the reign of Menkaurā (the Mycerinus of classical writers), a king of the fourth dynasty. It is certain, however, that the Egyptians possessed a Book of the Dead which was used for kings and royal personages, at least, early under the first dynasty, and that, in a form more or less complete, it was in use down to the time of the coming of Christianity into Egypt. The tombs of the officials of the third and fourth dynasties prove that the Book of Opening the Mouth and the Liturgy of Funerary Offerings (see pp. 13–18) were in use when they were made, and this being so it follows as a matter of course that at this period the Egyptians believed in the resurrection of the dead and in their immortality, that the religion of Osiris was generally accepted, that the efficacy of funerary offerings was unquestioned by the religious, and that men died believing that those who were righteous on earth would be rewarded in heaven, and that the evil-doer would be punished. The Pyramid Texts also prove that a Book of the Dead divided into chapters was in existence when they were written, for they mention the "Chapter of those who come forth (*i.e.* appear in heaven)," and the "Chapter of those who rise up" (Pepi I, l. 463), and the "Chapter of the *betu* incense," and the "Chapter of the natron incense" (Pepi I, 469). Whether these Chapters formed parts of the Pyramid Texts, or whether both they and the Pyramid Texts belonged to the Book of the Dead cannot be said, but it seems clear that the four Chapters

[1] *i.e.* before Menes became king of both Upper and Lower Egypt.

mentioned above formed part of a work belonging to a Book of the Dead that was older than the Pyramid Texts. This Book of the Dead was no doubt based upon the beliefs of the followers of the religion of Osiris, which began in the Delta and spread southwards into Upper Egypt. Its doctrines must have differed in many important particulars from those of the worshippers of the Sun-god of Heliopolis, whose priests preached the existence of a heaven of a solar character, and taught their followers to believe in the Sun-god Rā, and not in Temu, the ancient native god of Heliopolis, and not in the divine man Osiris. The exposition of the Heliopolitan creed is found in the Pyramid Texts, which also contain the proofs that before the close of the sixth dynasty the cult of Osiris had vanquished the cult of Rā, and that the religion of Osiris had triumphed.

Certain of the Chapters of the Book of the Dead (*e.g.* XXXB and LXIV) were written in the city of Thoth, or Khemenu, others were written in Anu, or Heliopolis, and others in Busiris and other towns of the Delta. Of the Book of the Dead that was in use under the fifth and sixth dynasties we have no copies, but many Chapters of the Recension in use under the eleventh and twelfth dynasties are found written in cursive hieroglyphs upon wooden sarcophagi, many of which may be seen in the British Museum. With the beginning of the eighteenth dynasty the Book of the Dead enters a new phase of its existence, and it became the custom to write it on rolls of papyrus, which were laid with the dead in their coffins, instead of on the coffins themselves. As the greater number of such rolls have been found in the tombs of priests and others at Thebes, the Recension that was in use from the eighteenth to the twenty-first dynasty (1600–900 B.C.) is commonly called the THEBAN RECENSION. This Recension, in its earliest form, is usually written with black ink in vertical columns of hieroglyphs, which are separated by black lines ; the titles of the Chapters, the opening words of each section, and the Rubrics are written with red ink. About the middle of the eighteenth dynasty pictures painted in bright colours, " vignettes," were added to the Chapters ; these are very valuable, because they sometimes explain or give a clue to the meaning of parts of the texts that are obscure. Under the twentieth and twenty-first dynasties the writing of copies of the Book of the Dead in hieroglyphs went out of fashion, and copies written in the hieratic, or cursive, character took their place. These were ornamented with vignettes drawn in outline with black ink, and although the scribes who made them wrote certain sections in hieroglyphs, it is clear that they did not possess the skill of the great scribes who flourished between 1600 and 1050 B.C. The last Recension of the Book of the Dead known to us in a complete form is the SAÏTE RECENSION, which came into existence about 600 B.C., and continued in use from that time to the Roman Period. In the Ptolemaic and Roman Periods the priests composed several small works such as the " Book of Breathings " and the " Book of Traversing Eternity," which were based upon the Book of the Dead, and were supposed to contain in a highly condensed form all the texts that were necessary for salvation. At a still later period even more abbreviated texts came into use, and the Book of the Dead ended its existence in the form of a series of almost illegible scrawls traced upon scraps of papyrus only a few inches square.

Rolls of papyrus containing the Book of the Dead were placed : (1) In a niche in the wall of the mummy chamber ; (2) in the coffin by the side of the deceased, or laid between the thighs or just above the ankles ; (3) in hollow wooden figures of the god Osiris, or Ptah-Seker-Osiris, or in the hollow pedestals on which such figures stood.

The Egyptians believed that the souls of the dead on leaving this world had to traverse a vast and difficult region called the Tuat, which was inhabited by gods, devils, fiends, demons, good spirits, bad spirits, and the souls of the wicked, to say nothing of snakes, serpents, savage animals, and monsters, before they could reach the Elysian Fields, and appear in the presence of Osiris. The Tuat was like the African " bush," and had no roads through it. In primitive times the Egyptians thought that only those souls that were provided with spells, incantations, prayers, charms, words of power, and amulets could ever hope to reach the Kingdom of Osiris. The spells and incantations were needed for the bewitchment of hostile beings of every kind ; the prayers, charms, and words of power were necessary for making other kinds of beings that possessed great powers to help the soul on its journey, and to deliver it from foes ; and the amulets gave the soul that was equipped with them strength, power, will, and knowledge to employ successfully every means of assistance that presented itself.

The OBJECT OF THE BOOK OF THE DEAD was to provide the dead man with all these spells, prayers, amulets, &c., and to enable him to overcome all the dangers and difficulties of the Tuat, and to reach Sekhet Aaru and Sekhet Hetep (the Elysian Fields), and to take his place among the subjects of Osiris in the Land of Everlasting Life. As time went on the beliefs of the Egyptians changed considerably about many important matters, but they never attempted to alter the Chapters of the Book of the Dead so as to bring them, if we may use the expression, " up to date." The religion of the eighteenth dynasty was far higher in its spiritual character generally than that of the twelfth dynasty, but the Chapters that were used under the twelfth dynasty were used under the eighteenth, and even under the twenty-sixth dynasty. In religion the Egyptian forgot nothing and abandoned nothing ; what was good enough for his ancestors was good enough for him, and he was content to go into the next world relying for his salvation on the texts which he thought had procured their salvation. Thus the Book of the Dead as a whole is a work that reflects all the religious beliefs of the Egyptians from the time when they were half savages to the period of the final downfall of their power.

The Theban Recension of the Book of the Dead contains about one hundred and ninety Chapters, many of which have Rubrics stating what effects will be produced by their recital, and describing ceremonies that must be performed whilst they are being recited. It is impossible to describe the contents of all the Chapters in our limited space, but

in the following brief summary the most important are enume-
rated. Chap. 1 contains the formulas that were recited on
the day of the funeral. Chap. 151 gives a picture of the
arrangement of the mummy chamber, and the texts to be
said in it. Chap. 137 describes certain magical ceremonies
that were performed in the mummy chamber, and describes
the objects of magical power that were placed in niches in
the four walls. Chap. 125 gives a picture of the Judgment
Hall of Osiris, and supplies the declarations of innocence
that the deceased made before the Forty-two Judges.
Chaps. 144–147, 149, and 150 describe the Halls, Pylons,
and Divisions of the Kingdom of Osiris, and supply the name
of the gods who guard them, and the formulas to be said by
the deceased as he comes to each. Chap. 110 gives a picture
of the Elysian Fields and a text describing all the towns
and places in them. Chap. 5 is a spell by the use of which
the deceased avoided doing work, and Chap. 6 is another,
the recital of which made a figure to work for him. Chap. 15
contains hymns to the rising and to the setting sun, and a
Litany of Osiris ; and Chap. 183 is a hymn to Osiris. Chaps.
2, 3, 12, 13, and others enabled a man to move about freely
in the Other World ; Chap. 9 secured his free passage in and
out of the tomb ; and Chap. 11 overthrew his enemies.
Chap. 17 deals with important beliefs as to the origin of God
and the gods, and of the heavens and the earth, and states
the different opinions which Egyptian theologians held
about many divine and mythological beings. The reason
for including it in the Book of the Dead is not quite clear,
but that it was a most important Chapter is beyond all
doubt. Chaps. 21 and 22 restored his mouth to the deceased,
and Chap. 23 enabled him to open it. Chap. 24 supplied
him with words of power, and Chap. 25 restored to him his
memory. Chaps. 26–30B gave to the deceased his heart,
and supplied the spells that prevented the stealers of hearts
from carrying it off, or from injuring it in any way. Two
of these Chapters (29 and 30B) were cut upon amulets made
in the form of a human heart. Chaps. 31 and 32 are spells
for driving away crocodiles, and Chaps. 33–38, and 40

Vignette and Part of the XCIInd Chapter of the Book of the Dead.
(Ani and his Soul are leaving the Tomb)

From the Papyrus of Ani in the British Museum.

are spells against snakes and serpents. Chaps. 41 and 42 preserved a man from slaughter in the Other World, Chap. 43 enabled him to avoid decapitation, and Chap. 44 preserved him from the second death. Chaps. 45, 46, and 154 protected the body from rot or decay and worms in the tomb. Chap. 50 saved the deceased from the headsman in the Tuat, and Chap. 51 enabled him to avoid stumbling. Chaps. 38, 52–60, and 62 ensured for him a supply of air and water in the Tuat, and Chap. 63 protected him from drinking boiling water there. Chaps. 64–74 gave him the power to leave the tomb, to overthrow enemies, and to " come forth by day." Chaps. 76–89 enabled a man to transform himself into the Light-god, the primeval soul of God, the gods Ptah and Osiris, a golden hawk, a divine hawk, a lotus, a *benu* bird, a heron, a swallow, a serpent, a crocodile, and into any being or thing he pleased. Chap. 89 enabled the soul of the deceased to rejoin its body at pleasure, and Chaps. 91 and 92 secured the egress of his soul and spirit from the tomb. Chaps. 94–97 made the deceased an associate of Thoth, and Chaps. 98 and 99 secured for him the use of the magical boat, and the services of the celestial ferryman, who would ferry him across the river in the Tuat to the Island of Fire, in which Osiris lived. Chaps. 101 and 102 provided access for him to the Boat of Rā. Chaps. 108, 109, 112, and 116 enabled him to know the Souls (*i.e.* gods) of the East and West, and of the towns of Pe,[1] Nekhen,[2] Khemenu,[3] and Anu.[4] Chaps. 117–119 enabled him to find his way through Rastau, a part of the kingdom of Seker, the god of Death. Chap. 152 enabled him to build a house, and Chap. 132 gave him power to return to the earth and see it. Chap. 153 provided for his escape from the fiend who went about to take souls in a net. Chaps. 155–160, 166, and 167 formed the spells that were engraved on amulets, *i.e.* the Tet (male), the Tet (female), the Vulture, the Collar, the Sceptre, the Pillow, the Pectoral, &c., and gave to the deceased the power of Osiris and Isis and other gods, and restored to him

---

[1] *i.e.* Pe Tep, or Buto.   [2] Eileithyiaspolis.
[3] Hermopolis.   [4] Heliopolis.

his heart, and lifted up his head. Chap. 162 kept heat in the body until the day of the resurrection. Chaps. 175 and 176 gave the deceased everlasting life and enabled him to escape the second death. Chap. 177 raised up the dead body, and Chap. 178 raised up the spirit-soul. The remaining Chapters perfected the spirit-soul, and gave it celestial powers, and enabled it to enjoy intercourse with the gods as an equal, and enabled it to participate in all their occupations and pleasures. We may now give a few extracts that will give an idea of the contents of some of the most important passages.

The following is the opening hymn to Osiris in the Papyrus of Ani :

" Glory be to Osiris Un-Nefer, the great god who dwelleth in Abydos, king of eternity, lord of everlastingness, whose existence endureth for millions of years. Eldest son of the womb of Nut,[1] begotten by Keb,[2] the Erpāt,[3] lord of the crowns of the South and North, lord of the lofty white crown, prince of gods and men : he hath received the sceptre, and the whip, and the rank of his divine fathers. Let thy heart in Semt-Ament [4] be content, for thy son Horus is established on thy throne. Thou art crowned lord of Tatu [5] and ruler in Abydos.[6] Through thee the world flourisheth in triumph before the power of Nebertcher.[7] He leadeth on that which is and that which is not yet, in his name of ' Taherstanef.' He toweth along the earth by Maāt [8] in his name of ' Seker ' ; he is exceedingly mighty and most terrible in his name of ' Osiris ' ; he endureth for ever and ever in his name of ' Un-Nefer.' Homage to thee, O King of kings, Lord of lords, Prince of princes, who from the womb of Nut hast ruled the world and Akert.[9] Thy body is [like] bright and shining metal, thy head is of azure blue,

---

[1] The Sky-goddess.
[2] The Earth-god.
[3] The hereditary chief of the gods.
[4] The other world.
[5] The town of Busiris on the Delta.
[6] Abydos in Upper Egypt.
[7] The Lord to the uttermost limit, *i.e.* Almighty God.
[8] The goddess of physical and moral law, and the personification of the conscience.
[9] A name of the Other World.

Her-Heru, the first Priest-King, and Queen Netchemet reciting a Hymn to the Rising Sun.
The Apes represent the Spirits of the Dawn.

From a papyrus (about 1050 B.C.) in the British Museum.

and the brilliance of the turquoise encircleth thee. O thou god An of millions of years, whose body pervadeth all things, whose face is beautiful in Ta-Tchesert,[1] grant thou to the Ka of the Osiris the scribe Ani splendour in heaven, power upon earth, and triumph in the Other World. Grant that I may sail down to Tatu in the form of a living soul, and sail up to Abydos in the form of the Benu bird ; [2] that I may go in and come out without being stopped at the pylons of the Lords of the Other World. May there be given unto me bread-cakes in the house of coolness, and offerings of food in Anu (Heliopolis), and a homestead for ever in Sekhet Aru,[3] with wheat and barley therefor."

In another Hymn to Osiris, which is found in the Papyrus of Hunefer, we have the following : " The gods come unto thee, bowing low before thee, and they hold thee in fear. They withdraw and depart when they see thee endued with the terror of Rā, and the victory of Thy Majesty is over their hearts. Life is with thee, and offerings of meat and drink follow thee, and that which is thy due is offered before thy face. I have come unto thee holding in my hands truth, and my heart hath in it no cunning (or deceit). I offer unto thee that which is thy due, and I know that whereon thou livest. I have not committed any kind of sin in the land ; I have defrauded no man of what is his. I am Thoth, the perfect scribe, whose hands are pure. I am the lord of purity, the destroyer of evil, the scribe of truth ; what I abominate is sin."

Here is an address, followed by a short Litany, which forms a kind of introduction to Chapter 15 in the Papyrus of Ani :

" Praise be unto thee, O Osiris, lord of eternity, Un-Nefer, Heru-Khuti, whose forms are manifold, whose attributes are majesty, [thou who art] Ptah-Seker-Tem in Heliopolis, lord of the Sheta shrine, creator of Het-ka-Ptah (Memphis) and

---

[1] The Holy Land, *i.e.* the Kingdom of Osiris.
[2] A bird which has been identified with the phœnix. The soul of Rā was incarnate in it.
[3] A name of the realm of Osiris, or the Elysian Fields.

of the gods who dwell therein, thou Guide of the Other World, whom the gods praise when thou settest in the sky. Isis embraceth thee contentedly, and she driveth away the fiends from the mouth of thy paths. Thou turnest thy face towards Amentet,[1] and thou makest the earth to shine like refined copper. The dead rise up to look upon thee, they breathe the air, and they behold thy face when [thy] disk riseth on the horizon. Their hearts are at peace, inasmuch as they behold thee, O thou who art Eternity and Everlastingness.

LITANY

" 1. Homage to thee, O [Lord of] the Dekans [2] in Heliopolis and of the heavenly beings in Kherāha,[3] thou god Unti, who art the most glorious of the gods hidden in Heliopolis.

" *Grant thou unto me a path whereon I may pass in peace, for I am just and true ; I have not spoken lies wittingly, nor have I done aught with deceit.*[4]

" 2. Homage to thee, O An [5] in Antes, Heru-Khuti,[6] with long strides dost thou stride over heaven, O Heru-Khuti.

" 3. Homage to thee, O Everlasting Soul, who dwellest in Tatu (Busiris), Un-Nefer,[7] son of Nut, who art the Lord of Akert.

" 4. Homage to thee in thy rule over Tatu. The Urrt Crown is fixed upon thy head. Thou art One, thou createst thy protection, thou dwellest in peace in Tatu.

" 5. Homage to thee, O Lord of the Acacia. The Seker Boat [8] is on its sledge ; thou turnest back the Fiend, the worker of evil ; thou makest the Eye of the Sun-god to rest upon its throne.

" 6. Homage to thee, mighty one in thine hour, Prince

---

[1] The "hidden" land, the West, the Other World.
[2] A group of thirty-six Star-gods.
[3] A town that stood on the site of Old Cairo.
[4] This response was to be repeated after each petition.
[5] A Light-god.   [6] Harmakhis of the Greeks.   [7] A form of Osiris.
[8] The Henu Boat of Seker was drawn round the sanctuary of Seker each morning.

great and mighty, dweller in Anrutef,[1] lord of eternity, creator of everlastingness. Thou art the lord of Hensu. [2]

" 7. Homage to thee, O thou who restest upon Truth. Thou art the Lord of Abydos; thy body is joined to Ta-Tchesert. Thou art he to whom fraud and deceit are abominable.

" 8. Homage to thee, O dweller in thy boat. Thou leadest the Nile from his source, the light shineth upon thy body ; thou art the dweller in Nekhen.[3]

" 9. Homage to thee, O Creator of the gods, King of the South, King of the North, Osiris, Conqueror, Governor of the world in thy gracious seasons ! Thou art the Lord of the heaven of Egypt (Atebui)."

The following passage illustrates the general character of a funerary hymn to Rā : " Homage to thee, O thou who art in the form of Khepera, Khepera the creator of the gods. Thou risest, thou shinest, thou illuminest thy mother [the sky]. Thou art crowned King of the Gods. Mother Nut [4] welcometh thee with bowings. The Land of Sunset (Manu) receiveth thee with satisfaction, and the goddess Maāt [5] embraceth thee at morn and at eve. Hail, ye gods of the Temple of the Soul (*i.e.* heaven), who weigh heaven and earth in a balance, who provide celestial food ! And hail, Tatunen,[6] One, Creator of man, Maker of the gods of the south and of the north, of the west and of the east ! Come ye and acclaim Rā, the Lord of heaven, the Prince—life, health, strength be to him !—the Creator of the gods, and adore ye him in his beautiful form as he riseth in his Morning Boat (Āntchet).

" Those who dwell in the heights and those who dwell in the depths worship thee. Thoth and the goddess Maāt have laid down thy course for thee daily for ever. Thine Enemy the Serpent hath been cast into the fire, the fiend hath fallen down into it headlong. His arms have been bound in chains, and Rā hath hacked off his legs ; the

---

[1] A district of Hensu.
[2] Herakleopolis in Upper Egypt.
[3] Eileithyiaspolis in Upper Egypt.
[4] The Sky-goddess.
[5] Goddess of Law.
[6] An ancient Earth-god,

Mesu Betshet [1] shall never more rise up. The Temple of the Aged God [in Anu] keepeth festival, and the sound of those who rejoice is in the Great House. The gods shout for joy when they see Rā rising, and when his beams are filling the world with light. The Majesty of the Holy God goeth forth and advanceth even unto the Land of Sunset (Manu). He maketh bright the earth at his birth daily, he journeyeth to the place where he was yesterday. O be thou at peace with me, and let me behold thy beauties! Let me appear on the earth. Let me smite [the Eater of] the Ass. [2] Let me crush the Serpent Seba. [3] Let me destroy Āapep [4] when he is most strong. Let me see the Abtu Fish in its season and the Ant Fish [5] in its lake. Let me see Horus steering thy boat, with Thoth and Maāt standing one on each side of him. Let me have hold of the bows of [thy] Evening Boat and the stern of thy Morning Boat. [6] Grant thou unto the Ka of me, the Osiris the scribe Ani, to behold the disk of the Sun, and to see the Moon-god regularly and daily. Let my soul come forth and walk hither and thither and whithersoever it pleaseth. Let my name be read from the list of those who are to receive offerings, and may offerings be set before me, even as they are set before the Followers of Horus. Let there be prepared for me a seat in the Boat of Rā on the day when the god goeth forth. Let me be received into the presence of Osiris, in the Land where Truth is spoken."

The prayers of the Book of the Dead consist usually of a string of petitions for sepulchral offerings to be offered in the tombs of the petitioners, and the fundamental idea under-

[1] The associates of Set, the god of Evil.

[2] The Ass was a form of the Sun-god, and its eater was a mythological monster-serpent.

[3] Another mythological serpent.

[4] The serpent that tried to swallow the sun each morning, but the Sun-god cast a spell on it and rendered it powerless.

[5] The Abtu and the Ant were two fishes that swam before the boat of the sun to warn the god of danger.

[6] *i.e.* Ani wishes to be sure of a seat in both boats.

lying them is that by their transmutation, which was effected by the words of the priests, the spirits of the offerings became available as the food of the dead. Many prayers contain requests for the things that tend to the comfort and general well-being of the dead, but here and there we find a prayer for forgiveness of sins committed in the body. The best example of such is the prayer that forms Chapter CXXVI. It reads : " Hail, ye four Ape-gods who sit in the bows of the Boat of Rā, who convey truth to Nebertchet, who sit in judgment on my weakness and on my strength, who make the gods to rest contented by means of the flame of your mouths, who offer holy offerings to the gods, and sepulchral meals to the spirit-souls, who live upon truth, who feed upon truth of heart, who are without deceit and fraud, and to whom wickedness is an abomination, do ye away with my evil deeds, and put ye away my sin, which deserved stripes upon earth, and destroy ye every evil thing whatsoever that clingeth to me, and let there be no bar whatsoever on my part towards you. Grant ye that I may make my way through the Amhet [1] chamber, let me enter into Rastau,[2] and let me pass through the secret places of Amentet. Grant that cakes, and ale, and sweetmeats may be given to me as they are given to the spirit-souls, and grant that I may enter in and come forth from Rastau." The four Ape-gods reply : " Come, for we have done away with thy wickedness, and we have put away thy sin, which deserved stripes, which thou didst commit upon earth, and we have destroyed all the evil that clung to thee. Enter, therefore, into Rastau, and pass in through the secret gates of Amentet, and cakes, and ale, and sweetmeats shall be given unto thee, and thou shalt go in and come out at thy desire, even as do those whose spirit-souls are praised [by the god], and [thy name] shall be proclaimed each day in the horizon."

Another prayer of special interest is that which forms Chapter XXXB. This is put into the mouth of the deceased

---

[1] A chamber in the kingdom of Seker in which the dead were examined.
[2] The corridors in the kingdom of Seker.

when he is standing in the Hall of Judgment watching the weighing of his heart in the Great Scales by Anubis and Thoth, in the presence of the Great Company of the gods and Osiris. He says : " My heart, my mother. My heart, my mother. My heart whereby I came into being. Let none stand up to oppose me at my judgment. May there be no opposition to me in the presence of the Tchatchau.[1] Mayest thou not be separated from me in the presence of the Keeper of the Balance. Thou art my Ka (*i.e.* Double, or vital power), that dwelleth in my body ; the god Khnemu who knitteth together and strengtheneth my limbs. Mayest thou come forth into the place of happiness whither we go. May the Shenit officers who decide the destinies of the lives of men not cause my name to stink [before Osiris]. Let it (*i.e.* the weighing) be satisfactory unto us, and let there be joy of heart to us at the weighing of words (*i.e.* the Great Judgment). Let not that which is false be uttered against me before the Great God, the Lord of Amentet (*i.e.* Osiris). Verily thou shalt be great when thou risest up [having been declared] a speaker of the truth."

In many papyri this prayer is followed by a Rubric, which orders that it is to be said over a green stone scarab set in a band of *tchamu* metal (*i.e.* silver-gold), which is to be hung by a ring from the neck of the deceased. Some Rubrics order it to be placed in the breast of a mummy, where it is to take the place of the heart, and say that it will " open the mouth " of the deceased. A tradition which is as old as the twelfth dynasty says that the Chapter was discovered in the town of Khemenu (Hermopolis Magna) by Herutataf, the son of Khufu, in the reign of Menkaurā, a king of the fourth dynasty. It was cut in hieroglyphs, inlaid with lapis-lazuli on a block of alabaster, which was set under the feet of Thoth, and was therefore believed to be a most powerful prayer. We know that this prayer was recited by the Egyptians in the Ptolemaic Period, and thus it is clear that it was in common use for a period of nearly four thousand years. It may well be the oldest prayer in the world.

---

[1] The chief officers of Osiris, the divine Taskmasters,

Under the Middle and New Empires this prayer was cut upon hard green stone scarabs, but the versions of it found on scarabs are often incomplete and full of mistakes. It is quite clear that the prayer was turned into a spell, and that it was used merely as a " word of power," and that the hard stone scarabs were regarded merely as amulets. On many of them spaces are found that have been left blank to receive the names of those with whom they were to be buried ; this proves that such scarabs once formed part of some undertaker's stock-in-trade, and that they were kept ready for those who were obliged to buy " heart scarabs " in a hurry.

Another remarkable composition in the Book of the Dead is the first part of Chapter CXXV, which well illustrates the lofty moral conceptions of the Egyptians of the eighteenth dynasty. The deceased is supposed to be standing in the " Usekht Maāti," or Hall of the Two Maāti goddesses, one for Upper Egypt and one for Lower Egypt, wherein Osiris and his Forty-two Judges judge the souls of the dead. Before judgment is given the deceased is allowed to make a declaration, which in form closely resembles that made in many parts of Africa at the present day by a man who is condemned to undergo the ordeal of drinking " red water," and in it he states that he has not committed offences against the moral and religious laws of his country. He says :

" Homage to thee, O Great God, thou Lord of Maāti. I have come to thee, O my Lord, and I have brought myself hither that I may behold thy beauties. I know thee. I know thy name. I know the names of the Forty-two [1] gods who live with thee in this Hall of Truth, who keep ward over sinners, and who feed upon their blood on the day when the lives of men are taken into account in the presence of Un-Nefer (*i.e.* the Good Being or Osiris). . . . Verily, I have come unto thee, I have brought truth unto thee. I have destroyed wickedness for thee. I have not done evil to men.

[1] The Forty-two gods represent the forty-two nomes, or counties, into which Egypt was divided.

I have not oppressed (or wronged) my family. I have not done wrong instead of right. I have not been a friend of worthless men. I have not wrought evil. I have not tried to make myself over-righteous. I have not put forward my name for exalted positions. I have not entreated servants evilly. I have not defrauded the man who was in trouble. I have not done what is hateful (or taboo) to the gods. I have not caused a servant to be ill-treated by his master. I have not caused pain [to any man]. I have not permitted any man to go hungry. I have made none to weep. I have not committed murder. I have not ordered any man to commit murder for me. I have inflicted pain on no man. I have not robbed the temples of their offerings. I have not stolen the cakes of the gods. I have not carried off the cakes offered to the spirits. I have not committed fornication. I have not committed acts of impurity in the holy places of the god of my town. I have not diminished the bushel. I have not added to or filched away land. I have not encroached upon the fields [of my neighbours]. I have not added to the weights of the scales. I have not falsified the pointer of the scales. I have not taken milk from the mouths of children. I have not driven away the cattle that were upon their pastures. I have not snared the feathered fowl in the preserves of the gods. I have not caught fish [with bait made of] fish of their kind. I have not stopped water at the time [when it should flow]. I have not breached a canal of running water. I have not extinguished a fire when it should burn. I have not violated the times [of offering] chosen meat-offerings. I have not driven off the cattle from the property of the gods. I have not repulsed the god in his manifestations. I am pure. I am pure. I am pure. I am pure."

In the second part of the Chapter the deceased repeats many of the above declarations of his innocence, but with each declaration the name of one of the Forty-two Judges is coupled. Thus we have :

1. " Hail, thou of the long strides, who comest forth from Heliopolis, I have not committed sin.

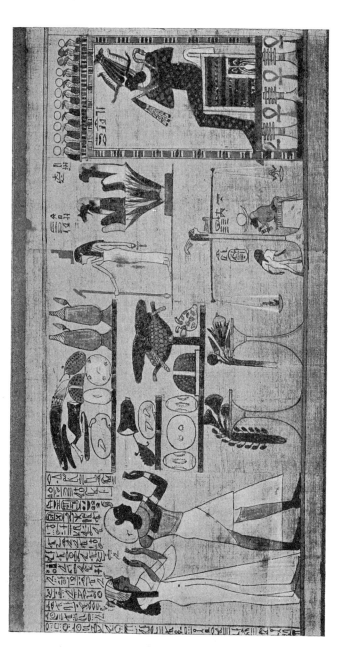

Her-Heru and Queen Netchemet standing in the Hall of Osiris and praying to the God, whilst the Heart of the Queen is being weighed in the Balance.

From a papyrus (about 1050 B.C.) *in the British Museum.*

2. " Hail, thou who art embraced by flame, who comest forth from Kherāha, I have not robbed with violence.

3. " Hail, Nose, who comest forth from Hermopolis, I have not done violence [to any man].

4. " Hail, Eater of shadows, who comest forth from the Qerti, I have not thieved.

5. " Hail, Stinking Face, who comest forth from Rastau, I have not slain man or woman.

9. " Hail, Crusher of bones, who comest forth from Hensu, I have not lied."

Nothing is known of the greater number of these Forty-two gods, but it is probable that they were local gods or spirits, each one representing a nome, whose names were added to the declarations with the view of making the Forty-two Judges represent all Egypt.

In the third part of the Chapter we find that the religious ideas expressed by the deceased have a far more personal character than those of the first and second parts. Thus, having declared his innocence of the forty-two sins or offences, " the heart which is righteous and sinless " says :

" Homage to you, O ye gods who dwell in your Hall of Maāti ! I know you and I know your names. Let me not fall under your knives, and bring ye not before the god whom ye follow my wickedness, and let not evil come upon me through you. Declare ye me innocent in the presence of Nebertcher,[1] because I have done that which is right in Tamera (Egypt), neither blaspheming God, nor imputing evil (?) to the king in his day. Homage to you, O ye gods, who live in your Hall of Maāti, who have no taint of sin in you, who live upon truth, who feed upon truth before Horus, the dweller in his disk. Deliver me from Baba, who liveth upon the entrails of the mighty ones, on the day of the Great Judgment. Let me come to you, for I have not committed offences [against you] ; I have not done evil, I have not borne false witness ; therefore let nothing [evil] be done unto me. I live upon truth. I feed upon truth. I have performed the commandments of men, and the things which

---

[1] The Lord to the uttermost limit, *i.e.* Almighty God.

make the gods contented. I have made the god to be at peace [with me by doing] that which is his will. I have given bread to the hungry man, and water to the thirsty man, and apparel to the naked man, and a ferry boat to him that had none. I have made offerings to the gods, and given funerary meals to the spirits. Therefore be ye my deliverers, be ye my protectors ; make ye no accusations against me in the presence [of the Great God]. I am clean of mouth and clean of hands ; therefore let be said unto me by those who shall see me : ' Come in peace, come in peace ' (*i.e.* Welcome ! Welcome !). . . . I have testified before Herfhaf,[1] and he hath approved me. I have seen the things over which the Persea tree spreadeth [its branches] in Rastau. I offer up my prayers to the gods, and I know their persons. I have come and have advanced to declare the truth and to set up the Balance [2] on its stand in Aukert." [3]

Then addressing the god Osiris the deceased says : " Hail, thou who art exalted upon thy standard, thou lord of the Atef crown, whose name is ' Lord of the Winds,' deliver me from thine envoys who inflict evils, who do harm, whose faces are uncovered, for I have done the right for the Lord of Truth. I have purified myself and my fore parts with holy water, and my hinder parts with the things that make clean, and my inward parts have been [immersed] in the Lake of Truth. There is not one member of mine wherein truth is lacking. I purified myself in the Pool of the South. I rested in the northern town in the Field of the Grass-hoppers, wherein the sailors of Rā bathe at the second hour of the night and at the third hour of the day." One would think that the moral worth of the deceased was such that he might then pass without delay into the most holy part of the Hall of Truth where Osiris was enthroned. But this is not the case, for before he went further he was obliged

---

[1] The celestial ferryman who ferried the souls of the righteous to the Island of Osiris. None but the righteous could enter his boat, and none but the righteous was allowed to land on the Island of Osiris.

[2] The balance in which the heart was weighed.

[3] A name of a part of the Other World near Heliopolis.

to repeat the magical names of various parts of the Hall of Truth ; thus we find that the priest thrust his magic into the most sacred of texts. At length Thoth, the great Recorder of Egypt, being satisfied as to the good faith and veracity of the deceased, came to him and asked why he had come to the Hall of Truth, and the deceased replied that he had come in order to be " mentioned " to the god. Thoth then asked him, " Who is he whose heaven is fire, whose walls are serpents, and the floor of whose house is a stream of water ? " The deceased replied, " Osiris " ; and he was then bidden to advance so that he might be introduced to Osiris. As a reward for his righteous life sacred food, which proceeded from the Eye of Rā, was allotted to him, and, living on the food of the god, he became a counterpart of the god.

From first to last the Book of the Dead is filled with spells and prayers for the preservation of the mummy and for everlasting life. As instances of these the following passages are quoted from Chapters 154 and 175. " Homage to thee, O my divine father Osiris, thou livest with thy members. Thou didst not decay. Thou didst not turn into worms. Thou didst not waste away. Thou didst not suffer corruption. Thou didst not putrefy. I am the god Khepera, and my members shall have an everlasting existence. I shall not decay. I shall not rot. I shall not putrefy. I shall not turn into worms. I shall not see corruption before the eye of the god Shu. I shall have my being, I shall have my being. I shall live, I shall live. I shall flourish, I shall flourish. I shall wake up in peace. I shall not putrefy. My inward parts shall not perish. I shall not suffer injury. Mine eye shall not decay. The form of my visage shall not disappear. Mine ear shall not become deaf. My head shall not be separated from my neck. My tongue shall not be carried away. My hair shall not be cut off. Mine eyebrows shall not be shaved off. No baleful injury shall come upon me. My body shall be established, and it shall neither crumble away nor be destroyed on this earth." The passage that refers to everlasting life occurs in Chapter 175, wherein

the scribe Ani is made to converse with Thoth and Temu
in the Tuat, or Other World.   Ani, who is supposed to have
recently arrived there, says : " What manner of country is
this to which I have come ?   There is no water in it.   There
is no air.   It is depth unfathomable, it is black as the
blackest night, and men wander helplessly therein.   In it a
man may not live in quietness of heart ; nor may the
affections be gratified therein." After a short address
to Osiris, the deceased asks the god, " How long shall
I live ? "   And the god says, " It is decreed that thou shalt
live for millions of millions of years, a life of millions of
years."

As a specimen of a spell that was used in connection
with an amulet may be quoted Chapter 156.   The amulet
was the *tet*, which represented a portion of the body of Isis.
The spell reads : " The blood of Isis, the power of Isis, the
words of power of Isis shall be strong to protect this mighty
one (*i.e.* the mummy), and to guard him from him that would
do unto him anything which he abominateth (or, is taboo to
him)." The object of the spell is explained in the Rubric,
which reads : " [This spell] shall be said over a *tet* made of
carnelian, which hath been steeped in water of *ankham*
flowers, and set in a frame of sycamore wood, and placed
on the neck of the deceased on the day of the funeral.   If
these things be done for him the powers of Isis shall protect
his body, and Horus, the son of Isis, shall rejoice in him when
he seeth him.   And there shall be no places hidden from him
as he journeyeth.   And one hand of his shall be towards
heaven and the other towards earth, regularly and continu-
ally.   Thou shalt not let any person who is with thee see it
[a few words broken away]." Of the spells written in the
Book of the Dead to make crocodiles, serpents, and other
reptiles powerless, the following are specimens : " Away
with thee ! Retreat ! Get back, O thou accursed Crocodile
Sui.   Thou shalt not come nigh me, for I have life through
the words of power that are in me.   If I utter thy name to
the Great God he will make thee to come before the two
divine messengers Betti and Herkemmaāt.   Heaven ruleth

its seasons, and the spell hath power over what it mastereth, and my mouth ruleth the spell that is inside it. My teeth which bite are like flint knives, and my teeth which grind are like unto those of the Wolf-god. O thou who sittest spellbound with thine eyes fixed through my spell, thou shalt not carry off my spell, thou Crocodile that livest on spells " (Chap. XXXI).

" Get thee back, thou Crocodile of the West, that livest on the never-resting stars. That which is thy taboo is in me. I have eaten the brow (or, skull) of Osiris. I am set.

" Get thee back, thou Crocodile of the West. The serpent Nāu is inside me. I will set it on thee, thy flame shall not approach me.

" Get thee back, thou Crocodile of the East, that feedest upon the eaters of filth. That which is thy taboo is in me. I advance. I am Osiris.

" Get thee back, thou Crocodile of the East. The serpent Nāu is inside me. I will set it on thee ; thy flame shall not approach me.

" Get thee back, thou Crocodile of the South, that feedest upon waste, garbage, and filth. That which is thy taboo is in me. . . . I am Sept.[1]

" Get thee back, thou Crocodile of the South. I will fetter thee. My charm is among the reeds (?). I will not yield unto thee.

" Get thee back, thou Crocodile of the North, that feedest upon what is left by the hours. That which is thy taboo is in me. The emissions shall [not] fall upon my head. I am Tem.[2]

" Get thee back, thou Crocodile of the North, for the Scorpion-goddess [3] is inside me, unborn (?). I am Uatch-Merti (?).[4]

---

[1] A god of the Eastern Delta and a local form of the Sun-god early in the day.

[2] The primeval god, a form of Pautti, the oldest Egyptian god.

[3] She was called "Serqet."

[4] A green-eyed serpent-god, or goddess, equipped with great power to destroy.

" Created things are in the hollow of my hand, and the
things that are not yet made are inside me.   I am clothed
in and supplied with thy spells, O Rā, which are above me
and beneath me. . . . I am Rā, the self-protected, no evil
thing whatsoever shall overthrow me " (Chap. XXXII).

CHAPTER V

FROM what has been said in the preceding chapter it will be clear that only wealthy people could afford to bury copies of the great Book of the Dead with their deceased relatives. Whether the chapters that formed it were written on coffins or on papyrus the cost of copying the work by a competent scribe must have been relatively very great. Towards the close of the twenty-sixth dynasty a feeling spread among the Egyptians that only certain parts of the Book of the Dead were essential for the resurrection of the body and for the salvation of the soul, and men began to bury with their dead copies of the most important chapters of it in a very much abridged form. A little later the scribes produced a number of works, in which they included only such portions of the most important chapters as were considered necessary to effect the resurrection of the body. In other words, they rejected all the old magical elements in the Book of the Dead, and preserved only the texts and formulæ that appertained to the cult of Osiris, the first man who had risen from the dead. One of the oldest of these later substitutes for the Book of the Dead is the *Shai en Sensen,* or "Book of Breathings." Several copies of this work are extant in the funerary papyri, and the following sections, translated from a papyrus in the British Museum, will give an idea of the character of the Book :

" Hail, Osiris [1] Kersher, son of Tashenatit ! Thou art pure, thy heart is pure. Thy fore parts are pure, thy hind parts are cleansed ; thy interior is cleansed with incense and

---

[1] The deceased is always supposed to be identified with Osiris.

natron, and no member of thine hath any defect in it whatsoever. Kersher is washed in the waters of the Field of
Offerings, that lieth to the north of the Field of the Grass-
hoppers. The goddesses Uatchet and Nekhebet purify thee at
the eighth hour of the night and at the eighth hour of the day.
Come then, enter the Hall of Truth, for thou art free from
all offence and from every defect, and ' Stone of Truth ' is
thy name. Thou enterest the Tuat (Other World) as one
exceedingly pure. Thou art purified by the Goddesses of
Truth in the Great Hall. Holy water hath been poured
over thee in the Hall of Keb (*i.e.* the earth), and thy body
hath been made pure in the Hall of Shu (heaven). Thou
lookest upon Rā when he setteth in the form of Tem at
eventide. Amen is nigh unto thee and giveth thee air, and
Ptah likewise, who fashioned thy members for thee ; thou
enterest the horizon with Rā. Thy soul is received in the
Neshem Boat of Osiris, thy soul is made divine in the House
of Keb, and thou art made to be triumphant for ever and
ever."

" Hail, Osiris Kersher ! Thy name flourisheth, thy earthly
body is stablished, thy spirit body germinateth, and thou
art not repulsed either in heaven or on earth. Thy face
shineth before Rā, thy soul liveth before Amen, and thy
earthly body is renewed before Osiris. Thou breathest the
breath of life for ever and ever. Thy soul maketh offerings
unto thee in the course of each day. . . . Thy flesh is collected on thy bones, and thy form is even as it was upon
earth. Thou takest drink into thy body, thou eatest with
thy mouth, and thou receivest thy rations in company with
the souls of the gods. Anubis protecteth thee ; he is thy
protector, and thou art not turned away from the Gates of
the Tuat. Thoth, the most mighty god, the Lord of Khemenu (Hermopolis), cometh to thee, and he writeth the
' Book of Breathings ' with his own fingers. Then doth thy
soul breathe for ever and ever, and thy form is renewed with
life upon earth ; thou art made divine with the souls of the
gods, thy heart is the heart of Rā, and thy limbs are the
limbs of the great god. Amen is nigh unto thee to make thee

to live again. Upuat openeth a prosperous road for thee. Thou seest with thine eyes, thou hearest with thine ears, thou speakest with thy mouth, thou walkest with thy legs. Thy soul hath been made divine in the Tuat, so that it may change itself into any form it pleaseth. Thou canst snuff at will the odours of the holy Acacia of Anu (An, or Heliopolis). Thou wakest each day and seest the light of Rā ; thou appearest upon the earth each day, and the ' Book of Breathings ' of Thoth is thy protection, for through it dost thou draw thy breath each day, and through it do thine eyes behold the beams of the Sun-god Aten. The Goddess of Truth vindicateth thee before Osiris, and her writings are upon thy tongue. Rā vivifieth thy soul, the Soul of Shu is in thy nostrils. Thou art even as Osiris, and ' Osiris Khenti Amenti ' is thy name. Thy body liveth in Tatu (Busiris), and thy soul liveth in heaven. . . . Thy odour is that of the holy gods in Amentet, and thy name is magnified like the names of the Spirits of heaven. Thy soul liveth through the ' Book of Breathings,' and it is rejoined to thy body by the ' Book of Breathings.' These fine extracts are followed in the British Museum papyrus by the praises of Kersher by the gods, a prayer of Kersher himself for offerings, and an extract from the so-called Negative Confession, which has been already described. The work is closed by an address to the gods, in which it is said that Kersher is sinless, that he feeds and lives upon Truth, that his deeds have satisfied the hearts of the gods, and that he has fed the hungry and given water to the thirsty and clothes to the naked.[1]

Another late work of considerable interest is the " Book of Traversing Eternity," the fullest known form of which is found on a papyrus at Vienna. This work describes how the soul of the deceased, when armed with the power which the Book of Traversing Eternity will give it, shall be able to

---

[1] A papyrus at Florence contains a copy of Part II. of The Book of Breathings. The fundamental ideas are the same as those in Part I., but the forms in which they are expressed are different. The deceased is made to address several gods by name, and to declare that he himself is those gods. " I am Rā, I am Atem, I am Osiris, I am Horus, I am Thoth," &c.

travel from one end of Egypt to the other, and to visit all the holy places, and to assist at the festivals, and to enjoy communion not only with the gods and spirits who assemble there, but also with its kinsfolk and acquaintances whom it left behind alive on the earth. The object of the book was to secure for the deceased the resurrection of his body ; it opens with the following words : " Thy soul liveth in heaven in the presence of Rā. Thy Ka hath acquired the divine nature of the gods. Thy body remaineth in the deep house (*i.e.* tomb) in the presence of Osiris. Thy spirit-body becometh glorious among the living. Thy descendants flourish upon the earth, in the presence of Keb, upon thy seat among the living, and thy name is stablished by the utterance of those who have their being through the ' Book of Traversing Eternity.' Thou comest forth by day, thou art joined to the Sun-god Aten." The text goes on to state that the deceased breathes, speaks, eats, drinks, sees, hears, and walks, and that all the organs of his body are in their proper places, and that each is performing its proper functions. He floats in the air, hovers in the shadow, rises in the sky, follows the gods, travels with the stars, dekans, and planets, and moves about by night and by day on earth and in heaven at will.

Of the works that were originally composed for recitation on the days of the festivals of Osiris, and were specially connected with the cult of this god, three, which became very popular in the Graeco-Roman period, may be mentioned. These are : (1) The Lamentations of Isis and Nephthys ; (2) The Festival Songs of Isis and Nephthys ; (3) The Book of making splendid the Spirit of Osiris. The first of these works was recited on the twenty-fifth day of the fourth month of the season Akhet (October–November) by two " fair women," who personified Isis and Nephthys. One of these had the name of Isis on her shoulder, and the other the name of Nephthys, and each held a vessel of water in her right hand, and a " Memphis cake of bread " in her left. The object of the recital was to commemorate the resurrection of Osiris, and if the book were recited on behalf of any deceased person it would make his spirit to be glorious, and stablish his body, and cause his Ka to rejoice, and give breath to his nostrils and air to his throat. The two " fair women " sang the sections alternately in the presence of the Kher-heb and Setem priests. The two first sections, as they are found on a papyrus in Berlin, read thus:—Isis SAITH: "Come to thy house, come to thy house, O An, come to thy house. Thine enemy [Set] hath perished. O beautiful youth, come to thy house. Look thou upon me. I am the sister who loveth thee, go not far from me. O Beautiful Boy, come to thy house, straightway, straightway. I cannot see thee, and my heart weepeth for thee ; my eyes follow thee about. I am following thee about so that I may see thee. Lo, I wait to see thee, I wait to see thee ; behold, Prince, I wait to see thee. It is good to see thee, it is good to see thee ; O An, it is good to see thee. Come to thy beloved one, come to thy beloved one, O Un-Nefer, whose word is truth. Come to thy wife, O thou whose heart is still. Come to the lady of thy house ; I am thy sister from thy mother's [womb]. Go not thou far from me. The faces of gods and men are turned towards thee, they all weep for thee together. As soon as I saw thee I cried out to thee, weeping with a loud voice which pierced the heavens, and thou didst not hear my voice. I am thy sister who loved thee upon earth ; none other loved thee more than [thy] sister, thy sister."

NEPHTHYS SAITH: " O Beautiful Prince, come to thy house. Let thy heart rejoice and be glad, for thine enemies have ceased to be. Thy two Sisters are nigh unto thee ; they guard thy bier, they address thee with words [full of] tears as thou liest prone on thy bier. Look thou at the young women ; speak to us, O our Sovereign Lord. Destroy thou all the misery that is in our hearts ; the chiefs among gods and men look upon thee. Turn thou towards us thy face, O our Sovereign Lord. At the sight of thy face life cometh to our faces ; turn not thou thy face from us. The joy of our heart is in the sight of thee. O Beautiful Sovereign, our hearts would see thee. I am thy sister Nephthys who loveth thee. The fiend Seba hath fallen, he hath not being. I am

with thee, and I act as the protectress of thy members for
ever and ever."

The second work, the " Festival Songs of Isis and Nephthys," was sung during the great festival of Osiris, which
took place in the fourth month of the Season of Akhet and
lasted five days (from the twenty-second to the twenty-sixth
day). It was sung by two virgins who wore fillets of sheep's
wool on their heads, and held tambourines in their hands ;
one was called Isis and the other Nephthys. According to
the rubrical directions given in the British Museum papyrus,
the sections were sung by both women together. The following passage will illustrate the contents of the work :

" Come, come, run to me, O strong heart ! Let me see
thy divine face, for I do not see thee, and make thou clear
the path that we may see thee as we see Rā in heaven, when
the heavens unite with the earth, and cause darkness to fall
upon the earth each day. My heart burneth as with fire at
thy escape from the Fiend, even as my heart burneth with
fire when thou turnest thy side to me ; O that thou wouldst
never remove it from me ! O thou who unitest the Two
Domains (i.e. Egypt, North and South), and who turnest
back those who are on the roads, I seek to see thee because
of my love for thee. . . . Thou fliest like a living being, O
Everlasting King; thou hast destroyed the fiend Anrekh.
Thou art the King of the South and of the North, and thou
goest forth from Tatchesert. May there never be a moment
in thy life when I do not fill thy heart, O my divine brother,
my lord who goest forth from Aqert. . . . My arms are raised
to protect thee, O thou whom I love. I love thee, O Husband, Brother, lord of love ; come thou in peace into thy
house. . . . Thy hair is like turquoise as thou comest forth
from the Fields of Turquoise, thy hair is like unto the finest
lapis-lazuli, and thou thyself art more blue than thy hair.
Thy skin and body are like southern alabaster, and thy bones
are of silver. The perfume of thy hair is like unto new myrrh,
and thy skull is of lapis-lazuli."

The third work, " The Book of making splendid the
Spirit of Osiris," was also sung at the great festival of Osiris

that took place during the November–December at Abydos and other great towns in Egypt, and if it were sung on behalf of any man, the resurrection and life, constantly renewed, of that man were secured for his soul and spirit. This Book, written in hieratic, is found in a papyrus in Paris, and the following extract will illustrate its contents: " Come to thy house, come to thy house, O An. Come to thy house, O Beautiful Bull, lord of men and women, the beloved one, the lord of women. O Beautiful Face, Chief of Akert, Prince, Khenti Amentiu, are not all hearts drunk through the love of thee, O Un-Nefer, whose word is truth ? The hands of men and gods are lifted up and seek thee, even as the hands of a babe are stretched out to his mother. Come thou to them, for their hearts are sad, and make them to rejoice. The lands of Horus exult, the domains of Set are overthrown because of their fear of thee. Hail, Osiris Khenti Amentiu ! I am thy sister Isis. No god and no goddess have done for thee what I have done. I, a woman, made a man child for thee, because of my desire to make thy name to live upon the earth. Thy divine essence was in my body, I brought him forth on the ground. He pleaded thy case, he healed thy suffering, he decreed the destruction of him that caused it. Set fell under his knife, and the Smamiu fiends of Set followed him. The throne of the Earth-god is thine, O thou who art his beloved son. . . . There is health in thy members, thy wounds are healed, thy sufferings are relieved, thou shalt never groan again in pain. Come to us thy sisters, come to us ; our hearts will live when thou comest. Men shall cry out to thee, and women shall weep glad tears, at thy coming to them. . . . The Nile appeareth at the command of thy mouth ; thou makest men to live on the effluxes that proceed from thy members, and thou makest every field to flourish. When thou comest that which is dead springeth into life, and the plants in the marshes put forth blossoms. Thou art the Lord of millions of years, the sustainer of wild creatures, and the lord of cattle ; every created thing hath its existence from thee. What is in the earth is thine. What is in the heavens is thine. What is in the

waters is thine.   Thou art the Lord of Truth, the hater of
sinners, whom thou overthrowest in their sins.   The Goddesses of Truth are with thee ; they never leave thee.   No
sinful man can approach thee in the place where thou art.
Whatsoever appertaineth to life and to death belongeth to
thee, and to thee belongeth everything that concerneth man."

During the period of the occupation of Egypt by the
Romans, the three last-named works were still further
abridged, and eventually the texts that were considered
essential for salvation were written upon small sheets of
papyrus from 9 to 12 inches high, and from 5 to 10 inches
wide.

CHAPTER VI

THE EGYPTIAN STORY OF THE CREATION

IF we consider for a moment the vast amount of thought which the Egyptian gave to the problems of the future life, and their deep-seated belief in resurrection and immortality, we cannot fail to conclude that he must have theorised deeply about the constitution of the heaven in which he hoped to live everlastingly, and about its Maker. The translations given in the preceding pages prove that the theologians of Egypt were ready enough to describe heaven, and the life led by the blessed there, and the powers and the attributes of the gods, but they appear to have shrunk from writing down in a connected form their beliefs concerning the Creation and the origin of the Creator. The worshippers of each great god proclaimed him to be the Creator of All, and every great town had its own local belief on the subject. According to the Heliopolitans, Atem, or Tem, and at a later period Rā, was the Creator ; according to Memphite theology he was Ptah ; according to the Hermopolitans he was Thoth ; and according to the Thebans he was Amen (Ammon). In only one native Egyptian work up to the present has there been discovered any connected account of the Creation, and the means by which it was effected, namely, the British Museum Papyrus, No. 10,188. This papyrus was written about 305 B.C., and is therefore of a comparatively late date, but the subject matter of the works contained in it is thousands of years older, and it is only *their* forms which are of a late date. The Story of the Creation is found in the last work in the papyrus, which is called the " Book of overthrowing Āapep, the Enemy of Rā, the Enemy of Un-Nefer " (*i.e.* Osiris). This work is a liturgy, which was said at certain times of the day and night in the great temple of Amen-Rā at Thebes, with the view of preventing the monster Āapep from obstructing the sunrise. Āapep was supposed to lie in wait for the sun daily just before sunrise, with the view of doing battle with him and overthrowing him. When the Sun-god arrived at the place where Āapep was, he first of all cast a spell upon the monster, which rendered him helpless, and then he cast his fiery rays upon him, which shrivelled him up, and the fire of the god consumed him entirely. In the temple of Amen-Rā the priests recited the spells that were supposed to help the Sun-god to burn up Āapep, and they burnt waxen figures of the monster in specially prepared fires, and, uttering curses, they trampled them under foot and defiled them. These spells and burnings were also believed to break up rain clouds, and to scatter fog and mist and to dissipate thunder-storms, and to help the sun to rise on this world in a cloudless sky. Āapep was a form of Set, the god of evil of every kind, and his allies were the "Red Fiends" and the "Black Fiends," and every power of darkness. In the midst of the magical spells of this papyrus we find two copies of the "Book of knowing how Rā came into being, and of overthrowing Āapep." One copy is a little fuller than the other, but they agree substantially. The words of this book are said in the opening line to have been spoken by the god Nebertcher, *i.e.* the "Lord to the uttermost limit," or God Himself. The Egyptian Christians, or Copts, in their religious writings use this name as an equivalent of God Almighty, the Lord of All, the God of the Universe. Nebertcher says: "I am the creator of what hath come into being. I myself came into being under the form of the god Khepera. I came into being under the form of Pautti (or, in primeval time), I formed myself out of the primeval matter, I made myself out of the substance that was in primeval time." [1] Nothing existed at that time except the great primeval watery mass called Nu, but in this there were the germs of everything that came into being

---

[1] The second version here states that the name of Nebertcher is Ausares (Osiris), who is the oldest god of all.

subsequently. There was no heaven, and no earth, and the god found no place on which to stand ; nothing, in fact, existed except the god. He says, "I was alone." He first created himself by uttering his own name as a word of power, and when this was uttered his visible form appeared. He then uttered another kind of word of power, and as a result of this his soul (*ba*) came into being, and it worked in connection with his heart or mind (*ab*). Before every act of creation Nebertcher, or his visible form Khepera, thought out what form the thing to be created was to take, and when he had uttered its name the thing itself appeared in heaven or earth. To fill the heaven, or place where he lived, the god next produced from his body and its shadow the two gods Shu and Tefnut. These with Nebertcher, or Khepera, formed the first triad of gods, and the "one god became three," or, as we should say, the one god had three aspects, each of which was quite distinct from the other. The tradition of the begetting of Shu and Tefnut is as old as the time of the pyramids, for it is mentioned in the text of Pepi I, l. 466. The next act of creation resulted in the emerging of the Eye of Nebertcher (later identified with Rā) from the watery mass (Nu), and light shone upon its waters. Shu and Tefnut then united and they produced Keb, the Earth-god, and Nut, the Sky-goddess. The text then refers to some calamity which befell the Eye of Nebertcher or of Khepera, but what it was is not clear ; at all events the Eye became obscured, and it ceased to give light. This period of darkness is, of course, the night, and to obviate the inconvenience caused by this recurring period of darkness, the god made a second Eye, *i.e.* the Moon, and set it in the heavens. The greater Eye ruled the day, and the lesser Eye the night. One of the results of the daily darkness was the descent of the Sky-goddess Nut to the Earth-god Keb each evening.

The gods and goddesses next created were five, namely, Osiris, Horus, Set, Isis, and Nephthys. Osiris married Isis, and their son was called Horus ; Set married Nephthys, but their son Anpu, or Anubis, is not mentioned in our text.

Osiris became the great Ancestor-god of Egypt, and was a reincarnation of his great-grandfather. Men and women were first formed from the tears that fell from the Eye of Khepera, or the Sun-god, upon his body ; the old Egyptian word for " men " very closely resembles in form and sound the word for " tears." Plants, vegetables, herbs, and trees owe their origin to the light of the moon falling upon the earth. Our text contains no mention of a special creation of the " beasts of the field," but the god states distinctly that he created the children of the earth, or creeping things of all kinds, and among this class quadrupeds are probably included. The men and women, and all the other living creatures that were made at that time by Nebertcher, or Khepera, reproduced their species, each in his own way, and thus the earth became filled with their descendants as we see at the present time. The elements of this Creation legend are very, very old, and the form in which they are grouped in our text suggests the influence of the priests of Heliopolis. It is interesting to note that only very ancient gods appear as Powers of creation, and these were certainly worshipped for many centuries before the priests of Heliopolis invented their cult of the Sun-god, and identified their god with the older gods of the country. We may note, too, that gods like Ptah and Amen, whose reputation was so great in later times, and even when our text was copied in 305 B.C., find no mention at all.

CHAPTER VII

LEGENDS OF THE GODS

THE Egyptians believed that at one time all the great gods and goddesses lived upon earth, and that they ruled Egypt in much the same way as the Pharaohs with whom they were more or less acquainted. They went about among men and took a real personal interest in their affairs, and, according to tradition, they spared no pains in promoting their wishes and well-being. Their rule was on the whole beneficent, chiefly because in addition to their divine attributes they possessed natures, and apparently bodily constitutions that were similar to those of men. Like men also they were supposed to feel emotions and passions, and to be liable to the accidents that befell men, and to grow old, and even to die. The greatest of all the gods was Rā, and he reigned over Egypt for very many years. His reign was marked by justice and righteousness, and he was in all periods of Egyptian history regarded as the type of what a king should be. When men instead of gods reigned over Egypt they all delighted to call themselves sons of Rā, and every king believed that Rā was his true father, and regarded his mother's husband as his father only in name. This belief was always common in Egypt, and even Alexander the Great found it expedient to adopt it, for he made a journey to the sanctuary of Amen (Ammon) in the Oasis of Sīwāh in order to be officially acknowledged by the god. Having obtained this recognition, he became the rightful lord of Egypt.

THE DESTRUCTION OF MANKIND

This Legend is cut in hieroglyphs on the walls of a small chamber in the tomb of Seti I about 1350 B.C. When Rā, the self-begotten and self-formed god, had been ruling gods and men for some time, men began to complain about him, saying, "His Majesty hath become old. His bones have turned into silver, his flesh into gold, and his hair into real lapis-lazuli." His Majesty heard these murmurings and commanded his followers to summon to his presence his Eye (*i.e.* the goddess Hathor), Shu, Tefnut, Keb, Nut, and the father and mother gods and goddesses who were with him in the watery abyss of Nu, and also the god of this water, Nu. They were to come to him with all their followers secretly, so that men should not suspect the reason for their coming, and take flight, and they were to assemble in the Great House in Heliopolis, where Rā would take counsel with them. In due course all the gods assembled in the Great House, and they ranged themselves down the sides of the House, and they bowed down in homage before Rā until their heads touched the ground, and said, "Speak, for we are listening." Then Rā addressing Nu, the father of the first-born gods, told him to give heed to what men were doing, for they whom he had created were murmuring against him. And he said, "Tell me what ye would do. Consider the matter, invent a plan for me, and I will not slay them until I have heard what ye shall say concerning this thing." Nu replied, "Thou, O my son Rā, art greater than the god who made thee (*i.e.* Nu himself), thou art the king of those who were created with thee, thy throne is established, and the fear of thee is great. Let thine Eye (Hathor) attack those who blaspheme thee." And Rā said, "Lo, they have fled to the mountains, for their hearts are afraid because of what they have said." The gods replied, "Let thine Eye go forth and destroy those who blasphemed thee, for no eye can resist thine when it goeth forth in the form of Hathor." Thereupon the Eye of Rā, or Hathor, went in pursuit of the blasphemers in the mountains, and slew them all. On her return Rā welcomed her, and the goddess said that the work of vanquishing men was dear to her heart. Rā then said that he would be the master of men as their king, and that he would destroy them. For three nights the goddess Hathor-Sekhmet waded about in the blood of men, the slaughter beginning at Hensu (Hera-kleopolis Magna).

Then the Majesty of Rā ordered that messengers should be sent to Abu, a town at the foot of the First Cataract, to fetch mandrakes (?), and when they were brought he gave them to the god Sekti to crush. When the women slaves were bruising grain for making beer, the crushed mandrakes (?) were placed in the vessels that were to hold the beer, together with some of the blood of those who had been slain by Hathor. The beer was then made, and seven thousand vessels were filled with it. When Rā saw the beer he ordered it to be taken to the scene of slaughter, and poured out on the meadows of the four quarters of heaven. The object of putting mandrakes (?) in the beer was to make those who drank fall asleep quickly, and when the goddess Hathor came and drank the beer mixed with blood and mandrakes (?) she became very merry, and, the sleepy stage of drunkenness coming on her, she forgot all about men, and slew no more. At every festival of Hathor ever after " sleepy beer " was made, and it was drunk by those who celebrated the feast.

Now, although the blasphemers of Rā had been put to death, the heart of the god was not satisfied, and he complained to the gods that he was smitten with the " pain of the fire of sickness." He said, " My heart is weary because I have to live with men ; I have slain some of them, but worthless men still live, and I did not slay as many as I ought to have done considering my power." To this the gods replied, " Trouble not about thy lack of action, for thy power is in proportion to thy will." Here the text becomes fragmentary, but it seems that the goddess Nut took the form of a cow, and that the other gods lifted Rā on to her back. When men saw that Rā was leaving the earth, they repented of their murmurings, and the next morning they went out with bows and arrows to fight the enemies of the Sun-god. As a reward for this Rā forgave those men their former blasphemies, but persisted in his intention of retiring from the earth. He ascended into the heights of heaven, being still on the back of the Cow-goddess Nut, and he created there Sekhet-hetep and Sekhet-Aaru as abodes for the blessed, and the flowers that blossomed therein he turned into stars. He also created the millions of beings who lived there in order that they might praise him. The height to which Rā had ascended was now so great that the legs of the Cow-goddess on which he was enthroned trembled, and to give her strength he ordained that Nut should be held up in her position by the godhead and upraised arms of the god Shu. This is why we see pictures of the body of Nut being supported by Shu. The legs of the Cow-goddess were supported by the various gods, and thus the seat of the throne of Rā became stable. When this was done Rā caused the Earth-god Keb to be summoned to his presence, and when he came he spake to him about the venomous reptiles that lived in the earth and were hostile to him. Then turning to Thoth, he bade him to prepare a series of spells and words of power, which would enable those who knew them to overcome snakes and serpents and deadly reptiles of all kinds. Thoth did so, and the spells which he wrote under the direction of Rā served as a protection of the servants of Rā ever after, and secured for them the help of Keb, who became sole lord of all the beings that lived and moved on and in his body, the earth. Before finally relinquishing his active rule on earth, Rā summoned Thoth and told him of his desire to create a Light-soul in the Tuat and in the Land of the Caves. Over this region he appointed Thoth to rule, and he ordered him to keep a register of those who were there, and to mete out just punishments to them. In fact, Thoth was to be ever after the representative of Rā in the Other World.

THE LEGEND OF RĀ AND ISIS

This Legend is found written in the hieratic character upon a papyrus preserved in Turin, and it illustrates a portion of the preceding Legend. We have seen that Rā instructed Thoth to draw up a series of spells to be used against venomous reptiles of all kinds, and the reader will perceive from the following summary that Rā had good reason for doing this. The Legend opens with a list of the titles of Rā, the "self-created god," creator of heaven, earth, breath of life, fire, gods, men, beasts, cattle, reptiles, feathered fowl, and fish, the King of gods and men, to whom cycles of 120 years are as years, whose manifold names are unknown even by the gods. The text continues : "Isis had the form of a woman, and knew words of power, but she was disgusted with men, and she yearned for the companionship of the gods and the spirits, and she meditated and asked herself whether, supposing she had the knowledge of the Name of Rā, it was not possible to make herself as great as Rā was in heaven and on the earth ? Meanwhile Rā appeared in heaven each day upon his throne, but he had become old, and he dribbled at the mouth, and his spittle fell on the ground. One day Isis took some of the spittle and kneaded up dust in it, and made this paste into the form of a serpent with a forked tongue, so that if it struck anyone the person struck would find it impossible to escape death. This figure she placed on the path on which Rā walked as he came into heaven after his daily survey of the Two Lands (*i.e.* Egypt). Soon after this Rā rose up, and attended by his gods he came into heaven, but as he went along the serpent drove its fangs into him. As soon as he was bitten Rā felt the living fire leaving his body, and he cried out so loudly that his voice reached the uttermost parts of heaven. The gods rushed to him in great alarm, saying, "What is the matter ? " At first Rā was speechless, and found himself unable to answer, for his jaws shook, his lips trembled, and the poison continued to run through every part of his body. When he was able to regain a little strength, he told the gods that some deadly creature had bitten him, something the like of which he had never seen, something which his hand had never made. He said, "Never before have I felt such pain ; there is no pain worse than this." Rā then went on to describe his greatness and power, and told the listening gods that his father and mother had hidden his name in his body so that no one might be able to master him by means of any spell or word of power. In spite of this something had struck him, and he knew not

what it was. " Is it fire ? " he asked. " Is it water ? My
heart is full of burning fire, my limbs are shivering, shooting
pains are in all my members." All the gods round about
him uttered cries of lamentation, and at this moment Isis
appeared. Going to Rā she said, " What is this, O divine
father ? What is this ? Hath a serpent bitten thee ? Hath
something made by thee lifted up its head against thee ?
Verily my words of power shall overthrow it ; I will make it
depart in the sight of thy light." Rā then repeated to Isis
the story of the incident, adding, " I am colder than water,
I am hotter than fire. All my members sweat. My body
quaketh. Mine eye is unsteady. I cannot look on the sky,
and my face is bedewed with water as in the time of the
Inundation." [1] Then Isis said, " Father, tell me thy name,
for he who can utter his own name liveth."

Rā replied, " I am the maker of heaven and earth. I
knit together the mountains and whatsoever liveth on them.
I made the waters. I made Mehturit [2] to come into being.
I made Kamutef.[3] I made heaven, and the two hidden gods
of the horizon, and put souls into the gods. I open my eyes,
and there is light ; I shut my eyes, and there is darkness.
I speak the word[s], and the waters of the Nile appear. I am
he whom the gods know not. I make the hours. I create
the days. I open the year. I make the river [Nile]. I
create the living fire whereby works in the foundries and work-
shops are carried out. I am Khepera in the morning, Rā at
noon, and Temu in the evening." Meanwhile the poison
of the serpent was coursing through the veins of Rā, and the
enumeration of his works afforded the god no relief from it.
Then Isis said to Rā, " Among all the things which thou hast
named to me thou hast not named thy name. Tell me thy
name, and the poison shall come forth from thee." Rā still
hesitated, but the poison was burning in his blood, and the
heat thereof was stronger than that of a fierce fire. At
length he said, " Isis shall search me through, and my name

---

[1] *i.e.* in the period of summer. The season Shemmu began in April and
ended about July 15.

[2] An ancient Cow-goddess of heaven.　　　　[3] A form of Amen-Rā.

shall come forth from my body and pass into hers." Then Rā hid himself from the gods, and for a season his throne in the Boat of Millions of Years was empty. When the time came for the heart of the god to pass into Isis, the goddess said to Horus, her son, " The great god shall bind himself by an oath to give us his two eyes (*i.e.* the sun and the moon)." When the great god had yielded up his name Isis pronounced the following spell : " Flow poison, come out of Rā. Eye of Horus, come out of the god, and sparkle as thou comest through his mouth. I am the worker. I make the poison to fall on the ground. The poison is conquered. Truly the name of the great god hath been taken from him. Rā liveth ! The poison dieth ! If the poison live Rā shall die." These were the words which Isis spoke, Isis the great lady, the Queen of the gods, who knew Rā by his own name.

In late times magicians used to write the above Legend on papyrus above figures of Temu and Heru-Hekenu, who gave Rā his secret name, and over figures of Isis and Horus, and sell the rolls as charms against snake bites.

The Legend of Horus of Behutet and the Winged Disk

The text of this Legend is cut in hieroglyphs on the walls of the temple of Edfu, in Upper Egypt, and some of the incidents described in it are illustrated by large bas-reliefs The form of the Legend here given dates from the Ptolemaic Period, but the subject matter is some thousands of years older. The great historical fact underlying the Legend is the Conquest of Egypt by some very early king who invaded Egypt from the south, and who succeeded in conquering every part of it, even the northern part of the Delta. The events described are supposed to have taken place whilst Rā was still reigning on the earth. The Legend states that in the three hundred and sixty-third year of the reign of Rā-Harmakhis, the ever living, His Majesty was in Ta-sti (*i.e.* the Land of the Bow, or Nubia) with his soldiers ; the enemy had reviled him, and for this reason the land is called " Uau-

atet " to this day.   From Nubia Rā sailed down the river
to Apollinopolis (Edfu), and Heru-Behutet, or Horus of
Edfu, was with him.   On arriving there Horus told Rā that
the enemy were plotting against him, and Rā told him to go
out and slay them.   Horus took the form of a great winged
disk, which flew up into the air and pursued the enemy, and
it attacked them with such terrific force that they could
neither see nor hear, and they fell upon each other, and slew
each other, and in a moment not a single foe was left alive.
Then Horus returned to the Boat of Rā-Harmakhis, in the
form of the winged disk which shone with many colours, and
said, " Advance, O Rā, and look upon thine enemies who
are lying under thee in this land."   Rā set out on the journey,
taking with him the goddess Ashtoreth, and he saw his
enemies lying on the ground, each of them being fettered.
After looking upon his slaughtered foes Rā said to the gods
who were with him, " Behold, let us sail in our boat on the
water, for our hearts are glad because our enemies have been
overthrown on the earth."   So the Boat of Rā moved onwards
towards the north, and the enemies of the god who were on
the banks took the form of crocodiles and hippopotami, and
tried to frighten the god, for as his boat came near them they
opened their jaws wide, intending to swallow it up together
with the gods who were in it.   Among the crew were the
Followers of Horus of Edfu, who were skilled workers in metal,
and each of these had in his hands an iron spear and a chain.
These " Blacksmiths " threw out their chains into the river
and allowed the crocodiles and hippopotami to entangle
their legs in them, and then they dragged the beasts towards
the bows of the Boat, and driving their spears into their
bodies, slew them there.   After the slaughter the bodies of
six hundred and fifty-one crocodiles were brought and laid
out before the town of Edfu.   When Thoth saw these he said,
" Let your hearts rejoice, O gods of heaven. Let your hearts
rejoice, O ye gods who dwell on the earth. The Young Horus
cometh in peace. On his way he hath made manifest deeds of
valour, according to the Book of slaying the Hippopotamus."
And from that day they made figures of Horus in metal.

Then Horus of Edfu took the form of the winged disk, and set himself on the prow of the Boat of Rā. He took with him Nekhebet, goddess of the South, and Uatchet, goddess of the North, in the form of serpents, so that they might make all the enemies of the Sun-god to quake in the South and in the North. His foes who had fled to the north doubled back towards the south, for they were in deadly fear of the god. Horus pursued and overtook them, and he and his blacksmiths had in their hands spears and chains, and they slew large numbers of them to the south-east of the town of Thebes in Upper Egypt. Many succeeded in escaping towards the north once more, but after pursuing them for a whole day Horus overtook them, and made a great slaughter among them. Meanwhile the other foes of the god, who had heard of the defeats of their allies, fled into Lower Egypt, and took refuge among the swamps of the Delta. Horus set out after them, and came up with them, and spent four days in the water slaying his foes, who tried to escape in the forms of crocodiles and hippopotami. He captured one hundred and forty-two of the enemy and a male hippopotamus, and took them to the fore part of the Boat of Rā. There he hacked them in pieces, and gave their inward parts to his followers, and their mutilated bodies to the gods and goddesses who were in the Boat of Rā and on the river banks in the town of Heben.

Then the remnant of the enemy turned their faces towards the Lake of the North, and they attempted to sail to the Mediterranean in boats ; but the terror of Horus filled their hearts, and they left their boats and fled to the district of Mertet-Ament, where they joined themselves to the worshippers of Set, the god of evil, who dwelt in the Western Delta. Horus pursued them in his boat for one day and one night without seeing them, and he arrived at the town of Per-Rehui. At length he discovered the position of the enemy, and he and his followers fell upon them, and slew a large number of them ; he captured three hundred and eighty-one of them alive, and these he took to the Boat of Rā, then, having slain them, he gave their carcases to his followers or bodyguard, who presumably devoured them. The custom of eating the bodies of enemies is very old in Egypt, and survives in some parts of Africa to this day.

Then Set, the great antagonist of Horus, came out and cursed him for the slaughter of his people, using most shameful words of abuse. Horus stood up and fought a duel with Set, the " Stinking Face," as the text calls him, and Horus succeeded in throwing him to the ground and spearing him. Horus smashed his mouth with a blow of his mace, and having fettered him with his chain, he brought him into the presence of Rā, who ordered that he was to be handed over to Isis and her son Horus, that they might work their will on him. Here we must note that the ancient editor of the Legend has confounded Horus the ancient Sun-god with Horus, son of Isis, son of Osiris. Then Horus, the son of Isis, cut off the heads of Set and his followers in the presence of Rā, and dragged Set by his feet round about throughout the district with his spear driven through his head and back, according to the order of Rā. The form which Horus of Edfu had at that time was that of a man of great strength, with the face and back of a hawk ; on his head he wore the Double Crown, with feathers and serpents attached, and in his hands he held a metal spear and a metal chain. And Horus, the son of Isis, took upon himself a similar form, and the two Horuses slew all the enemies on the bank of the river to the west of the town of Per-Rehui. This slaughter took place on the seventh day of the first month of the season Pert,[1] which was ever afterwards called the " Day of the Festival of Sailing."

Now, although Set in the form of a man had been slain, he reappeared in the form of a great hissing serpent, and took up his abode in a hole in the ground without being noticed by Horus. Rā, however, saw him, and gave orders that Horus, the son of Isis, in the form of a hawk-headed staff, should set himself at the mouth of the hole, so that the monster might never reappear among men. This Horus did, and Isis his mother lived there with him. Once again it became known to Rā that a remnant of the followers of

---

[1] About the middle of November.

Set had escaped, and that under the direction of the Smait fiends, and of Set, who had reappeared, they were hiding in the swamps of the Eastern Delta. Horus of Edfu, the winged disk, pursued them, speared them, and finally slew them in the presence of Rā. For the moment there were no more enemies of Rā to be found in the district on land, although Horus passed six days and six nights in looking for them ; but it seems that several of the followers of Set in the forms of water reptiles were lying on the ground under water, and that Horus saw them there. At this time Horus had strict guard kept over the tomb of Osiris in Anrutef,[1] because he learned that the Smait fiends wanted to come and wreck both it and the body of the god. Isis, too, never ceased to recite spells and incantations in order to keep away her husband's foes from his body. Meanwhile the " black-smiths " of Horus, who were in charge of the " middle regions " of Egypt, found a body of the enemy, and attacked them fiercely, slew many of them, and took one hundred and six of them prisoners. The " blacksmiths " of the west also took one hundred and six prisoners, and both groups of prisoners were slain before Rā. In return for their services Rā bestowed dwelling-places upon the " blacksmiths," and allowed them to have temples with images of their gods in them, and arranged for offerings and libations to be made to them by properly appointed priests of various classes.

Shortly after these events Rā discovered that a number of his enemies were still at large, and that they had sailed in boats to the swamps that lay round about the town of Tchal, or Tchar, better known as Zoan or Tanis. Once more Horus unmoored the Boat of Rā, and set out against them ; some took refuge in the waters, and others landed and escaped to the hilly land on the east. For some reason, which is not quite apparent, Horus took the form of a mighty lion with a man's face, and he wore on his head the triple crown. His claws were like flints, and he pursued the enemy on the hills, and chased them hither and thither, and captured one hundred and forty-two of them. He tore out their tongues,

---

[1] A district of Herakleopolis.

and ripped their bodies into strips with his claws, and gave them over to his allies in the mountains, who, no doubt, ate them. This was the last fight in the north of Egypt, and Rā proposed that they should sail up the river and return to the south. They had traversed all Egypt, and sailed over the lakes in the Delta, and down the arms of the Nile to the Mediterranean, and as no more of the enemy were to be seen the prow of the boat of Rā was turned southwards. Thoth recited the spells that produced fair weather, and said the words of power that prevented storms from rising, and in due course the Boat reached Nubia. When it arrived Horus found in the country of Uauatet men who were conspiring against him and cursing him, just as they had at one time blasphemed Rā. Horus, taking the form of the winged disk, and accompanied by the two serpent-goddesses, Nekhebet and Uatchet, attacked the rebels, but there was no fierce fighting this time, for the hearts of the enemy melted through fear of him. His foes cast themselves before him on the ground in submission, they offered no resistance, and they died straightway. Horus then returned to the town of Behutet (Edfu), and the gods acclaimed him, and praised his prowess. Rā was so pleased with him that he ordered Thoth to have a winged disk, with a serpent on each side of it, placed in every temple in Egypt in which he (*i.e.* Rā) was worshipped, so that it might act as a protector of the building, and drive away any and every fiend and devil that might wish to attack it. This is the reason why we find the winged disk, with a serpent on each side of it, above the doors of temples and religious buildings throughout the length and breadth of Egypt.

In many places in the text that contains the above Legend there are short passages in which attempts are made to explain the origins of the names of certain towns and gods. All these are interpolations in the narrative made by scribes at a late period of Egyptian history. As it would be quite useless to reproduce them without many explanatory notes, for which there is no room in this little book, they have been omitted.

THE LEGEND OF KHNEMU AND A SEVEN YEARS' FAMINE

This Legend is cut in hieroglyphs on a large rounded block of granite, which stands on the south-east portion of Sāhal, a little island in the First Cataract in Upper Egypt, two or three miles to the south of the modern town of Aswān, the ancient Syene. The form of the Legend, and the shapes of the hieroglyphs, and the late spelling of the words, prove that the inscription is the work of the Ptolemaic Period, though it is possible that the Legend in its simplest form is as old as the period to which it is ascribed in the Sāhal text, namely, the third dynasty, about 4100 B.C. The subject of the Legend is a terrible famine, which lasted for seven years, in the reign of King Tcheser, and which recalls the seven years' famine that took place in Egypt when Joseph was there. This famine was believed to have been caused by the king's neglect to worship properly the god Khnemu, who was supposed to control the springs of the Nile, which were asserted by the sages to be situated between two great rocks on the Island of Elephantine. The Legend sets forth that the Viceroy of Nubia, in the reign of Tcheser, was a nobleman called Meter, who was also the overseer of all the temple properties in the South. His residence was in Abu, or Elephantine, and in the eighteenth year of his reign the king sent him a despatch in which it was written thus : " This is to inform thee that misery hath laid hold upon me as I sit upon the great throne, and I grieve for those who dwell in the Great House.[1] My heart is grievously afflicted by reason of a very great calamity, which is due to the fact that the waters of the Nile have not risen to their proper height for seven years. Grain is exceedingly scarce, there are no garden herbs and vegetables to be had at all, and everything which men use for food hath come to an end. Every man robbeth

[1] An allusion to the royal title of Pharaoh, in Egyptian PER-AA, the " Great House," in whom and by whom all the Egyptians were supposed to live.

his neighbour. The people wish to walk about, but are unable to move. The baby waileth, the young man shuffleth
along on his feet through weakness. The hearts of the old men
are broken down with despair, their legs give way under them,
they sink down exhausted on the ground, and they lay their
hands on their bellies [in pain]. The officials are powerless
and have no counsel to give, and when the public granaries,
which ought to contain supplies, are opened, there cometh
forth from them nothing but wind. Everything is in a state
of ruin. I go back in my mind to the time when I had an
adviser, to the time of the gods, to the Ibis-god [Thoth],
and to the chief Kher-heb priest Imhetep (Imouthis),[1] the
son of Ptah of his South Wall.[2] [Tell me, I pray thee],
Where is the birthplace of the Nile ? What god or what
goddess presideth over it ? What kind of form hath the
god ? For it is he that maketh my revenue, and who filleth
the granaries with grain. I wish to go to [consult] the Chief
of Het-Sekhmet,[3] whose beneficence strengtheneth all men
in their works. I wish to go into the House of Life,[4] and to
take the rolls of the books in my own hands, so that I may
examine them [and find out these things]."

Having read the royal despatch the Viceroy Meter set out
to go to the king, and when he came to him he proceeded
to instruct the king in the matters about which he had asked
questions. The text makes the king say : " [Meter] gave me
information about the rise of the Nile, and he told me all
that men had written concerning it ; and he made clear to
me all the difficult passages [in the books], which my ancestors had consulted hastily, and which had never before been
explained to any king since the time when Rā [reigned].
And he said to me : There is a town in the river wherefrom
the Nile maketh his appearance. ' Abu ' was its name in
the beginning : it is the City of the Beginning, it is the Name
of the City of the Beginning. It reacheth to Uauatet,
which is the first land [on the south]. There is a long flight

---

[1] A famous priest and magician of Memphis, who was subsequently
deified.　　　　　　　　　　　　　　　　[2] A part of Memphis.
[3] *i.e.* Hermopolis, the town of Thoth.　　[4] *i.e.* the library of the temple.

of steps there (a nilometer ?), on which Rā resteth when he
determineth to prolong life to mankind. It is called ' Netch-
emtchem ānkh.' Here are the ' Two Qerti,' [1] which are
the two breasts wherefrom every good thing cometh. Here
is the bed of the Nile, here the Nile-god reneweth his youth,
and here he sendeth out the flood on the land. Here his
waters rise to a height of twenty-eight cubits ; at Hermopolis
(in the Delta) their height is seven cubits. Here the Nile-
god smiteth the ground with his sandals, and here he draweth
the bolts and throweth open the two doors through which
the water poureth forth. In this town the Nile-god dwelleth
in the form of Shu, and he keepeth the account of the products of all Egypt, in order to give to each his due. Here
are kept the cord for measuring land and the register of the
estates. Here the god liveth in a wooden house with a door
made of reeds, and branches of trees form the roof; its
entrance is to the south-east. Round about it are mountains
of stone to which quarrymen come with their tools when they
want stone to build temples to the gods, shrines for sacred
animals, and pyramids for kings, or to make statues. Here
they offer sacrifices of all kinds in the sanctuary, and here
their sweet-smelling gifts are presented before the face of
the god Khnemu. In the quarries on the river bank is
granite, which is called the ' stone of Abu.' The names of
its gods are : Sept (Sothis, the dog-star), Ānqet, Hep (the
Nile-god), Shu, Keb, Nut, Osiris, Horus, Isis, and Nephthys.
Here are found precious stones (a list is given), gold, silver,
copper, iron, lapis-lazuli, emerald, crystal, ruby, &c., alabaster, mother-of-emerald, and seeds of plants that are used in
making incense. These were the things which I learned
from Meter [the Viceroy]."

Having informed the king concerning the rise of the Nile
and the other matters mentioned in his despatch, Meter
made arrangements for the king to visit the temple of Khnemu
in person. This he did, and the Legend gives us the king's
own description of his visit. He says : I entered the temple,
and the keepers of the rolls untied them and showed them

---

[1] The two caverns which contained the springs of the Nile.

to me. I was purified by the sprinkling of holy water, and I passed through the places that were prohibited to ordinary folk, and a great offering of cakes, ale, geese, oxen, &c., was offered up on my behalf to the gods and goddesses of Abu. Then I found the god [Khnemu] standing in front of me, and I propitiated him with the offerings that I made unto him, and I made prayer and supplication before him. Then he opened his eyes,[1] and his heart inclined to me, and in a majestic manner he said unto me: "I am Khnemu who fashioned thee. My two hands grasped thee and knitted together thy body; I made thy members sound, and I gave thee thy heart. Yet the stones have been lying under the ground for ages, and no man hath worked them in order to build a god-house, to repair the [sacred] buildings which are in ruins, or to make shrines for the gods of the South and North, or to do what he ought to do for his lord, even though I am the Lord [the Creator]. I am Nu, the self-created, the Great God, who came into being in the beginning. [I am] Hep [the Nile-god] who riseth at will to give health to him that worketh for me. I am the Governor and Guide of all men, in all their periods, the Most Great, the Father of the gods, Shu, the Great One, the Chief of the earth. The two halves of heaven are my abode. The Nile is poured out in a stream by me, and it goeth round about the tilled lands, and its embrace produceth life for every one that breatheth, according to the extent of its embrace. . . . I will make the Nile to rise for thee, and in no year shall it fail, and it shall spread its water out and cover every land satisfactorily. Plants, herbs, and trees shall bend beneath [the weight of] their produce. The goddess Rennet (the Harvest goddess) shall be at the head of everything, and every product shall increase a hundred thousandfold, according to the cubit of the year.[2] The people shall be filled, verily to their hearts' desire, yea, everyone. Want shall cease, and the emptiness of the granaries shall come to an end. The Land of Mera (*i.e.* Egypt) shall be one cultivated land, the districts shall

---

[1] The king was standing before a statue with movable eyes.

[2] *i.e.* the number of the cubits which the waters of the Nile shall rise.

be yellow with crops of grain, and the grain shall be good. The fertility of the land shall be according to the desire [of the husbandman], and it shall be greater than it hath ever been before." At the sound of the word " crops " the king awoke, and the courage that then filled his heart was as great as his former despair had been.

Having left the chamber of the god the king made a decree by which he endowed the temple of Khnemu with lands and gifts, and he drew up a code of laws under which every farmer was compelled to pay certain dues to it. Every fisherman and hunter had to pay a tithe. Of the calves cast one tenth were to be sent to the temple to be offered up as the daily offering. Gold, ivory, ebony, spices, precious stones, and woods were tithed, whether their owners were Egyptians or not, but no local tribe was to levy duty on these things on their road to Abu. Every artisan also was to pay tithe, with the exception of those who were employed in the foundry attached to the temple, and whose occupation con- sisted in making the images of the gods. The king further ordered that a copy of this decree, the original of which was cut in wood, should be engraved on a stele to be set up in the sanctuary, with figures of Khnemu and his companion gods cut above it. The man who spat upon the stele [if discovered] was to be " admonished with a rope."

THE LEGEND OF THE WANDERINGS OF ISIS

The god Osiris, as we have seen in the chapter on the Egyptian Religion in the accompanying volume, lived and reigned at one time upon earth in the form of a man. His twin-brother Set was jealous of his popularity, and hated him to such a degree that he contrived a plan whereby he succeeded in putting Osiris to death. Set then tried to usurp his brother's kingdom and to make himself sole lord of Egypt, and, although no text states it distinctly, it is clear that he seized his brother's wife, Isis, and shut her up in his house. Isis was, however, under the protection of the god Thoth, and she escaped with her unborn child, and the

following Legend describes the incidents that befell her, and
the death and revivification of Horus. It is cut in hieroglyphs upon a large stone stele which was made for Ānkh-
Psemthek, a prophet of Nebun in the reign of Nectanebus I,
who reigned from 373 B.C. to 360 B.C. The stele was dug
up in 1828 at Alexandria, and was given to Prince Metternich by Muhammad Alī Pāsha ; it is now commonly known
as the " Metternich Stele." The Legend is narrated by the
goddess herself, who says :

I am Isis. I escaped from the dwelling wherein my brother
Set placed me. Thoth, the great god, the Prince of Truth
in heaven and on earth, said unto me : " Come, O goddess
Isis [hearken thou], it is a good thing to hearken, for he who
is guided by another liveth. Hide thyself with thy child,
and these things shall happen unto him. His body shall
grow and flourish, and strength of every kind shall be in him.
He shall sit upon his father's throne, he shall avenge him,
and he shall hold the exalted position of ' Governor of the
Two Lands.' " I left the house of Set in the evening, and
there accompanied me Seven Scorpions, that were to travel
with me, and sting with their stings on my behalf. Two of
them, Tefen and Befen, followed behind me, two of them,
Mestet and Mestetef, went one on each side of me, and three,
Petet, Thetet, and Maatet, prepared the way for me. I
charged them very carefully and adjured them to make no
acquaintance with any one, to speak to none of the Red
Fiends, to pay no heed to a servant (?), and to keep their
gaze towards the ground so that they might show me the
way. And their leader brought me to Pa-Sui, the town of
the Sacred Sandals,[1] at the head of the district of the Papyrus
Swamps. When I arrived at Teb I came to a quarter of the
town where women dwelt. And a certain woman of quality
spied me as I was journeying along the road, and she shut her
door in my face, for she was afraid because of the Seven
Scorpions that were with me. Then they took counsel concerning her, and they shot out their poison on the tail of
Tefen. As for me, a peasant woman called Taha opened

[1] These places were in the seventh nome of Lower Egypt (Metelites).

her door, and I went into the house of this humble woman. Then the scorpion Tefen crawled in under the door of the woman Usert [who had shut it in my face], and stung her son, and a fire broke out in it ; there was no water to put it out, but the sky sent down rain, though it was not the time of rain.   And the heart of Usert was sore within her, and she was very sad, for she knew not whether her son would live or die ; and she went through the town shrieking for help, but none came out at the sound of her voice.   And I was sad for the child's sake, and I wished the innocent one to live again.   So I cried out to her, saying, Come to me ! Come to me ! There is life in my mouth.   I am a woman well known in her town.   I can destroy the devil of death by a spell which my father taught me.   I am his daughter, his beloved one.

Then Isis laid her hands on the child and recited this spell : " O poison of Tefent, come forth, fall on the ground ; go no further.   O poison of Befent, come forth, fall on the ground. I am Isis, the goddess, the mistress of words of power.   I am a weaver of spells, I know how to utter words so that they take effect.   Hearken to me, O every reptile that biteth (or stingeth), and fall on the ground.   O poison of Mestet, go no further.   O poison of Mestetef, rise not up in his body. O poison of Petet and Thetet, enter not his body.   O poison of Maatet, fall on the ground.   Ascend not into heaven, I command you by the beloved of Rā, the egg of the goose which appeareth from the sycamore.   My words indeed rule to the uttermost limit of the night.   I speak to you, O scorpions.   I am alone and in sorrow, and our names will stink throughout the nomes. . . . The child shall live ! The poison shall die ! For Rā liveth and the poison dieth. Horus shall be saved through his mother Isis, and he who is stricken shall likewise be saved."   Meanwhile the fire in the house of Usert was extinguished, and heaven was content with the utterance of Isis.   Then the lady Usert was filled with sorrow because she had shut her door in the face of Isis, and she brought to the house of the peasant woman gifts for the goddess, whom she had apparently not recognised.

The spells of the goddess produced, of course, the desired
effect on the poison, and we may assume that the life of the
child was restored to him.　The second lot of gifts made to
Isis represented his mother's gratitude.

Exactly when and how Isis made her way to a hiding
place cannot be said, but she reached it in safety, and her son
Horus was born there.　The story of the death of Horus she
tells in the following words :　" I am Isis.　I conceived a child,
Horus, and I brought him forth in a cluster of papyrus plants
(or, bulrushes).　I rejoiced exceedingly, for in him I saw
one who would make answer for his father.　I hid him, and
I covered him up carefully, being afraid of that foul one
[Set], and then I went to the town of Am, where the people
gave thanks for me because they knew I could cause them
trouble.　I passed the day in collecting food for the child,
and when I returned and took Horus into my arms, I found
him, Horus, the beautiful one of gold, the boy, the child,
lifeless !　He had bedewed the ground with the water of his
eye and with the foam of his lips.　His body was motionless,
his heart did not beat, and his muscles were relaxed."　Then
Isis sent forth a bitter cry, and lamented loudly her misfor-
tune, for now that Horus was dead she had none to protect
her, or to take vengeance on Set.　When the people heard
her voice they went out to her, and they bewailed with her
the greatness of her affliction.　But though all lamented on
her behalf there was none who could bring back Horus to
life.　Then a " woman who was well known in her town, a
lady who was the mistress of property in her own right,"
went out to Isis, and consoled her, and assured her that the
child should live through his mother.　And she said, " A
scorpion hath stung him, the reptile Āunab hath wounded
him."　Then Isis bent her face over the child to find out if
he breathed, and she examined the wound, and found that
there was poison in it, and then taking him in her arms, " she
leaped about with him like a fish that is put upon hot coals,"
uttering loud cries of lamentation.　During this outburst
of grief the goddess Nephthys, her sister, arrived, and she
too lamented and cried bitterly over her sister's loss ; with

her came the Scorpion-goddess Serqet. Nephthys at once advised Isis to cry out for help to Rā, for, said she, it is wholly impossible for the Boat of Rā to travel across the sky whilst Horus is lying dead. Then Isis cried out, and made supplication to the Boat of Millions of Years, and the Sun-god stopped the Boat. Out of it came down Thoth, who was provided with powerful spells, and, going to Isis, he inquired concerning her trouble. " What is it, what is it, O Isis, thou goddess of spells, whose mouth hath skill to utter them with supreme effect ? Surely no evil thing hath befallen Horus, for the Boat of Rā hath him under its protection. I have come from the Boat of the Disk to heal Horus." Then Thoth told Isis not to fear, but to put away all anxiety from her heart, for he had come to heal her child, and he told her that Horus was fully protected because he was the Dweller in his disk, and the firstborn son of heaven, and the Great Dwarf, and the Mighty Ram, and the Great Hawk, and the Holy Beetle, and the Hidden Body, and the Governor of the Other World, and the Holy Benu Bird, and by the spells of Isis and the names of Osiris and the weeping of his mother and brethren, and by his own name and heart. Turning towards the child Thoth began to recite his spells and said, " Wake up, Horus ! Thy protection is established. Make thou happy the heart of thy mother Isis. The words of Horus bind up hearts and he comforteth him that is in affliction. Let your hearts rejoice, O ye dwellers in the heavens. Horus who avenged his father shall make the poison to retreat. That which is in the mouth of Rā shall circulate, and the tongue of the Great God shall overcome [opposition]. The Boat of Rā standeth still and moveth not, and the Disk (*i.e.* the Sun-god) is in the place where it was yesterday to heal Horus for his mother Isis. Come to earth, draw nigh, O Boat of Rā, O ye mariners of Rā ; make the boat to move and convey food of the town of Sekhem (*i.e.* Letopolis) hither, to heal Horus for his mother Isis. . . . Come to earth, O poison ! I am Thoth, the firstborn son, the son of Rā. Tem and the company of the gods have commanded me to heal Horus for his mother Isis. O Horus, O Horus, thy Ka protecteth thee, and thy Image worketh protection for thee. The poison is as the daughter of its own flame ; it is destroyed because it smote the strong son. Your temples are safe, for Horus liveth for his mother." Then the child Horus returned to life, to the great joy of his mother, and Thoth went back to the Boat of Millions of Years, which at once proceeded on its majestic course, and all the gods from one end of heaven to the other rejoiced. Isis entreated either Rā or Thoth that Horus might be nursed and brought up by the goddesses of the town of Pe-Tep, or Buto, in the Delta, and at once Thoth committed the child to their care, and instructed them about his future. Horus grew up in Buto under their protection, and in due course fought a duel with Set, and vanquished him, and so avenged the wrong done to his father by Set.

The Legend of Khensu-Nefer-hetep and the Princess of Bekhten

Here for convenience' sake may be inserted the story of the Possessed Princess of Bekhten and the driving out of the evil spirit that was in her by Khensu-Nefer-hetep. The text of the Legend is cut in hieroglyphs on a large sandstone tablet which was discovered by J. F. Champollion in the temple of Khensu at Thebes, and was removed by Prisse d'Avennes in 1846 to Paris, where it is now preserved in the Bibliothèque Nationale. The form of the Legend which we have is probably the work of the priests of Khensu, about 1000 B.C., who wished to magnify their god, but the incidents recorded are supposed to have taken place at the end of the fourteenth century B.C., and there may indeed be historical facts underlying the Legend. The text states that the king of Egypt, Usermaātrā-setepenrā Rāmeses-meri-Amen, *i.e.* Rameses II, a king of the nineteenth dynasty about 1300 B.C., was in the country of Nehern, or Mesopotamia, according to his yearly custom, and that the chiefs of the country, even those of the remotest districts from Egypt, came to do homage to him, and to bring him gifts, *i.e.* to pay tribute. Their gifts consisted of gold, lapis-lazuli, turquoise, and costly woods from the land of the god,[1] and each chief tried to outdo his neighbour in the magnificence of his gifts. Among these tributary chiefs was the Prince of Bekhten, who, in addition to his usual gift, presented to the king his eldest daughter, and he spake words of praise to the king, and prayed for his life. His daughter was beautiful, and the king thought her the most beautiful maiden in the world, and he gave her the name of Neferu-Rā and the rank of " chief royal wife," *i.e.* the chief wife of Pharaoh. When His Majesty brought her to Egypt she was treated as the Queen of Egypt.

One day in the late summer, in the fifteenth year of his reign, his Majesty was in Thebes celebrating a festival in honour of Father Amen, the King of the gods, in the temple now known as the Temple of Luxor, when an official came and informed the king that " an ambassador of the Prince of Bekhten had arrived bearing many gifts for the Royal Wife." The ambassador was brought into the presence with his gifts, and having addressed the king in suitable words of honour, and smelt the ground before His Majesty, he told him that he had come to present a petition to him on behalf of the Queen's sister, who was called Bentresht (*i.e.* daughter of joy). The princess had been attacked by a disease, and the Prince of Bekhten asked His Majesty to send a skilled physician to see her. Straightway the king ordered his magicians (or medicine men) to appear before him, and also his nobles, and when they came he told them that he had sent for them to come and hear the ambassador's request. And, he added, choose one of your number who is both wise and skilful ; their choice fell upon the royal scribe Tehuti-em-heb, and the king ordered him to depart to Bekhten to heal the princess. When the magician arrived in Bekhten he found that Princess Bentresht was under the influence of a malignant spirit, and that this spirit refused to be influenced in any way by him ; in fact all his

---

[1] *i.e.* Southern Arabia and a portion of the east coast of Africa near Somaliland,

Stele relating the Story of the Healing of Bentresht,
Princess of Bekhten.

wisdom and skill availed nothing, for the spirit was hostile to him.

Then the Prince of Bekhten sent a second messenger to His Majesty, beseeching him to send a god to Bekhten to overcome the evil spirit, and he arrived in Egypt nine years after the arrival of the first ambassador. Again the king was celebrating a festival of Amen, and when he heard of the request of the Prince of Bekhten he went and stood before the statue of Khensu, called " Nefer-hetep," and he said, " O my fair lord, I present myself a second time before thee on behalf of the daughter of the Prince of Bekhten." He then went on to ask the god to transmit his power to Khensu, " Pa-ari-sekher-em-Uast," the god who drives out the evil spirits which attack men, and to permit him to go to Bekhten and release the Princess from the power of the evil spirit. And the statue of Khensu Nefer-hetep bowed its head twice at each part of the petition, and this god bestowed a fourfold portion of his spirit and power on Khensu Pa-ari-sekher-em-Uast. Then the king ordered that the god should set out on his journey to Bekhten carried in a boat, which was accompanied by five smaller boats and by chariots and horses. The journey occupied seventeen months, and the god was welcomed on his arrival by the Prince of Bekhten and his nobles with suitable homage and many cries of joy. The god was taken to the place where Princess Bentresht was, and he used his magical power upon her with such good effect that she was made whole at once. The evil spirit who had possessed her came out of her and said to Khensu : " Welcome, welcome, O great god, who dost drive away the spirits who attack men. Bekhten is thine ; its people, both men and women, are thy servants, and I myself am thy servant. I am going to depart to the place whence I came, so that thy heart may be content concerning the matter about which thou hast come. I beseech Thy Majesty to give the order that thou and I and the Prince of Bekhten may celebrate a festival together." The god Khensu bowed his head as a sign that he approved of the proposal, and told his priest to make arrangements with the Prince of Bekhten for offering up a great offering. Whilst this conversation was passing between the evil spirit and the god the soldiers stood by in a state of great fear. The Prince of Bekhten made the great offering before Khensu and the evil spirit, and the Prince and the god and the spirit rejoiced greatly. When the festival was ended the evil spirit, by the command of Khensu, " departed to the place which he loved." The Prince and all his people were immeasurably glad at the happy result, and he decided that he would consider the god to be a gift to him, and that he would not let him return to Egypt. So the god Khensu stayed for three years and nine months in Bekhten, but one day, whilst the Prince was sleeping on his bed, he had a vision in which he saw Khensu in the form of a hawk leave his shrine and mount up into the air, and then depart to Egypt. When he awoke he said to the priest of Khensu, " The god who was staying with us hath departed to Egypt ; let his chariot also depart." And the Prince sent off the statue of the god to Egypt, with rich gifts of all kinds and a large escort of soldiers and horses. In due course the party arrived in Egypt, and ascended to Thebes, and the god Khensu Pa-ari-sekher-em-Uast went into the temple of Khensu Nefer-hetep, and laid all the gifts which he had received from the Prince of Bekhten before him, and kept nothing for his own temple. This he did as a proper act of gratitude to Khensu Nefer-hetep, whose gift of a fourfold portion of his spirit had enabled him to overcome the power of the evil spirit that possessed the Princess of Bekhten. Thus Khensu returned from Bekhten in safety, and he re-entered his temple in the winter, in the thirty-third year of the reign of Rameses II. The situation of Bekhten is unknown, but the name is probably not imaginary, and the country was perhaps a part of Western Asia. The time occupied by the god Khensu in getting there does not necessarily indicate that Bekhten was a very long way off, for a mission of the kind moved slowly in those leisurely days, and the priest of the god would probably be much delayed by the people in the towns and villages on the way, who would entreat him to ask the god to work cures on the diseased and afflicted that were brought to him. We must remember that when the Nubians made a treaty with Diocletian they stipulated that the goddess Isis should be allowed to leave her temple once a year, and to make a progress through the country so that men and women might ask her for boons, and receive them.

CHAPTER VIII

HISTORICAL LITERATURE

THE historical period of Egyptian history, that is to say, the period during which Egypt was ruled by kings, each one calling himself NESU-BATI, or " King of the South, King of the North," covers about 4400 years according to some Egyptologists, and 3300 years according to others. Of the kings of All Egypt who reigned during the period we know the names of about two hundred, but only about one hundred and fifty have left behind them monuments that enable us to judge of their power and greatness. There is no evidence to show that the Egyptians ever wrote history in our sense of the word, and there is not in existence any native work that can be regarded as a history of Egypt. The only known attempt in ancient times to write a history of Egypt was that made by Manetho, a skilled scribe and learned man, who, in the reign of Ptolemy II Philadelphus (289–246 B.C.), undertook to write a history of the country, which was to be placed in the Great Library at Alexandria. The only portion of this History that has come down to us is the List of Kings, which formed a section of it ; this List, in a form more or less accurate, is extant in the works of Africanus and Eusebius. According to the former 553 or 554 kings ruled over Egypt in 5380 years, and according to the latter 421 or 423 kings ruled over Egypt in 4547 or 4939 years. It is quite certain that the principal acts and wars of each king were recorded by the court scribes, or official " remembrancer " or " recorder " of the day, and there is no doubt that such records were preserved in the " House of Books," or Library, of the local temple for reference if necessary. If this were not so it would have been impossible for the scribes of the eighteenth and nineteenth dynasties to compile the lists of kings found on the Palermo Stone, and in the Turin Papyrus, and on the Tablets set up by Seti I and Rameses II at Abydos, and on the Tablet of Ancestors at Karnak. These Lists, however, seem to show that the learned scribes of the later period were not always sure of the true sequence of the names, and that when they were dealing with the names of the kings of the first two dynasties they were not always certain even about the correct spelling and reading of their names. The reason why the Egyptians did not write the history of their country from a general point of view is easily explained. Each king wished to be thought as great as possible, and each king's courtiers lost no opportunity of showing that they believed him to be the greatest king who had sat on the throne of Egypt. To magnify the deeds of his ancestors was neither politic nor safe, nor did it lead to favours or promotion. In no inscription of their descendants do we find the mighty deeds and great conquests of Amenemhāt III, or of Usertsen III, or of Thothmes III, praised or described, and no court scribe ever dared to draft a text stating that these were truly three of the greatest kings of Egypt. When a local chief succeeded in making himself king of All Egypt he did not concern himself with preserving records of the great deeds of the king whose throne he had seized. When foreign foes invaded Egypt and conquered it their followers raided the towns, burnt and destroyed all that could be got rid of, and smashed the monuments recording the prowess of the king they had overthrown. The net result of all this is that the history of Egypt can only be partially constructed, and that the sources of our information are a series of texts that were written to glorify individual kings, and not to describe the history of a dynasty, or the general development of the country, or the working out of a policy. In attempting to draw up a connected account of a reign or period the funerary inscriptions of high officials are often more useful than the royal inscriptions. In the following pages are given extracts from annals, building inscriptions, narratives of conquests, and "triumph inscriptions" of an official character; specimens of the funerary inscriptions that describe military expeditions, and supply valuable information about the general history of events, will be given in the chapter on Biographical Inscriptions.

The earliest known annals are found on a stone which is preserved in the Museum at Palermo, and which for this reason is called "The Palermo Stone"; the Egyptian text was first published by Signor A. Pellegrini in 1896. How the principal events of certain years of the reigns of kings from the Predynastic Period to the middle of the fifth dynasty are noted is shown by the following:

[Reign of] SENEFERU. Year . . .
The building of Tuataua ships of *mer* wood of a hundred capacity, and 60 royal boats of sixteen capacity.
Raid in the Land of the Blacks (*i.e.* the Sūdān), and the bringing in of seven thousand prisoners, men and women, and twenty thousand cattle, sheep, and goats.
Building of the Wall of the South and North [called] House of Seneferu.
The bringing of forty ships of cedar wood (or perhaps "laden with cedar wood").
[Height of the Nile.] Two cubits, two fingers.

[Reign of Seneferu.] Year . . .
The making of thirty-five . . . 122 cattle
The construction of one Tuataua ship of cedar wood of a hundred capacity, and two ships of *mer* wood of a hundred capacity.
The numbering for the seventh time.
[Height of the Nile.] Five cubits, one hand, one finger.

The royal historical inscriptions of the first eleven dynasties are very few, and their contents are meagre and unimportant. As specimens of historical documents of the twelfth dynasty the following may be quoted:

EDICT AGAINST THE BLACKS

This short inscription is dated in the eighth year of the reign of Usertsen III. " The southern frontier in the eighth year under the Majesty of the King of the South and North, Khākaurā (Usertsen III), endowed with life for ever. No Black whatsoever shall be permitted to pass [this stone] going down stream, whether travelling by land or sailing in a boat, with cattle, asses, goats, &c., belonging to the Blacks, with the exception of such as cometh to do business in the country of Aqen [1] or on an embassy. Such, however, shall be well entreated in every way. No boats belonging to the Blacks shall in future be permitted to pass down the river by the region of Heh." [2]

The methods of Usertsen III and his opinions of the Sūdānī folk are illustrated by the following inscription which he set up at Semnah, a fort built by him at the foot of the Second Cataract.

" In the third month [3] of the season Pert His Majesty fixed the boundary of Egypt on the south at Heh (Semnah). I made my boundary and went further up the river than my fathers. I added greatly to it. I give commands [therein]. I am the king, and what is said by me is done. What my heart conceiveth my hand bringeth to pass. I am [like] the crocodile which seizeth, carrieth off, and destroyeth without mercy. Words (or matters) do not remain dormant in my heart. To the coward soft talk suggesteth longsuffering ; this I give not to my enemies. Him who attacketh me I attack. I am silent in the matter that is for silence ; I answer as the matter demandeth. Silence after an attack maketh the heart of the enemy bold. The attack must be sudden like that of a crocodile. The man who hesitateth is a coward, and a wretched creature is he who is defeated on his own territory and turned into a slave. The Black understandeth talk only. Speak to him and he falleth prostrate.

[1] This district has not been identified.
[2] The district of Semnah and Kummah, about 40 miles south of Wādī Halfah. [3] =January–February.

He fleeth before a pursuer, and he pursueth only him that
fleeth.　The Blacks are not bold men; on the contrary,
they are timid and weak, and their hearts are cowed.　My
Majesty hath seen them, and [what I say] is no lie.

" I seized their women, I carried off their workers in the
fields, I came to their wells, I slew their bulls, I cut their corn
and I burnt it.　This I swear by the life of my father.　I
speak the truth; there is no doubt about the matter, and that
which cometh forth from my mouth cannot be gainsaid.
Furthermore, every son of mine who shall keep intact this
boundary which My Majesty hath made, is indeed my son;
he is the son who protecteth his father, if he keep intact the
boundary of him that begot him.　He who shall allow this
boundary to be removed, and shall not fight for it, is not my
son, and he hath not been begotten by me.　Moreover, My
Majesty hath caused to be made a statue of My Majesty on
this my boundary, not only with the desire that ye should
prosper thereby, but that ye should do battle for it."

Campaign of Thothmes II in the Sudān

The following extract illustrates the inscriptions in which
the king describes an expedition into a hostile country which
he has conducted with success.　It is taken from an inscription of Thothmes II, which is cut in hieroglyphs on a rock
by the side of the old road leading from Elephantine to
Philæ, and is dated in the first year of the king's reign.
The opening lines enumerate the names and titles of the king,
and proclaim his sovereignty over the Haunebu, or the
dwellers in the northern Delta and on the sea coast, Upper
and Lower Egypt, Nubia and the Eastern Desert, including
Sinai, Syria, the lands of the Fenkhu, and the countries that
lie to the south of the modern town of Khartum.　The next
section states: " A messenger came in and saluted His
Majesty and said: The vile people of Kash (i.e. Cush, Northern Nubia) are in revolt.　The subjects of the Lord of the
Two Lands (i.e. the King of Egypt) have become hostile to
him, and they have begun to fight.　The Egyptians [in Nubia]

are driving down their cattle from the shelter of the stronghold which thy father Thothmes [I] built to keep back the tribes of the South and the tribes of the Eastern Desert." The last part of the envoy's message seems to contain a statement that some of the Egyptians who had settled in Nubia had thrown in their lot with the Sūdānī folk who were in revolt. The text continues : " When His Majesty heard these words he became furious like a panther (or leopard), and he said : I swear by Rā, who loveth me, and by my father Amen, king of the gods, lord of the thrones of the Two Lands, that I will not leave any male alive among them. Then His Majesty sent a multitude of soldiers into Nubia, now this was his first war, to effect the overthrow of all those who had rebelled against the Lord of the Two Lands, and of all those who were disaffected towards His Majesty. And the soldiers of His Majesty arrived in the miserable land of Kash, and overthrew these savages, and according to the command of His Majesty they left no male alive, except one of the sons of the miserable Prince of Kash, who was carried away alive with some of their servants to the place where His Majesty was. His Majesty took his seat on his throne, and when the prisoners whom his soldiers had captured were brought to him they were placed under the feet of the good god. Their land was reduced to its former state of subjection, and the people rejoiced and their chiefs were glad. They ascribed praise to the Lord of the Two Lands, and they glorified the god for his divine beneficence. This took place because of the bravery of His Majesty, whom his father Amen loved more than any other king of Egypt from the very beginning, the King of the South and North, Āakheperenrā, the son of Rā, Thothmes (II), whose crowns are glorious, endowed with life, stability, and serenity, like Rā for ever."

CAPTURE OF MEGIDDO BY THOTHMES III

The following is the official account of the Battle of Megiddo in Syria, which was won by Thothmes III in the twenty-third year of his reign. The narrative is taken from the

Annals of Thothmes III. The king set out from Thebes and marched into Syria, and received the submission of several small towns, and having made his way with difficulty through the hilly region to the south of the city of Megiddo, he camped there to prepare for the battle. "Then the tents of His Majesty were pitched, and orders were sent out to the whole army, saying, Arm yourselves, get your weapons ready, for we shall set out to do battle with the miserable enemy at daybreak. The king sat in his tent, the officers made their preparations, and the rations of the servants were provided. The military sentries went about crying, Be firm of heart. Be firm of heart. Keep watch, keep watch. Keep watch over the life of the king in his tent. And a report was brought to His Majesty that the country was quiet, and that the foot soldiers of the south and north were ready. On the twenty-first day of the first month of the season Shemu (March–April) of the twenty-third year of the reign of His Majesty, and the day of the festival of the new moon, which was also the anniversary of the king's coronation, at dawn, behold, the order was given to set the whole army in motion. His Majesty set out in his chariot of silvergold, and he had girded on himself the weapons of battle, like Horus the Slayer, the lord of might, and he was like unto Menthu [the War-god] of Thebes, and Amen his father gave strength to his arms. The southern half of the army was stationed on a hill to the south of the stream Kīnā, and the northern half lay to the south-west of Megiddo ; His Majesty was between them, and Amen was protecting him and giving strength to his body. His Majesty at the head of his army attacked his enemies, and broke their line, and when they saw that he was overwhelming them they broke and fled to Megiddo in a panic, leaving their horses and their gold and silver chariots on the field. [The fugitives] were pulled up by the people over the walls into the city ; now they let down their clothes by which to pull them up. If the soldiers of His Majesty had not devoted themselves to securing loot of the enemy, they would have been able to capture the city of Megiddo at the moment when the vile foes from Kadesh and the vile foes from this city were being dragged up hurriedly over the walls into this city ; for the terror of His Majesty had entered into them, and their arms dropped helplessly, and the serpent on his crown overthrew them. Their horses and their chariots [which were decorated] with gold and silver were seized as spoil, and their mighty men of war lay stretched out dead upon the ground like fishes, and the conquering soldiers of His Majesty went about counting their shares. And behold, the tent of the vile chief of the enemy, wherein was his son, was also captured. Then all the soldiers rejoiced greatly, and they glorified Amen, because he had made his son (*i.e.* the king) victorious on that day, and they praised His Majesty greatly, and acclaimed his triumph. And they collected the loot which they had taken, viz. hands [cut off the dead], prisoners, horses, chariots [decorated with] gold and silver," etc.

In spite of the joy of the army Thothmes was angry with his troops for having failed to capture the city. Every rebel chief was in Megiddo, and its capture would have been worth more than the capture of a thousand other cities, for he could have slain all the rebel chiefs, and the revolt would have collapsed completely. Thothmes then laid siege to the city, and he threw up a strong wall round about it, through which none might pass, and the daily progress of the siege was recorded on a leather roll, which was subsequently preserved in the temple of Amen at Thebes. After a time the chiefs in Megiddo left their city and advanced to the gate in the siege-wall and reported that they had come to tender their submission to His Majesty, and it was accepted. They brought to him rich gifts of gold, silver, lapis-lazuli, turquoise, wheat, wine, cattle, sheep, goats, &c., and he reappointed many of the penitent chiefs to their former towns as vassals of Egypt. Among the gifts were 340 prisoners, 83 hands, 2041 mares, 191 foals, 6 stallions, a royal chariot with a golden pole, a second royal chariot, 892 chariots, total 924 chariots ; 2 royal coats of mail, 200 ordinary coats of mail, 502 bows, 7 tent poles inlaid with gold, 1929 cattle, 2000 goats, and 20,500 sheep.

THE CONQUESTS OF THOTHMES III SUMMARISED BY AMEN-RĀ, KING OF THE GODS

The conquests of Thothmes III were indeed splendid achievements, and the scribes of his time summarised them very skilfully in a fine text which they had cut in hieroglyphs on a large stele at Karnak. The treatment is, of course, somewhat poetical, but there are enough historical facts underlying the statements to justify a rendering of it being given in this chapter. The text is supposed to be a speech of Amen-Rā, the lord of the thrones of the Two Lands, to the king. He says :

"Thou hast come to me, thou hast rejoiced in beholding my beneficence, O my son, my advocate, Menkheperrā, living for ever ! I rise upon thee through my love for thee. My heart rejoiceth at thy auspicious comings to my temple. My hands knit together thy limbs with the fluid of life ; sweet unto me are thy gracious acts towards my person. I have stablished thee in my sanctuary. I have made thee to be a source of wonder [to men]. I have given unto thee strength and conquests over all lands. I have set thy Souls and the fear of thee in all lands. The terror of thee hath penetrated to the four pillars of the sky. I have made great the awe of thee in all bodies. I have set the roar of Thy Majesty everywhere [in the lands of] the Nine Bows (i.e. Nubia). The Chiefs of all lands are grouped in a bunch within thy fist. I put out my two hands ; I tied them in a bundle for thee. I collected the Antiu of Ta-sti [1] in tens of thousands and thousands, and I made captives by the hundred thousand of the Northern Nations. I have cast down thy foes under thy sandals, thou hast trampled upon the hateful and vile-hearted foes even as I commanded thee. The length and breadth of the earth are thine, and those who dwell in the East and the West are vassals unto thee. Thou hast trodden upon all countries, thy heart is expanded (i.e. glad). No one dareth to approach Thy Majesty with

---

[1] The natives of the Eastern Desert of Nubia.

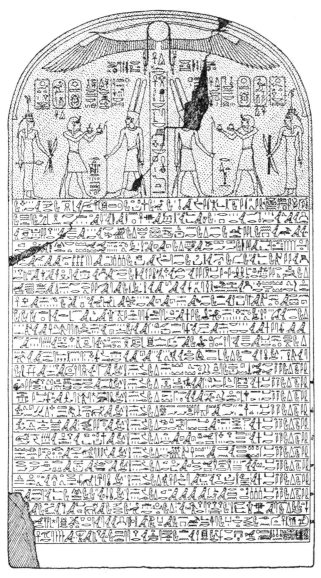

Stele on which is cut the Speech of Amen-Rā,
summarising the Conquests of Thothmes III.

hostility, because I am thy guide to conduct thee to them. Thou didst sail over the Great Circuit of water (the Euphrates) of Nehren (Aram Naharayim, or Mesopotamia) with strength and power. I have commanded for thee that they should hear thy roarings, and run away into holes in the ground. I stopped up their nostrils [shutting out] the breath of life. I have set the victories of Thy Majesty in their minds. The fiery serpent Khut which is on thy forehead burnt them up. It made thee to grasp as an easy prey the Ketu peoples, it burnt up the dwellers in their marshes with its fire. The Princes of the Āamu (Asiatics) have been slaughtered, not one of them remains, and the sons of the mighty men have fallen. I have made thy mighty deeds to go throughout all lands, the serpent on my crown hath illumined thy territory, nothing that is an abomination unto thee existeth in all the wide heaven, and the people come bearing offerings upon their backs, bowing to the ground before Thy Majesty, in accordance with my decree. I made impotent those who dared to attack thee, their hearts melted and their limbs quaked.

" I have come, making thee to trample under foot the Chief of Tchah (Syria), I have cast them down under thy feet in all the lands, I have made them to behold Thy Majesty as the ' lord of beams ' (*i.e.* the Sun-god), thou hast shone on their faces as the image of me.

" I have come, making thee to trample under foot the people of Asia, thou hast led away captive the Chiefs of the Āamu of Retenu, I have made them to behold Thy Majesty arrayed in thy decorations, grasping the weapons for battle, [mounted] on thy chariot.

" I have come, making thee to trample under foot the land of the East, thou hast trodden upon those who dwell in the districts of the Land of the God, I have made them to see thee as the brilliant star that shooteth out light and fire and scattereth its dew.

" I have come, making thee to trample under foot the land of the West, Kefti (Phœnicia) and Asi (Cyprus) are in awe of thee. I have made them to see Thy Majesty as a young bull, steady-hearted, with horns ready to strike, invincible.

" I have come, making thee to trample under foot those who are in their marshes, the Lands of Methen (Mitani) quake through their fear of thee.   I have made them to see Thy Majesty as the crocodile, the lord of terror in the water, unassailable.

" I have come, making thee to trample under foot those who dwell in the Islands, those who live in the Great Green (Mediterranean) hear thy roarings, I have made them to see Thy Majesty as the slayer when he mounteth on the back of his sacrificial animal.

" I have come, making thee to trample under foot the Thehenu (Libyans), the Islands of the Uthentiu [have sub-mitted to] the power of thy Souls.   I have made them to see Thy Majesty as a savage lion, which hath scattered the dead bodies of the people throughout their valleys.

" I have come, making thee to trample under foot the utter-most ends of the earth, the Circuit of the Great Circuit is in thy grasp, I have made them to see Thy Majesty as the hawk, which seizeth what it seeth when it pleaseth.

" I have come, making thee to trample upon those who are on their frontiers (?), thou hast smitten ' those on their sand ' (*i.e.* the desert dwellers), making them living captives.   I have made them to see Thy Majesty as a jackal of the south, moving fleetly and stealthily, and traversing the Two Lands.

" I have come, making thee to trample under foot the Antiu of Ta-sti, as far as . . . they are in thy grasp.   I have made them to see Thy Majesty as the Two Brothers (Set and Horus), I have gathered together their arms about thee with [strength].

" I have placed thy Two Sisters (Isis and Nephthys) near thee as protectresses for thee, the arms of Thy Majesty are [lifted] upwards to drive away evil.   I have made thee strong and glorious, O my beloved Son, thou Mighty Bull, crowned in Thebes, begotten by me . . ., Thothmes, the everliving, who hast performed for me all that my Ka wished. Thou hast set up my sanctuary with work that shall endure for ever, thou hast lengthened it and broadened it more than ever was done before.   The great pylon . . . Thou hast celebrated the festival of the beauties of Amen-Rā, thy monuments are greater than those of any king who hath existed, I commanded thee to do it.   I am satisfied with it.   I have stablished thee upon the throne of Horus for hundreds of thousands of years.   Thou shalt guide life . . ."

Summary of the Reign of Rameses III

The reign of Rameses III is remarkable in the annals of the New Empire, and the great works which this king carried out, and his princely benefactions to the temples of Egypt, are described at great length in his famous papyrus in the British Museum (Harris, No. 1, No. 9999).   The last section of the papyrus contains an excellent historical summary of the reign of Rameses III, and as it is one of the finest examples of this class of literature a translation of it is here given. The text is written in the hieratic character and reads :

King Usermaātrā-meri-Amen (Rameses III), life, strength, health [be to him !] the great god, said unto the princes, and the chiefs of the land, and the soldiers, and the charioteers, and the Shartanau soldiers, and the multitudes of the bowmen, and all those who lived in the land of Ta-mera (Egypt), Hearken ye, and I will cause you to know the splendid deeds which I did when I was king of men.   The land of Kamt was laid open to the foreigner, every man [was ejected] from his rightful holding, there was no " chief mouth " (*i.e.* ruler) for many years in olden times until the new period [came].   The land of Egypt [was divided among] chiefs and governors of towns, each one slew his neighbour. . . . Another period followed with years of nothingness (famine ?).   Arsu, a certain Syrian, was with them as governor, he made the whole land to be one holding before him. He collected his vassals, and mulcted them of their possessions heavily.   They treated the gods as if they were men, and they offered up no propitiatory offerings in their temples. Now when the gods turned themselves back to peace, and

A Page of the Hieratic Text, from the Great Harris Papyrus in the British Museum, describing the great Works carried out by Rameses III about 1200 B.C.

to the restoration of what was right in the land, according
to its accustomed and proper form, they established their
son who proceeded from their body to be Governor, life,
strength, health [be to him !], of every land, upon their great
throne, namely, Userkhārā-setep-en-Amen-meri-Amen, life
strength, health [be to him !], the son of Rā, Set-nekht-
merr-Rā-meri-Amen, life, strength, health [be to him !].
He was like Khepra-Set when he is wroth. He quieted the
whole country which had been in rebellion. He slew the
evil-hearted ones who were in Ta-mera (Egypt). He purified
the great throne of Egypt. He was the Governor, life,
strength, health [be to him !], of the Two Lands, on the
throne of Amen. He made to appear the faces that had
withdrawn themselves. Of those who had been behind
walls every man recognised his fellow. He endowed the
temples with offerings to offer as was right to the Nine Gods,
according to use and wont. He made me by a decree to be
the Hereditary Chief in the seat of Keb. I became the
" Great High Mouth " of the lands of Egypt, I directed the
affairs of the whole land, which had been made one. He
set on his double horizon (*i.e.* he died) like the Nine Gods.
There was performed for him what was performed for Osiris ;
sailing in his royal boat on the river, and resting [finally] in
his house of eternity (*i.e.* the tomb) in Western Thebes.

My father Amen, the lord of the gods, Rā, Tem, and Ptah
of the Beautiful Face made me to be crowned lord of the
Two Lands in the place of my begetter. I received the rank
of my father with cries of joy. The land had peace, being
fed with offerings, and men rejoiced in seeing me, Governor,
life, strength, health [be to him !], of the Two Lands, like
Horus when he was made to be Governor of the Two Lands
on the throne of Osiris. I was crowned with the Atef crown
with the serpents, I bound on the crown with plumes, like
Tatenn. I sat on the throne of Heru-Khuti (Harmakhis).
I was arrayed in the ornaments [of sovereignty] like Tem.
I made Ta-mera to possess many [different] kinds of men,
the officers of the palace, the great chiefs, large numbers of
horse and chariot soldiers, hundreds of thousands of them,

the Shartanau and the Qehequ, who were numberless, soldiers of the bodyguard in tens of thousands, and the peasants belonging to Ta-mera.

I enlarged all the frontiers of Egypt, I conquered those who crossed over them in their [own] lands. I slaughtered the Tanauna in their islands ; the Thakra and the Purastau were made into a holocaust. The Shartanau and the Uasheshu of the sea were made non-existent ; they were seized [by me] at one time, and were brought as captives to Egypt, like the sand in the furrows. I provided fortresses for them to dwell in, and they were kept in check by my name. Their companies were very numerous, like hundreds of thousands. I assessed every one of them for taxes yearly, in apparel and wheat from the stores and granaries. I crushed the Sāara and the tribes of the Shasu (nomad shepherds). I carried off their tents from their men, and the equipment thereof, and their flocks and herds likewise, which were without number. They were put in fetters and brought along as captives, as offerings to Egypt, and I gave them to the Nine Gods as slaves for their temples.

Behold, I will also make you to know concerning the other schemes that have been carried out in Ta-mera during my reign. The Labu (Libyans) and the Mashuashau had made their dwelling in Egypt, for they had captured the towns on the west bank of the Nile from Hetkaptah (Memphis) to Qarabana. They had occupied also both banks of the " Great River," and they had been in possession of the towns (or villages) of Kutut [1] for very, very many years whilst they were [lords] over Egypt. Behold, I crushed them and slaughtered them at one time (i.e. in one engagement). I overthrew the Mashuashau, the Libyans, the Asbatau, the Qaiqashau, the Shaiu, the Hasau, and the Baqanau. [I] slaughtered them in their blood, and they became piles of dead bodies. [Thus] I drove them away from marching over the border of Egypt. The rest of them I carried away, a vast multitude of prisoners, trussed like geese in front of my horses, their women and their children in tens of thousands,

---

[1] Perhaps the district of Canopus.

and their flocks and herds in hundreds of thousands. I allotted to their chiefs fortresses, and they lived there under my name. I made them officers of the bowmen, and captains of the tribes ; they were branded with my name and became my slaves ; their wives and their children were likewise turned into slaves. Their flocks and herds I brought into the House of Amen, and they became his live-stock for ever.

I made a very large well in the desert of Āina. It had a girdle wall like a mountain of basalt (?), with twenty buttresses (?) in the foundation [on] the ground, and its height was thirty cubits, and it had bastions. The frame-work and the doors were cut out of cedar, and the bolts thereof and their sockets were of copper. I cut out large sea-going boats, with smaller boats before them, and they were manned with large crews, and large numbers of serving-men. With them were the officers of the bowmen of the boats, and there were trained captains and mates to inspect them. They were loaded with the products of Egypt which were without number, and they were in very large numbers, like tens of thousands. These were despatched to the Great Sea of the water of Qett (*i.e.* the Red Sea), they arrived at the lands of Punt, no disaster followed them, and they were in an effective state and were awe-inspiring. Both the large boats and the little boats were laden with the products of the Land of the God, and with all kinds of wonderful and mysterious things which are produced in those lands, and with vast quantities of the *ānti* (myrrh) of Punt, which was loaded on to them by tens of thousands [of measures] that were without number. The sons of the chief of the Land of the God went in front of their offerings, their faces towards Egypt. They arrived and were sound and well at the mountain of Qebtit (Coptos),[1] they moored their boats in peace, with the things which they had brought as offerings. To cross the desert they were loaded upon asses and on [the backs of] men, and they were [re]loaded into river-barges at the quay of Coptos. They were despatched down the river, they arrived during a festi-

---

[1] *i.e.* the part at the Red Sea end of the Valley of Hammāmāt.

val, and some of the most wonderful of the offerings were carried into the presence of [My Majesty]. The children of their chiefs adored my face, they smelt the earth before my face, and rolled on the ground. I gave them to all the gods of this land to propitiate the two gods in front of me every morning.

I despatched my envoys to the desert of Āataka to the great copper workings that are in this place. Their sea-going boats were laden with [some of] them, whilst those who went through the desert rode on asses. Such a thing as this was never heard of before, from the time when kings began to reign. Their copper workings were found, and they were full of copper, and the metal was loaded by ten thousands [of measures] into their sea-going boats. They were despatched with their faces towards Egypt, and they arrived safely. The metal was lifted out and piled up under the veranda in the form of blocks (or ingots) of copper, vast numbers of them, as it were tens of thousands. They were in colour like gold of three refinings. I allowed everybody to see them, as they were wonderful things.

I despatched inspectors and overseers to the turquoise desert (*i.e.* Sinai) of my mother, the goddess Hathor, the lady of the turquoise. [They] carried to her silver, gold, byssus, fine (?) linen, and many things as numerous as the sand-grains, and laid them before her. And there were brought unto me most wonderfully fine turquoises, real stones, in large numbers of bags, and laid out before me. The like had never been seen before—since kings began to reign.

I caused the whole country to be planted with groves of trees and with flowering shrubs, and I made the people to sit under the shade thereof. I made it possible for an Egyptian woman to walk with a bold step to the place whither she wished to go ; no strange man attacked her, and no one on the road. I made the foot-soldiers and the charioteers sit down in my time, and the Shartanau and the Qehequ were in their towns lying at full length on their backs ; they were unafraid, for there was no fighting man [to come] from Kash (Nubia), [and no] enemy from Syria. Their bows and their weapons of war lay idle in their barracks, and they ate their fill and drank their fill with shouts of joy. Their wives were with them, [their] children were by their side ; there was no need to keep their eyes looking about them, their hearts were bold, for I was with them as strength and protection for their bodies. I kept alive (*i.e.* fed) the whole country, aliens, artisans, gentle and simple, men and women. I delivered a man from his foe and I gave him air. I rescued him from the strong man, him who was more honourable than the strong man. I made all men to have their rightful positions in their towns. Some I made to live [taking them] in the very chamber of the Tuat.[1] Where the land was bare I covered it over again ; the land was well filled during my reign. I performed deeds of beneficence towards the gods as well as towards men ; I had no property that belonged to the people. I served my office of king upon earth, as Governor of the Two Lands, and ye were slaves under my feet without [complaint ?]. Ye were satisfactory to my heart, as were your good actions, and ye performed my decrees and my words.

Behold, I have set in Akert (the Other World) like my father Rā. I am among the Great Companies of the gods of heaven, earth, and the Tuat. Amen-Rā hath stablished my son upon my throne, he hath received my rank in peace, as Governor of the Two Lands, and he is sitting upon the throne of Horus as Lord of the Two Nile-banks. He hath put on himself the Atef crown like Ta-Tenn, Usermaātrā-setep-en-Amen, life, strength, health [be to him !], the eldest-born son of Rā, the self-begotten, Rameses (IV)-heq-maāt-meri-Amen, life, strength, health [be to him !], the divine child, the son of Amen, who came forth from his body, rising as the Lord of the Two Lands, like Ta-Tenn. He is like a real son, favoured for his father's sake. Tie ye yourselves to his sandals. Smell the earth before him. Do homage to him. Follow him at every moment. Praise him. Worship him. Magnify his beneficent actions as ye do those of Rā every morning. Present ye before him your

---

[1] The sick and needy who were at death's door.

offerings [in] his Great House (*i.e.* palace), which is holy.
Carry ye to him the "blessings" (?) of the [tilled] lands and
the deserts. Be strong to fulfil his words and the decrees
that are uttered among you. Follow (?) his utterances, and
ye shall be safe under his Souls. Work all together for
him in every work. Haul monuments for him, excavate
canals for him, work for him in the work of your hands, and
there will accrue unto you his favour as well as his food
daily. Amen hath decreed for him his sovereignty upon
earth, he hath made this period of his life twice as long as
that of any other king, the King of the South and North,
the Lord of the Two Lands, Usermaātrā-setep-en-Amen,
life, strength, health [be to him !], the son of Rā, the lord of
crowns, Rameses (IV)-heqmaāt-meri-Amen, life, strength,
health [be to him !], who is endowed with life for ever.

The Invasion and Conquest of Egypt by Piānkhi, King of Nubia

The text describing the invasion and conquest of Egypt
by Piānkhi, King of Nubia, is cut in hieroglyphs upon a
massive stone stele which was found among the ruins of
Piānkhi's temple at Gebel Barkal, near the foot of the
Fourth Cataract, and which is now preserved in the Egyptian
Museum, Cairo. Although this composition does not belong
to the best period of Egyptian Literature, it is a very fine
work. The narrative is vivid, and the aim of the writer was
rather to state the facts of this splendid expedition than to
heap up empty compliments on the king ; both the subject-
matter and the dress in which it appears are well worthy of
reproduction in an English form. The inscription is dated
in the twenty-first year of Piānkhi's reign, and the king says :
"Hearken ye to [the account of] what I have done more
than my ancestors. I am a king, the emanation of the god,
the living offspring of the god Tem, who at birth was ordained
the Governor whom princes were to fear." His mother
knew before his birth that he was to be the Governor, he the
beneficent god, the beloved of the gods, the son of Rā who

was made by his (the god's) hands, Piānkhi-meri-Amen. One came and reported to His Majesty that the great prince Tafnekht had taken possession of all the country on the west bank of the Nile in the Delta, from the swamps even to Athi-taui,[1] that he had sailed up the river with a large force, that all the people on both sides of the river had attached themselves to him, and that all the princes and governors and heads of temple-towns had flocked to him, and that they were " about his feet like dogs." No city had shut its gates before him, on the contrary, Mer-Tem, Per-sekhem-kheper-Rā, Het-neter-Sebek, Per-Metchet, Thekansh, and all the towns in the west had opened their gates to him. In the east Het-benu, Taiutchait, Het-suten, and Pernebtepahet had opened to him, and he had besieged Hensu (Herakleopolis) and closely invested it. He had enclosed it like a serpent with its tail in its mouth. " Those who would come out he will not allow to come out, and those who would go in he will not allow to go in, by reason of the fighting that taketh place every day. He hath thrown soldiers round about it everywhere." Piānkhi listened to the report undismayed, and he smiled, for his heart was glad. Presently further reports of the uprising came, and the king learned that Nemart, another great prince, had joined his forces to those of Taf-nekht. Nemart had thrown down the fortifications of Nefrus, he had laid waste his own town, and had thrown off his allegiance to Piānkhi completely.

Then Piānkhi sent orders to Puarma and Las(?)-mer-sekni, the Nubian generals stationed in Egypt, and told them to assemble the troops, to seize the territory of Hermopolis, to besiege the city itself, to seize all the people, and cattle, and the boats on the river, and to stop all the agricultural operations that were going on ; these orders were obeyed. At the same time he despatched a body of troops to Egypt, with careful instructions as to the way in which they were to fight, and he bade them remember that they were fighting under the protection of Amen. He added, " When ye arrive

---

[1] A fortress a few miles south of Memphis.

at Thebes, opposite the Apts,[1] go into the waters of the river
and wash yourselves, then array yourselves in your finest
apparel, unstring your bows, and lay down your spears. Let
no chief imagine that he is as strong as the Lord of strength
(*i.e.* Amen), for without him there is no strength. The weak
of arm he maketh strong of arm. Though the enemy be many
they shall turn their backs in flight before the weak man,
and one shall take captive a thousand. Wet yourselves
with the water of his altars, smell the earth before him, and
say : O make a way for us ! Let us fight under the shadow
of thy sword, for a child, if he be but sent forth by thee, shall
vanquish multitudes when he attacketh." Then the soldiers
threw themselves flat on their faces before His Majesty,
saying, " Behold, thy name breedeth strength in us. Thy
counsel guideth thy soldiers into port (*i.e.* to success). Thy
bread is in our bodies on every road, thy beer quencheth our
thirst. Behold, thy bravery hath given us strength, and at
the mere mention of thy name there shall be victory. The
soldiers who are led by a coward cannot stand firm. Who
is like unto thee ? Thou art the mighty king who workest
with thy hands, thou art a master of the operations of war."

" Then the soldiers set out on their journey, and they
sailed down the river and arrived at Thebes, and they did
everything according to His Majesty's commands. And
again they set out, and they sailed down the river, and they
met many large boats sailing up the river, and they were full
of soldiers and sailors, and mighty captains from the North
land, every one fully armed to fight, and the soldiers of His
Majesty inflicted a great defeat on them ; they killed a very
large but unknown number, they captured the boats, made
the soldiers prisoners, whom they brought alive to the place
where His Majesty was." This done they proceeded on their
way to the region opposite Herakleopolis, to continue the
battle. Again the soldiers of Piānkhi attacked the troops
of the allies, and defeated and routed them utterly, and captured their boats on the river. A large number of the enemy
succeeded in escaping, and landed on the west bank of the

---

[1] *i.e.* the temples of Karnak and Luxor.

river at Per-pek. At dawn these were attacked by Piānkhi's troops, who slew large numbers of them, and [captured] many horses ; the remainder, utterly terror-stricken, fled northwards, carrying with them the news of the worst defeat which they had ever experienced.

Nemart, one of the rebel princes, fled up the river in a boat, and landed near the town of Un (Hermopolis), wherein he took refuge. The Nubians promptly beleaguered the town with such rigour that no one could go out of it or come in. Then they reported their action to Piānkhi, and when he had read their report, he growled like a panther, and said, " Is it possible that they have permitted any of the North- men to live and escape to tell the tale of his flight, and have not killed them to the very last man ? I swear by my life, and by my love for Rā, and by the grace which Father Amen hath bestowed upon me, that I will myself sail down the river, and destroy what the enemy hath done, and I will make him to retreat from the fight for ever." Piānkhi also declared his intention of stopping at Thebes on his way down the river, so that he might assist at the Festival of the New Year, and might look upon the face of the god Amen in his shrine at Karnak and, said he, " After that I will make the Lands of the North to taste my fingers." When the soldiers in Egypt heard of their lord's wrath, they attacked Per-Metchet (Ox- yrrhynchus), and they " overran it like a water-flood " ; a report of the success was sent to Piānkhi, but he was not satisfied. Then they attacked Ta-tehen (Tehnah ?), which was filled with northern soldiers. The Nubians built a tower with a battering ram and breached the walls, and they poured into the town and slew every one they found. Among the dead was the son of the rebel prince Tafnekht. This success was also reported to Piānkhi, but still he was not satisfied. Het-Benu was also captured, and still he was not satisfied.

In the middle of the summer Piānkhi left Napata (Gebel Barkal) and sailed down to Thebes, where he celebrated the New Year Festival. From there he went down the river to Un (Hermopolis), where he landed and mounted his war chariot ;

he was furiously angry because his troops had not destroyed the enemy utterly, and he growled at them like a panther. Having pitched his camp to the south-west of the city, he began to besiege it. He threw up a mound round about the city, he built wooden stages on it which he filled with archers and slingers, and these succeeded in killing the people of the city daily. After three days " the city stank," and envoys came bearing rich gifts to sue for peace. With the envoys came the wife of Nemart and her ladies, who cast themselves flat on their faces before the ladies of Piānkhi's palace, saying, " We come to you, O ye royal wives, ye royal daughters, and royal sisters. Pacify ye for us Horus (*i.e.* the King), the Lord of the Palace, whose Souls are mighty, and whose word of truth is great." A break of fifteen lines occurs in the text here, and the words that immediately follow the break indicate that Piānkhi is upbraiding Nemart for his folly and wickedness in destroying his country, wherein " not a full-grown son is seen with his father, all the districts round about being filled with children." Nemart acknowledged his folly, and then swore fealty to Piānkhi, promising to give him more gifts than any other prince in the country. Gold, silver, lapis-lazuli, turquoise, copper, and precious stones of all kinds were then presented, and Nemart himself led a horse with his right hand, and held a sistrum made of gold and lapis-lazuli in his left.

Piānkhi then arose and went into the temple of Thoth, and offered up oxen, and calves, and geese to the god, and to the Eight Gods of the city. After this he went through Nemart's palace, and then visited the stables " where the horses were, and the stalls of the young horses, and he perceived that they had been suffering from hunger. And he said, ' I swear by my own life, and by the love which I have for Rā, who reneweth the breath of life in my nostrils, that, in my opinion, to have allowed my horses to suffer hunger is the worst of all the evil things which thou hast done in the perversity of thy heart.' " A list was made of the goods that were handed over to Piānkhi, and a portion of them was reserved for the temple of Amen at Thebes.

The next prince to submit was the Governor of Herakleopolis, and when he had laid before Piānkhi his gifts he said : " Homage to thee, Horus, mighty king, Bull, conqueror of bulls. I was in a pit in hell. I was sunk deep in the depths of darkness, but now light shineth on me. I had no friend in the evil day, and none to support me in the day of battle. Thou only, O mighty king, who hast rolled away the darkness that was on me [art my friend]. Henceforward I am thy servant, and all my possessions are thine. The city of Hensu shall pay tribute to thee. Thou art the image of Rā, and art the master of the imperishable stars. He was a king, and thou art a king ; he perished not, and thou shalt not perish." From Hensu Piānkhi went down to the canal leading to the Fayyūm and to Illahūn and found the town gates shut in his face. The inhabitants, however, speedily changed their minds, and opened the gates to Piānkhi, who entered with his troops, and received tribute, and slew no one. Town after town submitted as Piānkhi advanced northwards, and none barred his progress until he reached Memphis, the gates of which were shut fast. When Piānkhi saw this he sent a message to the Memphites, saying : " Shut not your gates, and fight not in the city that hath belonged to Shu [1] for ever. He who wisheth to enter may do so, he who wisheth to come out may do so, and he who wisheth to travel about may do so. I will make an offering to Ptah and the gods of White Wall (Memphis). I will perform the ceremonies of Seker in the Hidden Shrine. I will look upon the god of his South Wall (*i.e.* Ptah), and I will sail down the river in peace. No man of Memphis shall be harmed, not a child shall cry out in distress. Look at the homes of the South ! None hath been slain except those who blasphemed the face of the god, and only the rebels have suffered at the block." These pacific words of Piānkhi were not believed, and the people of Memphis not only kept their gates shut, but manned the city walls with soldiers, and they were foolish enough to slay a small company of Nubian artisans and boatmen whom they found on the quay of Memphis. Tafnekht,

---

[1] The son of Khepera, or Tem, or Nebertcher.

the rebel prince of Saïs, entered Memphis by night, and addressed eight thousand of his troops who were there, and encouraged them to resist Piānkhi. He said to them: "Memphis is filled with the bravest men of war in all the Northland, and its granaries are filled with wheat, barley, and grain of all kinds. The arsenal is full of weapons. A wall goeth round the city, and the great fort is as strong as the mason could make it. The river floweth along the east side, and no attack can be made there. The byres are full of cattle, and the treasury is well filled with gold, silver, copper, apparel, incense, honey, and unguents. . . . Defend ye the city till I return." Tafnekht mounted a horse and rode away to the north.

At daybreak Piānkhi went forth to reconnoitre, and he found that the waters of the Nile were lapping the city walls on the north side of the city, where the sailing craft were tied up. He also saw that the city was extremely well fortified, and that there was no means whereby he could effect an entrance into the city through the walls. Some of his officers advised him to throw up a mound of earth about the city, but this counsel was rejected angrily by Piānkhi, for he had thought out a simpler plan. He ordered all his boats and barges to be taken to the quay of Memphis, with their bows towards the city wall; as the water lapped the foot of the wall, the boats were able to come quite close to it, and their bows were nearly on a level with the top of the wall. Then Piānkhi's men crowded into the boats, and, when the word of command was given, they jumped from the bows of the boats on to the wall, entered the houses built near it, and then poured into the city. They rushed through the city like a waterflood, and large numbers of the natives were slain, and large numbers taken prisoners. Next morning Piānkhi set guards over the temples to protect the property of the gods, then he went into the great temple of Ptah and reinstated the priests, and they purified the holy place with natron and incense, and offered up many offerings. When the report of the capture of Memphis spread abroad, numerous local chiefs came to Piānkhi, and did homage, and gave him tribute.

From Memphis he passed over to the east bank of the Nile to make an offering to Temu of Heliopolis. He bathed his face in the water of the famous " Fountain of the Sun," he offered white bulls to Rā at Shaiqaem-Anu, and he went into the great temple of the Sun-god. The chief priest welcomed him and blessed him ; " he performed the ceremonies of the Tuat chamber, he girded on the *seteb* garment, he censed himself, he was sprinkled with holy water, and he offered (?) flowers in the chamber in which the stone, wherein the spirit of the Sun-god abode at certain times, was preserved. He went up the step leading to the shrine to look upon Rā, and stood there. He broke the seal, unbolted and opened the doors of the shrine, and looked upon Father Rā in Het-benben. He paid adoration to the two Boats of Rā (Mātet and Sektet), and then closed the doors of the shrine and sealed them with his own seal." Piānkhi returned to the west bank of the Nile, and pitched his camp at Kaheni, whither came a number of princes to tender their submission and offer gifts to him. After a time it was reported to Piānkhi that Tafnekht, the head of the rebellion, had laid waste his town, burnt his treasury and his boats, and had entrenched himself at Mest with the remainder of his army. Thereupon Piānkhi sent troops to Mest, and they slew all its inhabitants. Then Tafnekht sent an envoy to Piānkhi asking for peace, and he said, " Be at peace [with me]. I have not seen thy face during the days of shame. I cannot resist thy fire, the terror of thee hath conquered me. Be-hold, thou art Nubti,[1] the Governor of the South, and Menth,[2] the Bull with strong arms. Thou didst not find thy servant in any town towards which thou hast turned thy face. I went as far as the swamps of the Great Green (*i.e.* the Medi-terranean), because I was afraid of thy Souls, and because thy word is a fire that worketh evil for me. Is not the heart of Thy Majesty cooled by reason of what thou hast done unto me ? Behold, I am indeed a most wretched man. Punish me not according to my abominable deeds, weigh

[1] The war-god of Ombos in Upper Egypt.
[2] The war-god of Hermonthis in Upper Epypt.

them not in a balance as against weights ; thy punishment of me is already threefold. Leave the seed, and thou shalt find it again in due season. Dig not up the young root which is about to put forth shoots. Thy Ka and the terror of thee are in my body, and the fear of thee is in my bones. I have not sat in the house of drinking beer, and no one hath brought to me the harp. I have only eaten the bread which hunger demanded, and I have only drunk the water needed [to slake] my thirst. From the day in which thou didst hear my name misery hath been in my bones, and my head hath lost its hair. My apparel shall be rags until Neith [1] is at peace with me. Thou hast brought on me the full weight of misery ; O turn thou thy face towards me, for, behold, this year hath separated my Ka from me. Purge thy servant of his rebellion. Let my goods be received into thy treasury, gold, precious stones of all kinds, and the finest of my horses, and let these be my indemnity to thee for everything. I beseech thee to send an envoy to me quickly, so that he may make an end of the fear that is in my heart. Verily I will go into the temple, and in his presence I will purge myself, and swear an oath of allegiance to thee by the God." And Piānkhi sent to him General Puarma and General Petamennebnesttaui, and Tafnekht loaded them with gold, and silver, and raiment, and precious stones, and he went into the temple and took an oath by the God that he would never again disobey the king, or make war on a neighbour, or invade his territory without Piānkhi's knowledge. So Piānkhi was satisfied and forgave him. After this the town of Crocodilopolis tendered its submission, and Piānkhi was master of all Egypt. Then two Governors of the South and two Governors of the North came and smelt the ground before Piānkhi, and these were followed by all the kings and princes of the North, " and their legs were [weak] like those of women." As they were uncircumcised and were eaters of fish they could not enter the king's palace ; only one, Nemart, who was ceremonially pure, entered the palace. Piānkhi was now tired of conquests, and he had all the loot which he

---

[1] The chief goddess of Saïs, the city of Tafnekht.

had collected loaded on his barges, together with goods from Syria and the Land of the God, and he sailed up the river towards Nubia. The people on both banks rejoiced at the sight of His Majesty, and they sang hymns of praise to him as he journeyed southwards, and acclaimed him as the Conqueror of Egypt. They also invoked blessings on his father and mother, and wished him long life. When he returned to Gebel Barkal (Napata) he had the account of his invasion and conquest of Egypt cut upon a large grey granite stele about 6 feet high and 4 feet 8 inches wide, and set up in his temple, among the ruins of which it was discovered accidentally by an Egyptian officer who was serving in the Egyptian Sūdān in 1862.

CHAPTER IX

ATTENTION has already been called to the very great importance of the autobiographies of the military and administrative officials of the Pharaohs, and a selection of them must now be given. They are, in many cases, the only sources of information which we possess about certain wars and about the social conditions of the periods during which they were composed, and they often describe events about which official Egyptian history is altogether silent. Most of these autobiographies are found cut upon the walls of tombs, and, though according to modern notions their writers may seem to have been very conceited, and their language exaggerated and bombastic, the inscriptions bear throughout the impress of truth, and the facts recorded in them have therefore especial value. The narratives are usually simple and clear, and as long as they deal with matters of fact they are easily understood, but when the writers describe their own personal characters and their moral excellences their meaning is sometimes not plain. Such autobiographies are sometimes very useful in settling the chronology of a doubtful period of history, and as an example of such may be quoted the autobiography of Ptah-shepses, preserved in the British Museum. This distinguished man was born in the reign of Menkaurā, the builder of the Third Pyramid at Gīzah, and he was educated with the king's children, being a great favourite of the king himself. The next king, Shepseskaf, gave him to wife Maātkhā, his eldest daughter, in order to keep him about the Court. Under the succeeding kings Userkaf and Sahurā he was advanced to great honour,

and he became so great a favourite of the next king, Neferari-
karā, that he was allowed to kiss the king's foot instead of
the ground on which it rested when he did homage. He
was promoted to further honours by the next king, Neferefrā,
and he lived to see Userenrā ascend the throne. Thus Ptah-
shepses lived under eight kings, and his inscription makes
it possible to arrange their reigns in correct chronological
order.

The Autobiography of Una

This inscription was found cut in hieroglyphs upon a slab
of limestone fixed in Una's tomb at Abydos ; it is now in the
Egyptian Museum in Cairo. It reads :

The Duke, the Governor of the South, the judge belonging to Nekhen, prince of Nekheb, the *smer uat* vassal
of Osiris Khenti Amenti, Una, saith : " I was a child girded
with a girdle under the Majesty of King Teta. My rank
was that of overseer of tillage (?), and I was deputy inspector
of the estates of Pharaoh. . . . I was chief of the *teb* chamber
under the Majesty of Pepi. His Majesty gave me the rank
of *smer* and deputy priest of his pyramid—town. Whilst
I held the rank of . . . His Majesty made me a ' judge
belonging to Nekhen.' His heart was more satisfied with
me than with any other of his servants. Alone I heard
every kind of private case, there being with me only the
Chief Justice and the Governor of the town . . . in the
name of the king, of the royal household, and of the Six Great
Houses. The heart of the king was more satisfied with me
than with any other of his high officials, or any of his nobles,
or any of his servants. I asked the Majesty of [my] Lord
to permit a white stone sarcophagus to be brought for me
from Raau.[1] His Majesty made the keeper of the royal
seal, assisted by a body of workmen, bring this sarcophagus
over from Raau in a barge, and he came bringing with it in
a large boat, which was the property of the king, the cover
of the sarcophagus, the slabs for the door, and the slabs for

---

[1] On the east bank, opposite Memphis.

the setting of the stele, and a pair of stands for censers (?), and a tablet for offerings. Never before was the like of this done for any servant. [He did this for me] because I was perfect in the heart of His Majesty, because I was acceptable to the heart of His Majesty, and because the heart of His Majesty was satisfied with me.

"Behold, I was 'judge belonging to Nekhen' when His Majesty made me a *smer uāt*, and overseer of the estates of Pharaoh, and . . . of the four overseers of the estate of Pharaoh who were there. I performed my duties in such a way as to secure His Majesty's approval, both when the Court was in residence and when it was travelling, and in appointing officials for duty. I acted in such a way that His Majesty praised me for my work above everything. During the secret inquiry which was made in the king's household concerning the Chief Wife Amtes, His Majesty made me enter to hear the case by myself. There was no Chief Justice there, and no Town Governor, and no nobleman, only myself, and this was because I was able and acceptable to the heart of His Majesty, and because the heart of His Majesty was filled with me. I did the case into writing, I alone, with only one judge belonging to Nekhen, and yet my rank was only that of overseer of the estates of Pharaoh. Never before did a man of my rank hear the case of a secret of the royal household, and His Majesty only made me hear it because I was more perfect to the heart of His Majesty than any officer of his, or any nobleman of his, or any servant of his.

"His Majesty had to put down a revolt of the Āamu dwellers on the sand.[1] His Majesty collected an army of many thousands strong in the South everywhere, beyond Abu (Elephantine) and northwards of Aphroditopolis, in the Northland (Delta) everywhere, in both halves of the region, in Setcher, and in the towns like Setcher, in Arthet of the Blacks, in Matcha of the Blacks, in Amam of the Blacks, in Uauat of the Blacks, in Kaau of the Blacks, and in the Land of Themeh. His Majesty sent me at the head of this army. Behold, the

---

[1] *i.e.* the nomads on the Marches of the Eastern Desert.

dukes, the royal seal-bearers, the *smer uats* of the palace, the chiefs, the governors of the forts (?) of the South and the North, the *smeru*, the masters of caravans, the overseers of the priests of the South and North, and the overseers of the stewards, were commanding companies of the South and the North, and of the forts and towns which they ruled, and of the Blacks of these countries, but it was I who planned tactics for them, although my rank was only that of an overseer of the estates of Pharaoh of . . . . No one quarrelled with his fellow, no one stole the food or the sandals of the man on the road, no one stole bread from any town, and no one stole a goat from any encampment of people. I despatched them from North Island, the gate of Ihetep, the Uārt of Heru-neb-Maāt. Having this rank . . . I investigated (?) each of these companies (or regiments); never had any servant investigated (?) companies in this way before. This army returned in peace, having raided the Land of the dwellers on sand. This army returned in peace, having thrown down the fortresses thereof. This army returned in peace, having cut down its fig-trees and vines. This army returned in peace, having set fire [to the temples] of all its gods. This army returned in peace, having slain the soldiers there in many tens of thousands. This army returned in peace, bringing back with it vast numbers of the fighting men thereof as living prisoners. His Majesty praised me for this exceedingly. His Majesty sent me to lead this army five times, to raid the Land of the dwellers on sand, whensoever they rebelled with these companies. I acted in such a way that His Majesty praised me exceedingly. When it was reported that there was a revolt among the wild desert tribes of the Land of Shert[1] . . . I set out with these warriors in large transports, and sailed until I reached the end of the high land of Thest, to the north of the Land of the dwellers on sand, and when I had led the army up I advanced and attacked the whole body of them, and I slew every rebel among them.

"I was the . . . of the Palace, and bearer of the [royal]

[1] A part of Syria (?).

sandals, when His Majesty the King of the South and North, Merenrā, my ever living Lord, made me Duke and Governor of the South land beyond Abu (Elephantine) and of the district north of Aphroditopolis, because I was perfect to the heart of His Majesty, because I was acceptable to the heart of His Majesty, and because the heart of His Majesty was satisfied with me.   I was . . . [of the Palace], and sandal-bearer when His Majesty praised me for displaying more watchfulness (or attention) at Court in respect of the appointment of officials for duty than any of his princes, or nobles, or servants.   Never before was this rank bestowed on any servant.   I performed the duties of Governor of the South to the satisfaction [of every one].   No one complained of (or quarrelled with) his neighbour ; I carried out work of every kind.   I counted everything that was due to the Palace in the South twice, and all the labour that was due to the Palace in the South I counted twice.   I served the office of Prince, ruling as a Prince ought to rule in the South ; the like of this was never before done in the South.   I acted in such a way that His Majesty praised me for it.   His Majesty sent me to the Land of Abhat to bring back a sarcophagus, " the lord of the living one," with its cover, and a beautiful and magnificent pyramidion for the Queen's pyramid [which is called] Khānefer Merenrā.   His Majesty sent me to Abu to bring back a granite door and its table for offerings, with slabs of granite for the stele door and its framework, and to bring back granite doors and tables for offerings for the upper room in the Queen's pyramid, Khānefer Merenrā.   I sailed down the Nile to the pyramid Khānefer Merenrā with six lighters, and three barges, and three floats(?), accompanied by one war boat.   Never before had any [official] visited Abhat and Abu with [only] one war boat since kings have reigned.   Whensoever His Majesty gave an order for anything to be done I carried it out thoroughly according to the order which His Majesty gave concerning it.

" His Majesty sent me to Het-nub to bring back a great table for offerings of *rutt* stone (quartzite sandstone ?) of Het-nub.   I made this table for offerings reach him in seventeen days. It was quarried in Het-nub, and I caused it to float down the river in a lighter. I cut out the planks for him in acacia wood, sixty cubits long and thirty cubits broad ; they were put together in seventeen days in the third month (May–June) of the Summer Season. Behold, though there was no water in the basins (?) it arrived at the pyramid Khānefer Merenrā in peace. I performed the work throughout in accordance with the order which the Majesty of my Lord had given to me. His Majesty sent me to excavate five canals in the South, and to make three lighters, and four barges of the acacia wood of Uauat. Behold, the governors of Arthet, Uauat, and Matcha brought the wood for them, and I finished the whole of the work in one year. [When] they were floated they were loaded with huge slabs of granite for the pyramid Khānefer Merenrā ; moreover, all of them were passed through these five canals . . . because I ascribed more majesty, and praise (?), and worship to the Souls of the King of the South and North, Merenrā, the ever living, than to any of the gods. . . . I carried out everything according to the order which his divine Ka gave me.

" I was a person who was beloved by his father, and praised by his mother, and gracious to his brethren, I the Duke, a real Governor[1] of the South, the vassal of Osiris, Una."

THE AUTOBIOGRAPHY OF HERKHUF

This inscription is cut in hieroglyphs upon a slab of stone, which was originally in the tomb of Herkhuf at Aswân, and is now in the Egyptian Museum in Cairo and upon parts of the walls of his tomb. Herkhuf was a Duke, a *smer uat*, a Kher-heb priest, a judge belonging to Nekhen, the Lord of Nekheb, a bearer of the royal seal, the shēkh of the caravans, and an administrator of very high rank in the South. All these titles, and the following lines, together with prayers for offerings, are cut above the door of his tomb. He says :

" I came this day from my town. I descended from

---

[1] *i.e.* his title was not honorary.

my nome. I builded a house and set up doors. I dug a
lake and I planted sycamore trees. The King praised me.
My father made a will in my favour. I am perfect. . . .
[I am a person] who is beloved by his father, praised
by his mother, whom all his brethren loved. I gave bread
to the hungry man, raiment to the naked, and him who
had no boat I ferried over the river. O ye living men
and women who are on the earth, who shall pass by this
tomb in sailing down or up the river, and who shall say, ' A
thousand bread-cakes and a thousand vessels of beer to the
lord of this tomb,' I will offer them for you in Khert Nefer
(the Other World). I am a perfect spirit, equipped [with
spells], and a Kher-heb priest whose mouth hath knowledge.
If any young man shall come into this tomb as if it were his
own property I will seize him like a goose, and the Great God
shall pass judgment on him for it. I was a man who spoke
what was good, and repeated what was loved. I never
uttered any evil word concerning servants to a man of power,
for I wished that I might stand well with the Great God. I
never gave a decision in a dispute between brothers which
had the effect of robbing a son of the property of his father."

Herkhuf, the Duke, the *smer uat*, the chamberlain, the
Judge belonging to Nekhen, the Lord of Nekheb, bearer of
the royal seal, the *smer uat*, the Kher-heb priest, the governor
of the caravans, the member of council for the affairs of the
South, the beloved of his Lord, Herkhuf,[1] who bringeth the
things of every desert to his Lord, who bringeth the offering
of royal apparel, governor of the countries of the South, who
setteth the fear of Horus in the lands, who doeth what his
lord applaudeth, the vassal of Ptah-seker, saith :

" His Majesty Merenrā, my Lord, sent me with my father
Ara, the *smer uat* and Kher-heb priest, to the land of Amam
to open up a road into this country. I performed the journey in seven months. I brought back gifts of all kinds from
that place, making beautiful the region (?) ; there was very
great praise to me for it. His Majesty sent me a second
time by myself. I started on the road of Abu (Elephantine),

---

[1] Some titles are here repeated.

I came back from Arthet, Mekher, Terres, Artheth, in a period of eight months.   I came back and I brought very large quantities of offerings from this country.   Never were brought such things to this land.   I came back from the house of the Chief of Setu and Arthet, having opened up these countries.   Never before had any *smer* or governor of the caravan who had appeared in the country of Amam opened up a road.   Moreover, His Majesty sent me a third time to Amam.   I started from . . . on the Uhat road, and I found the Governor of Amam was then marching against the Land of Themeh, to fight the Themeh, in the western corner of the sky.   I set out after him to the Land of Themeh, and made him to keep the peace, whereupon he praised all the gods for the King (of Egypt).   [Here follow some broken lines.]   I came back from Amam with three hundred asses laden with incense, ebony, *heknu*, grain, panther skins, ivory, . . . boomerangs, and valuable products of every kind.   When the Chief of Arthet, Setu, and Uauat saw the strength and great number of the warriors of Amam who had come back with me to the Palace, and the soldiers who had been sent with me, this chief brought out and gave to me bulls, and sheep, and goats.   And he guided me on the roads of the plains of Arthet, because I was more perfect, and more watchful (or alert) than any other *smer* or governor of a caravan who had ever been despatched to Amam.   And when the servant (*i.e.* Herkhuf) was sailing down the river to the capital (or Court) the king made the duke, the *smer uat*, the overseer of the bath, Khuna (or Una) sail up the river with boats loaded with date wine, *mesuq* cakes, bread-cakes, and beer." [1]

Herkhuf made a fourth journey into the Sūdān, and when he came back he reported his successes to the new king, Pepi II, and told him that among other remarkable things he had brought back from Amam a dancing dwarf, or pygmy. The king then wrote a letter to Herkhuf and asked him to send the dwarf to him in Memphis.   The text of this letter Herkhuf had cut on the front of his tomb, and it reads thus :

---

[1] Herkhuf's titles are here repeated.

Royal seal. The fifteenth day of the third month of the Season Akhet (Sept.–Oct.) of the second year. Royal despatch to the *smer uat*, the Kher-heb priest, the governor of the caravan, Herkhuf. I have understood the words of this letter which thou hast made to the king in his chamber to make him to know that thou hast returned in peace from Amam, together with the soldiers who were with thee. Thou sayest in this thy letter that there have been brought back by thee great and beautiful offerings of all kinds, which Hathor, the Lady of Ammaau, hath given to the divine Ka of the King of the South and North, Neferkarā, the ever-living, for ever. Thou sayest in this thy letter that there hath been brought back by thee [also] a pygmy (or dwarf) who can dance the dance of the god, from the Land of the Spirits, like the pygmy whom the seal-bearer of the god Baurtet brought back from Punt in the time of Assa. Thou sayest to [my] Majesty, " The like of him hath never been brought back by any other person who hath visited Amam." Behold, every year thou performest what thy Lord wisheth and praiseth. Behold, thou passest thy days and thy nights meditating about doing what thy Lord ordereth, and wisheth, and praiseth. And His Majesty will confer on thee so many splendid honours, which shall give renown to thy grandson for ever, that all the people shall say when they have heard what [my] Majesty hath done for thee, " Was there ever anything like this that hath been done for the *smer uat* Herkhuf when he came back from Amam because of the sagacity (or attention) which he displayed in doing what his Lord commanded, and wished for, and praised ? " Come down the river at once to the Capital. Bring with thee this pygmy whom thou hast brought from the Land of the Spirits, alive, strong, and healthy, to dance the dance of the god, and to cheer and gratify the heart of the King of the South and North, Neferkarā, the everliving. When he cometh down with thee in the boat, cause trustworthy men to be about him on both sides of the boat, to prevent him from falling into the water. When he is asleep at night cause trustworthy men to sleep by his side on his bedding.

Sec [that he is there] ten times [each] night. [My] Majesty wisheth to see this pygmy more than any offering of the countries of Ba and Punt. If when thou arrivest at the Capital, this pygmy who is with thee is alive, and strong, and in good health, [My] Majesty will confer upon thee a greater honour than that which was conferred upon the bearer of the seal Baurtet in the time of Assa, and as great is the wish of [My] Majesty to see this pygmy orders have been brought to the *smer*, the overseer of the priests, the governor of the town . . . to arrange that rations for him shall be drawn from every station of supply, and from every temple without. . . .

The Autobiography of Ameni Amenemhāt

This inscription is cut in hieroglyphs on the doorposts of the tomb of Ameni at Beni-hasan in Upper Egypt. It is dated in the forty-third year of the reign of Usertsen I, a king of the twelfth dynasty, about 2400 B.C. After giving the date and a list of his titles, Ameni says :

" I followed my Lord when he sailed to the South to overthrow his enemies in the four countries of Nubia. I sailed to the south as the son of a duke, and as a bearer of the royal seal, and as a captain of the troops of the Nome of Mehetch, and as a man who took the place of his aged father, according to the favour which he enjoyed in the king's house and the love that was his at Court. I passed through Kash in sailing to the South. I set the frontier of Egypt further southwards, I brought back offerings, and the praise of me reached the skies. His Majesty set out and overthrew his enemies in the vile land of Kash. I returned, following him as an alert official. There was no loss among my soldiers. [And again] I sailed to the South to fetch gold ore for the Majesty of the King of the South, the King of the North, Kheperkarā (Usertsen I), the ever living. I sailed to the south with the Erpā and Duke, the eldest son of the king, of his body Ameni.[1] I sailed to the south with a company of four

---

[1] He afterwards reigned as Amenemhāt II.

hundred chosen men from my troops ; they returned in safety, none of them having been lost. I brought back the gold which I was expected to bring, and I was praised for it in the house of the king ; the prince [Ameni] praised God for me. [And again] I sailed to the south to bring back gold ore to the town of Qebti (Coptos) with the Erpā, the Duke, the governor of the town, and the chief officer of the Government, Usertsen, life, strength, health [be to him !]. I sailed to the south with a company of six hundred men, every one being a mighty man of war of the Nome of Mehetch. I returned in peace, with all my soldiers in good health (or safe), having performed everything which I had been commanded to do. I was a man who was of a conciliatory disposition, one whose love [for his fellows] was abundant, and I was a governor who loved his town. I passed [many] years as governor of the Mehetch Nome. All the works (*i.e.* the forced labour) due to the palace were performed under my direction. The overseers of the chiefs of the districts of the herdsmen of the Nome of Mehetch gave me three thousand bulls, together with their gear for ploughing, and I was praised because of it in the king's house every year of making [count] of the cattle. I took over all the products of their works to the king's house, and there were no liabilities against me in any house of the king. I worked the Nome of Mehetch to its farthest limit, travelling frequently [through it]. No peasant's daughter did I harm, no widow did I wrong, no field labourer did I oppress, no herdsman did I repulse. I did not seize the men of any master of five field labourers for the forced labour (corvée). There was no man in abject want during the period of my rule, and there was no man hungry in my time. When years of hunger came, I rose up and had ploughed all the fields of the Nome of Mehetch, as far as it extended to the south and to the north, [thus] keeping alive its people, and providing the food thereof, and there was no hungry man therein. I gave to the widow as to the woman who possessed a husband. I made no distinction between the elder and the younger in whatsoever I gave. When years of high Nile floods came, the lords (*i.e.* the producers) of wheat and barley, the lords of products of every kind, I did not cut off (or deduct) what was due on the land [from the years of low Nile floods], I Ameni, the vassal of Horus, the Smiter of the Rekhti,[1] generous of hand, stable of feet, lacking avarice because of his love for his town, learned in traditions (?), who appeareth at the right moment, without thought of guile, the vassal of Khnemu, highly favoured in the king's house, who boweth before ambassadors, who performeth the behests of the nobles, speaker of the truth, who judgeth righteously between two litigants, free from the word of deceit, skilled in the methods of the council chamber, who discovereth the solution of a difficult question, Ameni.

The Autobiography of Thetha

This inscription is cut in hieroglyphs upon a large rectangular slab of limestone now preserved in the British Museum (No. 100). It belongs to the period of the eleventh dynasty, when texts of the kind are very rare, and was made in the reign of Uahānkh, or Antef. It reads :

Thetha, the servant in truth of the Horus Uahānkh, the King of the South, the King of the North, the son of Rā, Antef, the doer of beneficent acts, living like Rā for ever, beloved by him from the bottom of his heart, holder of the chief place in the house of his lord, the great noble of his heart, who knoweth the matters of the heart of his lord, who attendeth him in all his goings, one in heart with His Majesty in very truth, the leader of the great men of the house of the king, the bearer of the royal seal in the seat of confidential affairs, keeping close the counsel of his lord more than the chiefs, who maketh to rejoice the Horus (i.e. the king) through what he wisheth, the favourite of his Lord, beloved by him as the mouth of the seal, the president of the place of confidential affairs, whom his lord loveth, the mouth of the seal, the chief after the king, the vassal, saith :

I was the beloved one of his Lord, I was he with whom

---

[1] Titles of Ameni repeated.

he was well pleased all day and every day. I passed a long period of my life [that is] years, under the Majesty of my Lord, the Horus, Uahānkh, the King of the South and North, the son of the Sun, Antef. Behold, this country was subject unto him in the south as far as Thes, and in the north as far as Abtu of Then (Abydos of This). Behold, I was in the position of body servant of his, and was an actual chief under him. He magnified me, and he made my position to be one of great prominence, and he set me in the place beloved (?) for the affairs of his heart, in his palace. Because of the singleness [of my heart] he appointed me to be a bearer of the royal seal, and the deputy of the registrary (?). [I] selected the good things of all kinds of the offerings brought to the Majesty of my Lord, from the South and from the North land whensoever a taxing was made, and I made him to rejoice at the assessment which was made everywhere throughout the country. Now His Majesty had been afraid that the tribute, which was brought to His Majesty, my Lord, from the princes who were the overlords of the Red Country (Lower Egypt), would dwindle away in this country, and he had been afraid that the same would be the case in the other countries also. He committed to me these matters, for he knew that my administration was able. I rendered to him information about them, and because of my great knowledge of affairs never did anything escape that was not replaced. I was one who lived in the heart of his Lord, in very truth, and I was a great noble after his own heart. I was as cool water and fire in the house of my Lord. The shoulders of the great ones bent [before me]. I did not thrust myself in the train of the wicked, for which men are hated. I was a lover of what was good, and a hater of what was evil. My disposition was that of one beloved in the house of my Lord. I carried out every course of action in accordance with the urgency that was in the heart of my Lord. Moreover, in the matter of every affair which His Majesty caused me to follow out, if any official obstructed me in truth I overthrew his opposition. I neither resisted his order, nor hesitated, but I carried it out in very truth. In making any computation which he ordered, I made no mistake. I did not set one thing in the place of another. I did not increase the flame of his wrath in its strength. I did not filch property from an inheritance. Moreover, as concerning all that His Majesty commanded to set before him in respect of the royal household (or *harim*), I kept accounts of everything which His Majesty desired, and I gave them unto him, and I made satisfactory all their statements. Because of the greatness of my knowledge nothing ever escaped me.

I made a *mekha* boat for my town, and a *sehi* boat, so that I might attend in the train of my Lord, and I was one of the number of the great ones on every occasion when travel or journeying had to be performed, and I was held in great esteem, and entreated most honourably. I provided my own equipment from the possessions which His Majesty, the Horus Uahānkh, the King of the South, the King of the North, the son of the Sun, Antef, who liveth like Rā for ever, gave unto me because of the greatness of his love for me, until he departed in peace to his horizon (*i.e.* the tomb). And when his son, that is to say, the Horus Nekhtneb-Tep-nefer, the King of the South, the King of the North, the son of Rā, Antef, the producer of beneficent acts, who liveth for ever like Rā, entered his house, I followed him as his body-companion into all his beautiful places that rejoiced [his] heart, and because of the greatness of my knowledge there was never anything wanting (?). He committed to me and gave into my hand every duty that had been mine in the time of his father, and I performed it effectively under His Majesty ; no matter connected with any duty escaped me. I lived the [remainder] of my days on the earth near the King, and was the chief of his body-companions. I was great and strong under His Majesty, and I performed everything which he decreed. I was one who was pleasing to his Lord all day and every day.

The Autobiography of Aahmes (Amasis), the Naval Officer

This inscription is cut in hieroglyphs on the walls of the tomb of Aahmes at Al-Kāb in Upper Egypt; this distinguished marine flourished in the reigns of the first kings of the eighteenth dynasty, about 1600 B.C. The text reads :

The captain of the transport men, Aahmes, the son of Abana, the truth-speaker, saith : O all men, I will declare unto you, and will inform you concerning the favours that were conferred upon me. Seven times was I given gold in the sight of the whole land, and likewise slaves, both male and female, and grants of land for estates to be held by me in perpetuity were also made to me. Thus the name of a man bold and brave in his deeds shall not be extinguished in this land for ever ! He saith :

I passed my childhood in the town of Nekheb (Eileithyias-polis, Al-Kāb). My father was a soldier in the army of the King of the South, the King of the North, Seqenn-Rā, whose word is truth ; Baba was his name, and he was the son of Reant. I performed military service as his substitute in the ship called the *Bull* in the reign of the Lord of the Two Lands, Nebpehtirā (Amasis I), whose word is truth. I was at that time a youth, and was unmarried, and I slept in the *shennu*. Afterwards I got a house (*i.e.* wife) for myself, and I was drafted off to a ship, the " North " (?), because of my bravery. Then it became my lot to follow after the king, life, strength, health [be to him !], on my feet whensoever he made a journey in his chariot. The king sat down (*i.e.* besieged) before the city of Hetuārt (Avaris), and it was my lot whilst I was on my two feet to do a deed of bravery in the presence of His Majesty, whereupon I was made an officer in the vessel [called] *Khā-em-Mennefer*. The king was fighting on the arm of the river of Avaris [called] Patchetku, and I rose up and engaged in the fight, and I brought back a hand.[1] The royal herald proclaimed the matter, and the king gave me the gift of gold [which was awarded] for

---

[1] He had cut it off from a vanquished foe.

bravery. The fighting was renewed at this place (*i.e.* Avaris), and I again joined in the fight, and I brought back a hand; and the king gave me the gift of gold [which was awarded] for bravery a second time.

Then the king fought a battle in Egypt, to the south of this place, and I made prisoner a man and brought him back alive; I went down into the water [1] and brought him along on the road to the town, being firmly bound, and I crossed the water with him in a boat. The royal herald proclaimed [this act], and indeed I was rewarded with a double portion of the gold [which is awarded] for bravery. Then the king captured Avaris, and I brought back prisoners from the town, one man and three women, in all four persons. His Majesty gave these to me for slaves. Then His Majesty sat down before (*i.e.* besieged) Sharhana [2] in the fifth year, and captured it. I brought back from thence two persons, women, and one hand. And the king gave me the gift of gold [awarded] for bravery, as well as the two prisoners for slaves.

Now after His Majesty had smitten the Mentiu of Satet, [3] he sailed up the river to Khenthennefer to crush the Antiu of Sti, [4] and His Majesty overthrew them completely, and slew very many of them. I rose up and made three prisoners, viz. two men, alive, and three hands. And the king rewarded me with a double portion of gold, and he gave me the two prisoners to be my slaves. Returning His Majesty sailed down the river. His heart was expanded with the bravery of strength, for he had [now] conquered the Lands of the South [as well as] the Lands of the North. [Then as for] Aatti, the accursed one, who came from the South, his destiny came upon him, and he perished. The gods of the South laid their hands upon him, and His Majesty found him in Thenttaāmu (?). His Majesty brought him back bound alive, and with him were all his people loaded with fetters. I

---

[1] The water of the arm of the Nile.
[2] The Syrian town mentioned in Joshua xix. 6.
[3] Tribes of the Eastern Desert (?).
[4] The tribes of the Nubian Desert.

captured two of the soldiers of the enemy, and I brought them back, firmly fettered, from the boat of the foe Aatti. And the king gave me five men and parcels of land, five *stat* [in area] in my city. This was likewise done for the sailors, one and all. Then that vanquished foe came, Tetaān (the accursed one !) was his name, and he had gathered together round about himself men with hearts hostile [to the king]. His Majesty smote him and his accursed servants, and they ceased to exist. His Majesty gave me three men and a parcel of land five *stat* [in area] in my town.

I transported the King of the South, the King of the North, Tcheserkarā (Amenhetep I), whose word is truth, when he sailed up the river to Kash (Cush, Nubia) to extend towards the south the frontiers of Egypt. His Majesty captured that accursed Anti of Nubia in the midst of his accursed bowmen ; he was brought back, fettered by the neck, and they could not escape. [They were] deported, and were not allowed [to remain] upon [their] own land, and they became as if they existed not. And behold, I was at the head of our bowmen ! I fought with all my strength and might, and His Majesty saw my bravery. I brought back two hands and carried them to His Majesty. And the king went and raided men, women, and cattle, and I rose up and captured a prisoner and brought him alive to His Majesty. I brought back His Majesty from Khnemet-heru,[1] and the king gave me a gift of gold. I brought back alive two women whom I had captured in addition to those I had already carried to His Majesty, and the king appointed me to be " Āhatiu-en-Heq " (*i.e.* " Warrior of the Princes," or " Crown-warrior "). I transported the King of the South, the King of the North, Āakheperkarā, whose word is truth, when he sailed up the river to Khent-hen-nefer, to put down the rebellion in Khet land, and to put an end to the incursions of the people of Asemt. I fought with great bravery in his presence in the troubled water during the towing (?) of the fighting barges over the rapids (?), and the king made me the " Captain of the Transport." His Majesty, life,

---

[1] The " Upper Pool," site unknown.

strength, health [be to him !] . . . raged like a panther, he shot his first arrow, [which] remained in the neck of the vanquished foe . . . [the enemies] were helpless before the flaming serpent on his crown ; [thus] were they made in the hour of defeat and slaughter, and their slaves were brought back prisoners alive. Returning His Majesty sailed down the river having all the mountains and deserts in his hand. And that accursed Anti of Nubia was hung up head downwards, at the prow of the boat of His Majesty, and [then] placed on the ground in the Apts (i.e. Karnak). After these things the king set out on an expedition against Rethenu (Northern Syria), to avenge himself on foreign lands. His Majesty went forth against Neharina, where he found that the wretched enemy had set his warriors in battle array. His Majesty defeated them with great slaughter, and those who were captured alive and brought back by him from his wars could not be counted. And behold, I was the captain of our soldiers, and His Majesty saw my deeds of might. I brought out of the fight a chariot with its horses, and he who had been driving it was fettered prisoner inside it, and I carried them to His Majesty, who gave me a gift of gold, a twofold portion. Then I waxed old, and I arrived at a great age, and the favours [bestowed upon] me were as [many as those] at the beginning [of my life] . . . a tomb in the mountain which I myself have made.

THE AUTOBIOGRAPHY OF AAHMES (AMASIS), SURNAMED
PEN-NEKHEB

This inscription is cut in hieroglyphs upon the walls of the tomb of Aahmes at Al-Kāb in Upper Egypt. Aahmes was a contemporary of Aahmes the transport officer, and served under several of the early kings of the eighteenth dynasty. The text reads :

The Erpā, the Duke, the bearer of the seal, the man who took prisoners with his own hands, Aahmes, saith : I accompanied the King of the South, the King of the North, Neb-pehtirā (Amasis I), whose word is truth, and I captured for him in Tchah (Syria) one prisoner alive and one hand. I accompanied the King of the South, the King of the North, Tcheserkarā, whose word is truth, and I captured for him in Kash (Nubia) one prisoner alive. On another occasion I captured for him three hands to the north of Aukehek. I accompanied the King of the South, the King of the North, whose word is truth, and I captured for him two prisoners alive, in addition to the three other prisoners who were alive, and who escaped (?) from me in Kash, and were not counted by me. And on another occasion I laboured for him, and I captured for him in the country of Neherina (Mesopotamia) twenty-one hands, one horse, and one chariot. I accompanied the King of the South, the King of the North, Āakheperenrā, whose word is law, and I brought away as tribute a very large number of the Shasu [1] alive, but I did not count them. I accompanied the Kings of the South, the Kings of the North, [those great] gods, and I was with them in the countries of the South and North, and in every place where they went, namely, King Nebpehtirā (Amasis I), King Tcheserkarā (Amenhetep I), Āakheperkarā (Thothmes I), Āakheperenrā (Thothmes II), and this beneficent god Menkheperrā [2] (Thothmes III), who is endowed with life for ever. I have reached a good old age, I have lived with kings, I have enjoyed favours under their Majesties, and affection hath been shown to me in the Palace, life, strength, health [be to them !]. The divine wife, the chief royal wife Māatkarā, whose word is truth, showed several favours to me. I held in my arms her eldest daughter, the Princess Neferurā, whose word is law, when she was a nursling, I the bearer of the royal seal, who captured my prisoners, Aahmes, who am surnamed Pen-Nekheb, did this. I was never absent from the king at the time of fighting, beginning with Nebpehtirā (Amasis I), and continuing until the reign of Menkheperrā (Thothmes III). Tcheserkarā (Amenhetep I) gave me in gold

---

[1] The nomads of the Syrian desert.

[2] The titles, King of the North, King of the South, and the words, "whose word is truth" occur with each name ; they are omitted in the translation.

two rings, two collars, one armlet, one dagger, one fan, and one pectoral (?). Āakheperkarā (Thothmes I) gave me in gold four hand rings, four collars, one armlet, six flies, three lions, two axe-heads. Āakheperenrā gave me in gold four hand rings, six collars, three armlets (?), one plaque, and in silver two axe-heads.

THE AUTOBIOGRAPHY OF TEHUTI, THE ERPĀ

The autobiographies given hitherto are those of soldiers, sailors, and officials who in the performance of their duties travelled in Nubia, the Egyptian Sūdān, the Eastern Sūdān, the Red Sea Littoral, Sinai, and Western Asia. The following autobiography is that of one of the great nobles, who in the eighteenth dynasty assisted in carrying out the great building schemes of Queen Hātshepset and Thothmes III. Tehuti was an hereditary chief (erpā), and a Duke, and the Director of the Department of the Government in which all the gold and silver that were brought to Thebes as tribute were kept, and he controlled the distribution of the same in connection with the Public Works Department. The text begins with the words of praise to Amen-Rā for the life of Hātshepset and of Thothmes III, thus : " Thanks be to Amen-[Rā, the King of the Gods], and praise be to His Majesty when he riseth in the eastern sky for the life, strength, and health of the King of the South, the King of the North, Maātkarā (Hātshepset), and of the King of the South, the King of the North, Menkheperrā (Thothmes III), who are endowed with life, stability, serenity, and health like Rā for ever. I performed the office of chief mouth (i.e. director), giving orders. I directed the artificers who were engaged on the work of the great boat of the head of the river [called] Userhatamen. It was inlaid (or overlaid) with the very best gold of the mountains, the splendour of which illumined all Egypt, and it was made by the King of the South, the King of the North, Maātkarā,[1] in connection with the monuments which he made for his father Amen-Rā, Lord of the Thrones

---

[1] This queen frequently ascribed to herself male attributes.

of the Two Lands, who is endowed with life like Rā for ever. I performed the office of chief mouth, giving orders. I directed the artificers who were engaged on the work of the God-house, the horizon of the god, and on the work of the great throne, which was [made] of the very best silver-gold[1] of the mountains, and of perfect work to last for ever, which was made by Maātkarā in connection with the monuments which he made for his father Amen-Rā, &c. I performed the office of chief mouth, giving orders. I directed the artificers who were engaged on the work of the shrine (?) of Truth, the framework of the doors of which was of silver-gold, made by Maātkarā, &c. I performed the office of chief mouth, giving orders. I directed the artificers who were engaged on the works of Tcheser-Tcheseru,[2] the Temple of Millions of Years, the great doors of which were made of copper inlaid with figures in silver-gold, which was made by Maātkarā, &c. I performed the office of chief mouth, giving orders. I directed the artificers who were engaged on the work of Khākhut, the great sanctuary of Amen, his horizon in Amentet, whereof all the doors [were made] of real cedar wood inlaid (or overlaid) with bronze, made by Maātkarā, &c. I performed the office of chief mouth, giving orders. I directed the artificers who were engaged on the works of the House of Amen, it shall flourish to all eternity! whereof the pavement was inlaid with blocks of gold and silver, and its beauties were like unto those of the horizon of heaven, made by Maātkarā, &c. I performed the office of chief mouth, giving orders. I directed the artificers who were engaged on the work of the great shrine, which was made of ebony from Kenset (Nubia), with a broad, high base, having steps, made of translucent alabaster [from the quarry] of Het-nub, made by Maātkarā, &c. I performed the office of chief mouth, giving orders. I directed the artificers who were engaged on the works of the Great House of the god, which was plated

---

[1] *i.e.* that kind of gold which is found in its natural state alloyed with silver.

[2] The "Holy of Holies," the name of Hātshepset's temple at Dēr al-Baharī.

with silver in which figures were inlaid in gold—its splendour lighted up the faces of all who beheld it—made by Maātkarā, &c. I performed the office of chief mouth, giving orders. I directed the artificers who were engaged on the work of the great broad, high doors of the temple of Karnak, which were covered with plates of copper inlaid with figures in silver-gold, made by Maātkarā, &c. I performed the office of chief mouth, giving orders. I directed the artificers who were engaged on the work of the holy necklaces and pectorals, and on the large talismans of the great sanctuary, which were made of silver-gold and many different kinds of precious stones, made by Maātkarā, &c. I performed the office of chief mouth, giving orders. I directed the artificers who were engaged on the works in connection with the two great obelisks, [each of which] was one hundred and eight cubits in height (about 162 feet) and was plated with silver-gold, the brilliance whereof filled all Egypt, made by Maātkarā, &c. I performed the office of chief mouth, giving orders. I directed the artificers who were engaged on the work of the holy gate [called] " Amen-shefit," which was made of a single slab of copper, and of the images (?) that belonged thereto, made by Maātkarā, &c. I directed the artificers who were engaged on the work of the altar-stands of Amen. These were made of an incalculable quantity of silver-gold, set with precious stones, by Maātkara, &c. I directed the artificers who were engaged on the work of the store-chests, which were plated with copper and silver-gold and inlaid with precious stones, made by Maātkarā, &c. I directed the artificers who were engaged on the works of the Great Throne, and the God-house, which is built of granite and shall last like the firmly fixed pillars of the sky, made by Maātkarā, &c.

And as for the wonderful things, and all the products of all the countries, and the best of the wonderful products of Punt, which His Majesty presented to Amen, Lord of the Apts, for the life, strength, and health of His Majesty, and with which he filled the house of this holy god, for Amen had given him Egypt because he knew that he would rule it wisely (?), behold, it was I who registered them, because I was of strict integrity. My favour was permanent before [His Majesty], it never diminished, and he conferred more distinctions on me than on any other official about him, for he knew my integrity in respect of him. He knew that I carried out works, and that I covered my mouth (*i.e.* held my tongue) concerning the affairs of his palace. He made me the director of his palace, knowing that I was experienced in affairs. I held the seal of the Two Treasuries, and of the store of all the precious stones of every kind that were in the God-house of Amen in the Apts,[1] which were filled up to their roofs with the tribute paid to the god. Such a thing never happened before, even from the time of the primeval god. His Majesty commanded to be made a silver-gold . . . for the Great Hall of the festivals. [The metal] was weighed by the *heqet* measure for Amen, before all the people, and it was estimated to contain 88½ *heqet* measures, which were equal to 8592½ *teben*.[2] It was offered to the god for the life, strength, and health of Maātkarā, the ever living. I received the *sennu* offerings which were made to Amen-Rā, Lord of the Apts ; these things, all of them, took place in very truth, and I exaggerate not. I was vigilant, and my heart was perfect in respect of my lord, for I wish to rest in peace in the mountain of the spirit-bodies who are in the Other World (Khert-Neter). I wish my memory to be perpetuated on the earth. I wish my soul to live before the Lord of Eternity. I wish that the doorkeepers of the gates of the Tuat (Other World) may not repulse my soul, and that it may come forth at the call of him that shall lay offerings in my tomb, that it may have bread in abundance and ale in full measure, and that it may drink of the water from the source of the river. I would go in and come out like the Spirits who do what the gods wish, that my name may be held in good repute by the people who shall come in after years, and that they may praise me at the two seasons (morning and evening) when they praise the god of my city.

---

[1] The temples of Karnak and Luxor.

[2] The *teben* = 90.959 grammes.

THE AUTOBIOGRAPHY OF THAIEMHETEP, THE DAUGHTER
OF HERĀNKH

This remarkable inscription is found on a stele which is
preserved in the British Museum (No. 1027), and which was
made in the ninth year of King Ptolemy Philopator Philadelphus (71 B.C.). The text opens with a prayer to all the
great gods of Memphis for funerary offerings, and after a
brief address to her husband's colleagues, Thaiemhetep
describes in detail the principal incidents of her life, and gives
the dates of her birth, death, &c., which are rarely found on
the funerary stelæ of the older period. Thaiemhetep was
an important member of the semi-royal, great high-priestly
family] of Memphis, and her funerary inscription throws
much light on the theology of the Ptolemaic Period.

1. SUTEN-TA-HETEP,[1] may Seker-Osiris, at the head of
the House of the KA of Seker, the great god in Rāqet ; and
Hap-Asar (Serapis), at the head of Amentet, the king of the
gods, King of Eternity and Governor of everlastingness ;
and Isis, the great Lady, the mother of the god, the eye of
Rā, the Lady of heaven, the mistress of all the gods ; and
Nephthys, the divine sister of Horus, the 2 avenger of his
father, the great god in Rāqetit ; and Anubis, who is on his
hill, the dweller in the chamber of embalmment, at the head
of the divine hall ; and all the gods and goddesses who dwell
in the mountain of Amentet the beautiful of Hetkaptah
(Memphis), give the offerings that come forth at the word,
beer, and bread, and oxen, and geese, and incense, and
unguents, and suits of apparel, and good things of all kinds
upon their altars, to the KA of 3 the Osiris, the great princess, the one who is adorned, the woman who is in the highest
favour, the possessor of pleasantness, beautiful of body,
sweet of love in the mouth of every man, who is greatly

[1] These words mean, " The king gives an offering," and the formula is
as old at least as the fourth dynasty. It is obvious that the king could not
make a funerary gift to every one who died, but the words are always found
in funerary texts down to the latest times.

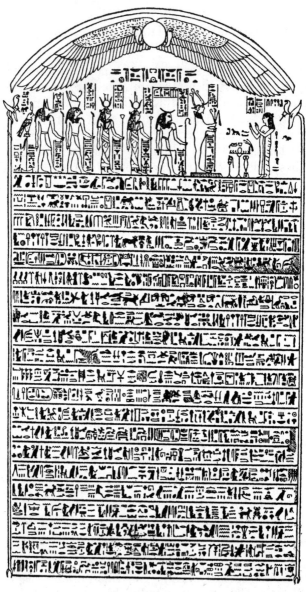

The Autobiography of Thaiemhetep, the daughter of Herānkh.

praised by her kinsfolk, the youthful one, excellent of disposition, always ready to speak her words of sweetness, whose counsel is excellent, Thaiemhetep, whose word (or voice) is truth, the beloved daughter of the royal kinsman, the priest of Ptah, libationer of the gods of 4 White Wall (Memphis), priest of Menu (or Amsu), the Lord of Senut (Panopolis), and of Khnemu, the Lord of Smen-Heru (Ptolemaïs), priest of Horus, the Lord of Sekhem (Letopolis), chief of the mysteries in Aat-Beqt, chief of the mysteries in Sekhem, and in It, and in Khā-Hap ; the daughter of the beautiful sistrum bearer of Ptah, the great one of his South Wall, the Lord of Ānkh-taui, Herānkh, 5 she saith :

" Hail, all ye judges and all ye men of learning, and all ye high officials, and all ye nobles, and all ye people, when ye enter into this tomb, come ye, I pray, and hearken unto what befell me.

" The ninth day of the fourth month [1] of the season Akhet of the ninth year under the Majesty of the King of the Two Lands, the god Philopator, Philadelphus, Osiris the Young, the Son of Rā, the lord of the Crowns of the South and of the North, Ptolemy, the ever living, beloved of Ptah and Isis, 6 [was] the day whereon I was born.

" On the . . . day of the third month [2] of the season Shemu of the twenty-third year under the Majesty of this same Lord of the Two Lands, my father gave me to wife to the priest of Ptah, the scribe of the library of divine books, the priest of the Tuat Chamber,[3] the libationer of the gods of the Wall, the superintendent of the priests of the gods and goddesses of the North and South, the two eyes of the King of Upper Egypt, the two ears of the King of Lower Egypt, the second of the king in raising up the Tet pillar,[4] the staff of the king [when] brought into the temples, 7 the Erpā in the throne chamber of Keb, the Kher-heb (precentor) in the seat of Thoth, the repeater (or herald) of the tillage of the

---

[1] October–November. [2] May–June.
[3] The Hall of Offerings in the tomb.
[4] The raising of the Tet pillar was an important ceremony, which was performed at the annual miracle-play of Osiris ; it symbolised resurrection.

Ram-god, who turneth aside the Utchat (sacred eye), who approacheth the Utchat by the great Ram of gold (?), who seeth the setting of the great god [who] is born when it is fettered, the Ur-kherp-hem,[1] Pa-sher-en-Ptah, the son of a man who held like offices, Peta-Bast, whose word (or voice) is truth, born of 8 the great decorated sistrum bearer and tambourine woman of Ptah, the great one of his South Wall, the Lord of Ānkh-taui, whose word (or voice) is truth.

" And the heart of the Ur-kherp-hem rejoiced in her exceedingly. I bore to him a child three times, but I did not bear a man child besides these three daughters. And I and the Ur-kherp-hem prayed to 9 the Majesty of this holy god, who [worketh] great wonders and bestoweth happiness (?), who giveth a son to him that hath one not, and Imhetep, the son of Ptah, hearkened unto our words, and he accepted his prayers. And the Majesty of this god came unto this Ur-kherp-hem during [his] sleep, and said unto him, 10 ' Let there be built a great building in the form of a large hall [for the lord of] Ānkh-taui, in the place where his body is wrapped up (or concealed), and in return for this I will give thee a man child.' And the Ur-kherp-hem woke up out of his sleep after these [words], and he smelt the ground before this holy god. And he laid them (*i.e.* the words) before the priests, 11 and the chief of the mysteries, and the libationers, and the artisans of the House of Gold, at one time, and he despatched them to make the building perfect in the form of a large, splendid funerary hall. And they did everything according as he had said. And he performed the ceremony of ' Opening the Mouth ' for this holy god, and he made to him a great offering of the beautiful offerings of every kind, and he bestowed upon him sculptured images 12 for the sake of this god, and he made happy their hearts with offerings of all kinds in return for this [promise].

" Then I conceived a man child, and I brought him forth on the fifteenth day of the third month [2] of the season Shemu of the sixth year, at the eighth hour of the day, under

[1] This was the official title of the high-priest of Memphis.
[2] May–June.

the Majesty of the Queen, the Lady of the Two Lands, Cleopatra, Life, Strength, Health [be to her !], 13 [the day] of the festival of ' things on the altar ' of this holy god, Imhetep, the son of Ptah, his form being like unto that of the son of Him that is south of his wall (*i.e.* Ptah), great rejoicings on account of him were made by the inhabitants of White Wall (Memphis), and there were given to him his name of Imhetep and the surname of Peta-Bast, and all the people rejoiced in him. 14

" The sixteenth day of the second month [1] of the season Pert of the tenth year was the day on which I died. My husband, the priest and divine father of Ptah, the priest of Osiris, Lord of Rastau, the priest of the King of the South, the King of the North, the Lord of the Two Lands, Ptolemy, whose word is truth, the chief of the mysteries of the House of Ptah, the chief of the mysteries of heaven, earth, and the Other World, the chief of the mysteries of Rastau, the chief of the mysteries of Rāqet, the Ur-kherp-hem, Pa-sher-en-Ptah, placed me in Am-urtet, 15 he performed for me all the rites and ceremonies which are [performed] for the dead who are buried in a fitting manner, he had me made into a beautiful mummy, and caused me to be laid to rest in his tomb behind Rāqet.

" Hail, brother, husband, friend ! O Ur-kherp-hem, cease not to drink, to eat, to drink wine, 16 to enjoy the love of women, and to pass thy days happily ; follow thy heart (or desire) day and night. Set not sorrow in thy heart, for oh, are the years [which we pass] so many on the earth [that we should do this] ? For Amentet is a land where black darkness cannot be pierced by the eye, and it is a place of restraint (or misery) for him that dwelleth therein. The holy ones [who are there] sleep in their forms. They wake not 17 up to look upon their friends, they see not their fathers [and] their mothers, and their heart hath no desire for their wives [and] their children. The living water of the earth is for those who are on it, stagnant water is for me. It cometh 18 to him that is upon the earth. Stagnant is

[1] December–January.

the water which is for me. I know not the place wherein I am. Since I arrived at this valley of the dead I long for running water. I say, ' Let not my attendant remove the pitcher from the stream.' 19. O that one would turn my face to the north wind on the bank of the stream, and I cry out for it to cool the pain that is in my heart. He whose name is ' Arniau '[1] calleth everyone to him, and they come to him with quaking hearts, and they are terrified through their fear of him. 20. By him is no distinction made between gods and men, with him princes are even as men of no account. His hand is not turned away from all those who love him, for he snatcheth away the babe from his mother's [breast] even as he doth the aged man. He goeth about on his way, and all men fear him, and [though] they make supplication before him, he turneth not his face away from them. Useless is it to make entreaty to him, 21 for he hearkeneth not unto him that maketh supplication unto him, and even though he shall present unto him offerings and funerary gifts of all kinds, he will not regard them.

" Hail, all ye who arrive in this funeral mountain, present ye unto me offerings, cast incense into the flame and pour out libations at every festival of Amentet."

The scribe and sculptor, the councillor, the chief of the mysteries of the House of Shent in Tenen, the priest of Horus, Imhetep, the son of the priest Khā-Hap, whose word (or voice) is truth, cut this inscription.

[1] The great Death-god.

CHAPTER X

THE STORY OF SANEHAT

THE text of this very interesting story is found written in the hieratic character upon papyri which are preserved in Berlin. The narrative describes events which are said to have taken place under one of the kings of the twelfth dynasty, and it is very possible that the foundation of this story is historical. The hero is himself supposed to relate his own adventures thus :

The Erpā, the Duke, the Chancellor of the King of the North, the *smer uati*, the judge, the Āntchmer of the marches, the King in the lands of the Nubians, the veritable royal kinsman loving him, the member of the royal bodyguard, Sanehat, saith : I am a member of the bodyguard of his lord, the servant of the King, and of the house of Neferit, the feudal chieftainess, the Erpāt princess, the highly favoured lady, the royal wife of Usertsen, whose word is truth in Khnemetast, the royal daughter of Amenemhāt, whose word is truth in Qanefer. On the seventh day of the third month of the season Akhet, in the thirtieth year [of his reign], the god drew nigh to his horizon, and the King of the South, the King of the North, Sehetepabrā,[1] ascended into heaven, and was invited to the Disk, and his divine members mingled with those of him that made him. The King's House was in silence, hearts were bowed down in sorrow, the two Great Gates were shut fast, the officials sat motionless, and the people mourned.

Now behold [before his death] His Majesty had despatched

---

[1] *i.e.* Amenemhāt II.

an army to the Land of the Themehu, under the command
of his eldest son, the beautiful god Usertsen.   And he went
and raided the desert lands in the south, and captured slaves
from the Thehenu (Libyans), and he was at that moment
returning and bringing back Libyan slaves and innumerable
beasts of every kind.   And the high officers of the Palace
sent messengers into the western country to inform the
King's son concerning what had taken place in the royal
abode.   And the messengers found him on the road, and they
came to him by night and asked him if it was not the proper
time for him to hasten his return, and to set out with his
bodyguard without letting his army in general know of his
departure.   They also told him that a message had been
sent to the princes who were in command of the soldiers in
his train not to proclaim [the matter of the King's death] to
any one else.

   Sanehat continues : When I heard his voice speaking I
rose up and fled.   My heart was cleft in twain, my arms
dropped by my side, and trembling seized all my limbs.   I
ran about distractedly, hither and thither, seeking a hiding-
place.   I went into the thickets in order to find a place
wherein I could travel without being seen.   I made my
way upstream, and I decided not to appear in the Palace,
for I did not know but that deeds of violence were taking
place there.   And I did not say, " Let life follow it," but I
went on my way to the district of the Sycamore.   Then I
came to the Lake (or Island) of Seneferu, and I passed the
whole day there on the edge of the plain.   On the following
morning I continued my journey, and a man rose up immediately in front of me on the road, and he cried for mercy ;
he was afraid of me.   When the night fell I walked into the
village of Nekau, and I crossed the river in an *usekht* boat
without a rudder, by the help of the wind from the west.
And I travelled eastwards of the district of Aku, by the pass
of the goddess Herit, the Lady of the Red Mountain.   Then
I allowed my feet to take the road downstream, and I travelled
on to Anebuheq, the fortress that had been built to drive
back the Satiu (nomad marauders), and to hold in check

the tribes that roamed the desert. I crouched down in the scrub during the day to avoid being seen by the watchmen on the top of the fortress. I set out again on the march, when the night fell, and when daylight fell on the earth I arrived at Peten, and I rested myself by the Lake of Kamur. Then thirst came upon me and overwhelmed me. I suffered torture. My throat was burnt up, and I said, "This indeed is the taste of death." But I took courage, and collected my members (i.e. myself), for I heard the sounds that are made by flocks and herds. Then the Satiu of the desert saw me, and the master of the caravan who had been in Egypt recognised me. And he rose up and gave me some water, and he warmed milk [for me], and I travelled with the men of his caravan, and thus I passed through one country after the other [in safety]. I avoided the land of Sunu and I journeyed to the land of Qetem, where I stayed for a year and a half.

And Āmmuiansha, the Shēkh of Upper Thennu, took me aside and said unto me, "Thou wilt be happy with me, for thou wilt hear the language of Egypt." Now he said this because he knew what manner of man I was, for he had heard the people of Egypt who were there with him bear testimony concerning my character. And he said unto me, "Why and wherefore hast thou come hither? Is it because the departure of King Sehetepabrā from the Palace to the horizon hath taken place, and thou didst not know what would be the result of it?" Then I spake unto him with words of deceit, saying, "I was among the soldiers who had gone to the land of Themeh. My heart cried out, my courage failed me utterly, it made me follow the ways over which I fled. I hesitated, but felt no regret. I did not hearken unto any evil counsel, and my name was not heard on the mouth of the herald. How I came to be brought into this country I know not; it was, perhaps, by the Providence of God."

And Āmmuiansha said unto me, "What will become of the land without that beneficent god the terror of whom passed through the lands like the goddess Sekhmet in a year of pestilence?" Then I made answer unto him, saying, "His son shall save us. He hath entered the Palace, and hath taken possession of the heritage of his father. Moreover, he is the god who hath no equal, and no other can exist beside him, the lord of wisdom, perfect in his plans, of good will when he passeth decrees, and one cometh forth and goeth in according to his ordinance. He reduced foreign lands to submission whilst his father [sat] in the Palace directing him in the matters which had to be carried out. He is mighty of valour, he slayeth with his sword, and in bravery he hath no compeer. One should see him attacking the nomads of the desert, and pouncing upon the robbers of the highway ! He beateth down opposition, he smiteth arms helpless, his enemies cannot be made to resist him. He taketh vengeance, he cleaveth skulls, none can stand up before him. His strides are long, he slayeth him that fleeth, and he who turneth his back upon him in flight never reacheth his goal. When attacked his courage standeth firm. He attacketh again and again, and he never yieldeth. His heart is bold when he seeth the battle array, he permitteth none to sit down behind. His face is fierce [as] he rusheth on the attacker. He rejoiceth when he taketh captive the chief of a band of desert robbers. He seizeth his shield, he raineth blows upon him, but he hath no need to repeat his attack, for he slayeth his foe before he can hurl his spear at him. Before he draweth his bow the nomads have fled, his arms are like the souls of the Great Goddess. He fighteth, and if he reacheth his object of attack he spareth not, and he leaveth no remnant. He is beloved, his pleasantness is great, he is the conqueror, and his town loveth him more than herself ; she rejoiceth in him more than in her god, and men throng about him with rejoicings. He was king and conqueror before his birth, and he hath worn his crowns since he was born. He hath multiplied births, and he it is whom God hath made to be the joy of this land, which he hath ruled, and the boundaries of which he hath enlarged. He hath conquered the Lands of the South, shall he not conquer the Lands of the North ? He hath been created to smite the hunters of the desert, and to crush the tribes that roam the sandy waste. . . ." Then the Shēkh of Upper Thennu said unto me, " Assuredly Egypt is a happy country in that it knoweth his vigour. Verily, as long as thou tarriest with me I will do good unto thee."

And he set me before his children, and he gave me his eldest daughter to wife, and he made me to choose for myself a very fine territory which belonged to him, and which lay on the border of a neighbouring country, and this beautiful region was called Aa. In it there are figs, and wine is more abundant than water. Honey is plentiful, oil existeth in large quantities, and fruits of every kind are on the trees thereof. Wheat, barley, herds of cattle, and flocks of sheep and goats are there in untold numbers. And the Shēkh showed me very great favour, and his affection for me was so great that he made me Shēkh of one of the best tribes in his country. Bread-cakes were made for me each day, and each day wine was brought to me with roasted flesh and wild fowl, and the wild creatures of the plain that were caught were laid before me, in addition to the game which my hunting dogs brought in. Food of all kinds was made for me, and milk was prepared for me in various ways. I passed many years in this manner, and my children grew up into fine strong men, and each one of them ruled his tribe. Every ambassador on his journey to and from Egypt visited me. I was kind to people of every class. I gave water to the thirsty man. I suppressed the highway robber. I directed the operations of the bowmen of the desert, who marched long distances to suppress the hostile Shēkhs, and to reduce their power, for the Shēkh of Thennu had appointed me General of his soldiers many years before this. Every country against which I marched I terrified into submission. I seized the crops by the wells, I looted the flocks and herds, I carried away the people and their slaves who ate their bread, I slew the men there. Through my sword and bow, and through my well-organised campaigns, I was highly esteemed in the mind of the Shēkh, and he loved me, for he knew my bravery, and he set me before his children when he saw the bravery of my arms.

Then a certain mighty man of valour of Thennu came and reviled me in my tent ; he was greatly renowned as a man of war, and he was unequalled in the whole country, which he had conquered. He challenged me to combat, being urged to fight by the men of his tribe, and he believed that he could conquer me, and he determined to take my flocks and herds as spoil. And the Shēkh took counsel with me about the challenge, and I said, " I am not an acquaintance of his, and I am by no means a friend of his. Have I ever visited him in his domain or entered his door, or passed through his compound ? [Never !] He is a man whose heart becometh full of evil thoughts, whensoever he seeth me, and he wisheth to carry out his fell design and plunder me. He is like a wild bull seeking to slay the bull of a herd of tame cattle so that he may make the cows his own. Or rather he is a mere braggart who wisheth to seize the property which I have collected by my prudence, and not an experienced warrior. Or rather he is a bull that loveth to fight, and that loveth to make attacks repeatedly, fearing that otherwise some other animal will prove to be his equal. If, however, his heart be set upon fighting, let him declare [to me] his intention. Is God, Who knoweth everything, ignorant of what he hath decided to do ? "

And I passed the night in stringing my bow, I made ready my arrows of war, I unsheathed my dagger, and I put all my weapons in order. At daybreak the tribes of the land of Thennu came, and the people who lived on both sides of it gathered themselves together, for they were greatly concerned about the combat, and they came and stood up round about me where I stood. Every heart burned for my success, and both men and women uttered cries (or exclamations), and every heart suffered anxiety on my behalf, saying, " Can there exist possibly any man who is a mightier fighter and more doughty as a man of war than he ? " Then mine adversary grasped his shield, and his battle-axe, and his spears, and after he had hurled his weapons at me, and I had succeeded in avoiding his short spears, which arrived harmlessly one after the other, he became filled with fury, and making up his mind to attack me at close quarters he threw himself upon me. And I hurled my javelin at him, which remained fast in his neck, and he uttered a long cry and fell on his face, and I slew him with his own weapons. And as I stood upon his back I shouted the cry of victory, and every Āamu man (*i.e.* Asiatic) applauded me, and I gave thanks to Menthu ;[1] and the slaves of my opponent mourned for their lord. And the Shēkh Āmmuiansha took me in his arms and embraced me. I carried off his (*i.e.* the opponent's) property. I seized his cattle as spoil, and what he meditated doing to me I did unto him. I took possession of the contents of his tent, I stripped his compound, I became rich, I increased my store of goods, and I added greatly to the number of my cattle.

Thus did God prosper the man who made Him his support. Thus that day was washed (*i.e.* satisfied) the heart of the man who was compelled to make his escape from his own into another country. Thus that day the integrity of the man who was once obliged to take to flight as a miserable fugitive was proven in the sight of all the Court. Once I was a wanderer wandering about hungry, and now I can give bread to my neighbours. Once I had to flee naked from my country, and now I am the possessor of splendid raiment, and of apparel made of the finest byssus. Once I was obliged to do my own errands and to fetch and carry for myself, and now I am the master of troops of servants. My house is beautiful, my estate is spacious, and my name is repeated in the Great House. O Lord of the gods, who hath ordered my goings, I will offer propitiatory offerings unto Thee : I beseech Thee to restore me to Egypt, and O be Thou pleased most graciously to let me once again look upon the spot where my mind dwelleth for hours [at a time]! How great a boon would it be for me to cleanse my body in the land of my birth ! Let, I pray, a period of happiness attend me, and may God give me peace. May He dispose events in such a way that the close of the career of the man who hath suffered misery, whose heart hath seen sorrow, who hath

---

[1] The War-god of Thebes.

wandered into a strange land, may be happy. Is He not at peace with me this day ? Surely He shall hearken to him that is afar off. . . . Let the King of Egypt be at peace with me, and may I live upon his offerings. Let me salute the Mistress of the Land (*i.e.* the Queen) who is in his palace, and let me hear the greetings of her children. O would that my members could become young again ! For now old age is stealing on me. Infirmity overtaketh me. Mine eyes refuse to see, my hands fall helpless, my knees shake, my heart standeth still, the funerary mourners approach and they will bear me away to the City of Eternity, wherein I shall become a follower of Nebertcher. She will declare to me the beauties of her children, and they shall traverse it with me.

Behold now, the Majesty of the King of Egypt, Kheperkarā, whose word is truth, having spoken concerning the various things that had happened to me, sent a messenger to me bearing royal gifts, such as he would send to the king of a foreign land, with the intention of making glad the heart of thy servant now [speaking], and the princes of his palace made me to hear their salutations. And here is a copy of the document, which was brought to thy servant [from the King] instructing him to return to Egypt.

" The royal command of the Horus, Ānkh-mestu, Lord of Nekhebet and Uatchet, Ānkh-mestu, King of the South, King of the North, Kheperkarā, the son of Rā, Amen-emhāt, the everliving, to my follower Sanehat. This royal order is despatched unto thee to inform thee. Thou hast travelled about everywhere, in one country after another, having set out from Qetem and reached Thennu, and thou hast journeyed from place to place at thine own will and pleasure. Observe now, what thou hast done [unto others, making them to obey thee], shall be done unto thee. Make no excuses, for they shall be set aside ; argue not with [my] officials, for thy arguments shall be refuted. Thy heart shall not reject the plans which thy mind hath formulated. Thy Heaven (*i.e.* the Queen), who is in the Palace, is stable and flourishing at this present time, her head is crowned with the sovereignty of the earth, and her children are in the royal chambers of the Palace. Lay aside the honours which thou hast, and thy life of abundance (or luxury), and journey to Egypt. Come and look upon thy native land, the land where thou wast born, smell the earth (*i.e.* do homage) before the Great Gate, and associate with the nobles thereof. For at this time thou art beginning to be an old man, and thou canst no longer produce sons, and thou hast [ever] in thy mind the day of [thy] burial, when thou wilt assume the form of a servant [of Osiris]. The unguents for thine embalmment on the night [of mummification] have been set apart for thee, together with thy mummy swathings, which are the work of the hands of the goddess Tait. Thy funerary procession, which will march on the day of thy union with the earth, hath been arranged, and there are prepared for thee a gilded mummy-case, the head whereof is painted blue, and a canopy made of *mesket* wood. Oxen shall draw thee [to the tomb], the wailing women shall precede thee, the funerary dances shall be performed, those who mourn thee shall be at the door of thy tomb, the funerary offerings dedicated to thee shall be proclaimed, sacrifices shall be offered for thee with thy oblations, and thy funerary edifice shall be built in white stone, side by side with those of the princes and princesses. Thy death must not take place in a foreign land, the Āamu folk shall not escort thee [to thy grave], thou shalt not be placed in the skin of a ram when thy burial is effected ; but at thy burial there shall be . . . and the smiting of the earth, and when thou departest lamentations shall be made over thy body."

When this royal letter reached me I was standing among the people of my tribe, and when it had been read to me I threw myself face downwards on the ground, and bowed until my head touched the dust, and I clasped the document reverently to my breast. Then [I rose up] and walked to and fro in my abode, rejoicing and saying, " How can these things possibly be done to thy servant who is now speaking, whose heart made him to fly into foreign lands [where dwell] peoples who stammer in their speech ? Assuredly it is a good and gracious thought [of the King] to deliver me from death

[here], for thy Ka (*i.e.* double) will make my body to end [its existence] in my native land."

Here is a copy of the reply that was made by the servant of the Palace, Sanehat, to the above royal document :

"In peace the most beautiful and greatest! Thy KA knoweth of the flight which thy servant, who is now speaking, made when he was in a state of ignorance, O thou beautiful god, Lord of Egypt, beloved of Rā, favoured of Menthu, the Lord of Thebes. May Amen-Rā, lord of the thrones of the Two Lands, and Sebek, and Rā, and Horus, and Hathor, and Tem and his Company of the Gods, and Neferbaiu, and Semsuu, and Horus of the East, and Nebt-Amehet, the goddess who is joined to thy head, and the Tchatchau gods who preside over the Nile flood, and Menu, and Heru-khenti-semti, and Urrit, the Lady of Punt, and Nut, and Heru-ur (Haroeris), and Rā, and all the gods of Tamera (Egypt), and of the Islands of the Great Green Sea (*i.e.* Mediterranean), bestow upon thee a full measure of their good gifts, and grant life and serenity to thy nostrils, and may they grant unto thee an eternity which hath no limit, and everlastingness which hath no bounds ! May thy fear penetrate and extend into all countries and mountains, and mayest thou be the possessor of all the region which the sun encircleth in his course. This is the prayer which thy servant who now speaketh maketh on behalf of his lord who hath delivered him from Ament.

"The lord of knowledge who knoweth men, the Majesty of the Setepsa abode (*i.e.* the Palace), knoweth well that his servant who is now speaking was afraid to declare the matter, and that to repeat it was a great thing. The great god (*i.e.* the King), who is the counterpart of Rā, hath done wisely in what he hath done, and thy servant who now speaketh hath meditated upon it in his mind, and hath made himself to conform to his plans. Thy Majesty is like unto Horus, and the victorious might of thine arms hath conquered the whole world. Let thy Majesty command that Maka [chief of] the country of Qetma, and Khentiaaush [chief of] Khent-Keshu, and Menus [chief of] the lands of the Fenkhu, be brought hither, and these Governors will testify that these things have come to pass at the desire of thy KA (*i.e.* double), and that Thenu doth not speak words of overboldness to thee, and that she is as [obedient as] thy hunting dogs. Behold, the flight, which thy servant who is now speaking made, was made by him as the result of ignorance ; it was not wilful, and I did not decide upon it after careful meditation. I cannot understand how I could ever have separated myself from my country. It seemeth to me now to have been the product of a dream wherein a man who is in the swamps of the Delta imagineth himself to be in Abu (Elephantine, or Syene), or of a man who whilst standing in fertile fields imagineth himself to be in the deserts of the Sūdān. I fear nothing and no man can make with truth [accusations] against me. I have never turned my ear to disloyal plottings, and my name hath never been in the mouth of the crier [of the names of proscribed folk] ; though my members quaked, and my legs shook, my heart guided me, and the God who ordained this flight of mine led me on. Behold, I am not a stiff-necked man (or rebel), nay, I held in honour [the King], for I knew the land of Egypt and that Rā hath made thy fear to exist everywhere in Egypt, and the awe of thee to permeate every foreign land. I beseech thee to let me enter my native land. I beseech thee to let me return to Egypt. Thou art the apparel of the horizon. The Disk (*i.e.* the Sun) shineth at thy wish. One drinketh the water of the river Nile at thy pleasure. One breatheth the air of heaven when thou givest the word of command. Thy servant who now speaketh will transfer the possessions which he hath gotten in this land to his kinsfolk. And as for the embassy of thy Majesty which hath been despatched to the servant who now speaketh, I will do according to thy Majesty's desire, for I live by the breath which thou givest, O thou beloved of Rā, Horus, and Hathor, and thy holy nostrils are beloved of Menthu, Lord of Thebes; mayest thou live for ever ! "

And I tarried one day in the country of Aa in order to transfer my possessions to my children. My eldest son attended to the affairs of the people of my settlement, and

the men and women thereof (*i.e.* the slaves), and all my possessions were in his hand, and all my children, and all my
cattle, and all my fruit trees, and all my palm plantations
and groves.   Then thy servant who is now speaking set
out on his journey and travelled towards the South.   When
I arrived at Heruuatu, the captain of the frontier patrol
sent a messenger to inform the Court of my arrival.   His
Majesty sent a courteous overseer of the servants of the
Palace, and following him came large boats laden with gifts
from the King for the soldiers of the desert who had escorted
me and guided me to the town of Heruuatu.   I addressed
each man among them by name and every toiler had that
which belonged to him.   I continued my journey, the wind
bore me along, food was prepared for me and drink made
ready for me, and the best of apparel (?), until I arrived at
Athettaui.[1]   On the morning of the day following my arrival,
five officials came to me, and they bore me to the Great House,
and I bowed low until my forehead touched the ground before
him.   And the princes and princesses were standing waiting
for me in the *umtet* chamber, and they advanced to meet me
and to receive me, and the *smeru* officials conducted me into
the hall, and led me to the privy chamber of the King, where
I found His Majesty [seated] upon the Great Throne in the
umtet chamber of silver-gold.   I arrived there, I raised myself
up after my prostrations, and I knew not that I was in his
presence.   Then this god (*i.e.* the King) spake unto me
harshly, and I became like unto a man who is confounded
in the darkness ; my intelligence left me, my limbs quaked,
my heart was no longer in my body, and I knew not whether
I was dead or alive.   Then His Majesty said unto one of his
high officials, " Raise him, and let him speak unto me."   And
His Majesty said unto me, " Thou hast come then !   Thou
hast smitten foreign lands and thou hast travelled, but now
weakness hath vanquished thee, thou hast become old, and
the infirmities of thy body are many.   The warriors of the
desert shall not escort thee [to thy grave] . . . wilt thou not
speak and declare thy name ? "   And I was afraid to con-

---

[1] A fortified town a little to the south of Memphis.

tradict him, and I answered him about these matters like a man who was stricken with fear. Thus did my Lord speak to me.

And I answered and said, " The matter was not of my doing, for, behold, it was done by the hand of God ; bodily terror made me to flee according to what was ordained. But, behold, I am here in thy presence ! Thou art life. Thy Majesty doeth as thou pleasest." And the King dismissed the royal children, and His Majesty said unto the Queen, " Look now, this is Sanehat who cometh in the guise of an Asiatic, and who hath turned himself into a nomad warrior of the desert." And the Queen laughed a loud hearty laugh, and the royal children cried out with one voice before His Majesty, saying, " O Lord King, this man cannot really be Sanehat " ; and His Majesty said, " It is indeed ! "

Then the royal children brought their instruments of music, their *menats* and their sistra, and they rattled their sistra, and they passed backwards and forwards before His Majesty, saying, " Thy hands perform beneficent acts, O King. The graces of the Lady of Heaven rest [upon thee]. The goddess Nubt giveth life to thy nostrils, and the Lady of the Stars joineth herself to thee, as thou sailest to the South wearing the Crown of the North, and to the North wearing the Crown of the South. Wisdom is stablished in the mouth of Thy Majesty, and health is on thy brow. Thou strikest terror into the miserable wretches who entreat thy mercy Men propitiate thee, O Lord of Egypt, [as they do] Rā, and thou art acclaimed with cries of joy like Nebertcher. Thy horn conquereth, thine arrow slayeth, [but] thou givest breath to him that is afflicted. For our sakes graciously give a boon to this traveller Sanehat, this desert warrior who was born in Tamera (Egypt). He fled through fear of thee, and he departed to a far country because of his terror of thee. Doth not the face that gazeth on thine blench ? Doth not the eye that gazeth into thine feel terrified ? " Then His Majesty said, " Let him fear not, and let him not utter a sound of fear. He shall be a *smer* official among the princes of the palace, he shall be a member of the company of the *shenit* officials.   Get ye gone to the refectory of the palace, and see to it that rations are provided for him."

Thereupon I came forth from the privy chamber of the King, and the royal children clasped my hands, and we passed on to the Great Door, and I was lodged in the house of one of the King's sons, which was beautifully furnished.   In it there was a bath, and it contained representations of the heavens and objects from the Treasury.   And there [I found] apparel made of royal linen, and myrrh of the finest quality which was used by the King, and every chamber was in charge of officials who were favourites of the King, and every officer had his own appointed duties.   And [there] the years were made to slide off my members.   I cut and combed my hair, I cast from me the dirt of a foreign land, together with the apparel of the nomads who live in the desert. I arrayed myself in apparel made of fine linen, I anointed my body with costly ointments, I slept upon a bedstead [instead of on the ground], I left the sand to those who dwelt on it, and the crude oil of wood wherewith they anoint them- selves.   I was allotted the house of a nobleman who had the title of *smer*, and many workmen laboured upon it, and its garden and its groves of trees were replanted with plants and trees.   Rations were brought to me from the palace three or four times each day, in additions to the gifts which the royal children gave me unceasingly.   And the site of a stone pyramid among the pyramids was marked out for me.   The surveyor-in-chief to His Majesty chose the site for it, the director of the funerary designers drafted the designs and inscriptions which were to be cut upon it, the chief of the masons of the necropolis cut the inscriptions, and the clerk of the works in the necropolis went about the country collecting the necessary funerary furniture.   I made the building to flourish, and provided everything that was necessary for its upkeep.   I acquired land round about it. I made a lake for the performance of funerary ceremonies, and the land about it contained gardens, and groves of trees, and I provided a place where the people on the estate might dwell similar to that which is provided for a *smeru* nobleman of the first rank. My statue, which was made for me by His Majesty, was plated with gold, and the tunic thereof was of silver-gold. Not for any ordinary person did he do such things. May I enjoy the favour of the King until the day of my death shall come !

Here endeth the book ; [given] from its beginning to its end, as it hath been found in writing.

THE STORY OF THE EDUCATED PEASANT KHUENANPU

The text of this most interesting story is written in the hieratic character on papyri which are preserved in the British Museum and in the Royal Library at Berlin. It is generally thought that the story is the product of the period that immediately followed the twelfth dynasty.

Once upon a time there lived a man whose name was Khuenanpu, a peasant of Sekhet-hemat,[1] and he had a wife whose name was Nefert. This peasant said to this wife of his, " Behold, I am going down into Egypt in order to bring back food for my children. Go thou and measure up the grain which remaineth in the granary, [and see how many] measures [there are]." Then she measured it, and there were eight measures. Then this peasant said unto this wife of his, " Behold, two measures of grain shall be for the support of thyself and thy children, but of the other six thou shalt make bread and beer whereon I am to live during the days on which I shall be travelling." And this peasant went down into Egypt, having laden his asses with *aaa* plants, and *retmet* plants, and soda and salt, and wood of the district of . . ., and *aunt* wood of the Land of Oxen,[2] and skins of panthers and wolves, and *neshau* plants, and *anu* stones, and *tenem* plants, and *kheperur* plants, and *sahut*, and *saksut* seeds (?), and *masut* plants, and *sent* and *abu* stones, and *absa* and *anba* plants, and doves and *naru* and *ukes* birds, and *tebu*, *uben* and *tebsu* plants, and *kenkent* seeds, and the plant " hair of the earth," and *anset* seeds, and all kinds of beautiful

---

[1] A district to the west of Cairo now known as Wādi an-Natrūn.
[2] The Oasis of Farāfrah.

products of the land of Sekhet-hemat. And when this peasant had marched to the south, to Hensu,[1] and had arrived
at the region of Perfefa, to the north of Metnat, he found a
man standing on the river bank whose name was Tehutinekht, who was the son of a man whose name was Asri ;
both father and son were serfs of Rensi, the son of Meru the
steward. When this man Tehutinekht saw the asses of this
peasant, of which his heart approved greatly, he said, " Would
that I had any kind of god with me to help me to seize for
myself the goods of this peasant ! " Now the house of this
Tehutinekht stood upon the upper edge of a sloping path
along the river bank, which was narrow and not wide. It
was about as wide as a sheet of linen cloth, and upon one
side of it was the water of the stream, and on the other was
a growing crop. Then this Tehutinekht said unto his slave,
" Run and bring me a sheet of linen out of my house " ; and
it was brought to him immediately. Then he shook out the
sheet of linen over the narrow sloping path in such a way
that its upper edge touched the water, and the fringed edge
the growing crop. And when this peasant was going along
the public path, this Tehutinekht said unto him, " Be careful, peasant, wouldst thou walk upon my clothes ? " And
this peasant said, " I will do as thou pleasest ; my way is
good." And when he turned to the upper part of the path,
this Tehutinekht said, " Is my corn to serve as a road for thee,
O peasant ? " Then this peasant said, " My way is good.
The river-bank is steep, and the road is covered up with thy
corn, and thou hast blocked up the path with thy linen
garment. Dost thou really intend not to let us pass ? Hath
it come to pass that he dareth to say such a thing ? " [At
that moment] one of the asses bit off a large mouthful of the
growing corn, and this Tehutinekht said, " Behold, thy ass
is eating my corn ! Behold, he shall come and tread it out."
Then this peasant said, " My way is good. Because one
side of the road was made impassable [by thee], I led my ass
to the other side (?), and now thou hast seized my ass because

[1] The Khānēs of the Hebrews and Herakleopolis of the Greeks, the
modern Ahnās al-Madīnah.

he bit off a large mouthful of the growing corn. However, I know the master of this estate, which belongeth to Rensi, the son of Meru. There is no doubt that he hath driven every robber out of the whole country, and shall I be robbed on his estate?" And this Tehutinekht said, "Is not this an illustration of the proverb which the people use, 'The name of the poor man is only mentioned because of his master?' It is I who speak to thee, but it is the steward [Rensi, the son of Meru] of whom thou art thinking." Then Tehutinekht seized a cudgel of green tamarisk wood, and beat cruelly with it every part of the peasant's body, and took his asses from him and carried them off into his compound. And this peasant wept and uttered loud shrieks of pain because of what was done to him. And this Tehutinekht said, "Howl not so loudly, peasant, or verily [thou shalt depart] to the domain of the Lord of Silence."[1] Then this peasant said, "Thou hast beaten me, and robbed me of my possessions, and now thou wishest to steal even the very complaint that cometh out of my mouth! Lord of Silence indeed! Give me back my goods. Do not make me to utter complaints about thy fearsome character."

And this peasant spent ten whole days in making entreaties to this Tehutinekht [for the restoration of his goods], but Tehutinekht paid no attention to them whatsoever. At the end of this time this peasant set out on a journey to the south, to the city of Hensu, in order to lay his complaint before Rensi, the son of Meru, the steward, and he found him just as he was coming forth from the door in the courtyard of his house which opened on the river bank, to embark in his official boat on the river. And this peasant said, "I earnestly wish that it may happen that I may make glad thy heart with the words which I am going to say! Peradventure thou wilt allow some one to call thy confidential servant to me, in order that I may send him back to thee thoroughly well informed as to my business." Then Rensi, the son of Meru, the steward, caused his confidential servant to go to this peasant, who sent him back to him thoroughly well

---

[1] *i.e.* Osiris. This was a threat to kill the peasant.

informed as to his business. And Rensi, the son of Meru, the steward, made inquiries about this Tehutinekht from the officials who were immediately connected with him, and they said unto him, " Lord, the matter is indeed only one that concerneth one of the peasants of Tehutinekht who went [to do business] with another man near him instead of with him. And, as a matter of fact, [officials like Tehutinekht] always treat their peasants in this manner whensoever they go to do business with other people instead of with them. Wouldst thou trouble thyself to inflict punishment upon Tehutinekht for the sake of a little soda and a little salt ? [It is unthinkable.] Just let Tehutinekht be ordered to restore the soda and the salt and he will do so [immediately]." And Rensi, the son of Meru, the steward, held his peace ; he made no answer to the words of these officials, and to this peasant he made no reply whatsoever.

And this peasant came to make his complaint to Rensi, the son of Meru, the steward, and on the first occasion he said, " O my lord steward, greatest one of the great ones, guide of the things that are not and of these that are, when thou goest down into the Sea of Truth,[1] and dost sail thereon, may the attachment (?) of thy sail not tear away, may thy boat not drift (?), may no accident befall thy mast, may the poles of thy boat not be broken, mayest thou not run aground when thou wouldst walk on the land, may the current not carry thee away, mayest thou not taste the calamities of the stream, mayest thou never see a face of fear, may the timid fish come to thee, and mayest thou obtain fine, fat waterfowl. O thou who art the father of the orphan, the husband of the widow, the brother of the woman who hath been put away by her husband, and the clother of the motherless, grant that I may place thy name in this land in connection with all good law. Guide in whom there is no avarice, great man in whom there is no meanness, who destroyest falsehood and makest what is true to exist, who comest to the word of my mouth, I speak that thou mayest hear. Perform justice, O thou

---

[1] The name of a lake in the Other World ; see *Book of the Dead*, Chap. 17, l. 24.

who art praised, to whom those who are most worthy of praise give praise. Do away the oppression that weigheth me down. Behold, I am weighted with sorrow, behold, I am sorely wronged. Try me, for behold, I suffer greatly."

Now this peasant spake these words in the time of the King of the South, the King of the North, Nebkaurā, whose word is truth. And Rensi, the son of Meru, the steward, went into the presence of His Majesty, and said, " My Lord, I have found one of these peasants who can really speak with true eloquence. His goods have been stolen from him by an official who is in my service, and behold, he hath come to lay before me a complaint concerning this." His Majesty said unto Rensi, the son of Meru, the steward, " If thou wouldst see me in a good state of health, keep him here, and do not make any answer at all to anything which he shall say, so that he may continue to speak. Then let that which he shall say be done into writing, and brought unto us, so that we may hear it. Take care that his wife and his children have food to live upon, and see that one of these peasants goeth to remove want from his house. Provide food for the peasant himself to live upon, but thou shalt make the provision in such a way that the food may be given to him without letting him know that it is thou who hast given it to him. Let the food be given to his friends and let them give it to him." So there were given unto him four bread-cakes and two pots of beer daily. These were provided by Rensi, the son of Meru, the steward, and he gave them to a friend, and it was this friend who gave them to the peasant. And Rensi, the son of Meru, the steward, sent instructions to the governor of [the Oasis of] Sekhet-hemat to supply the wife of the peasant with daily rations, and there were given unto her regularly the bread-cakes that were made from three measures of corn.

Then this peasant came a second time to lay his complaint [before Rensi], and he found him as he was coming out from the . . ., and he said, " O steward, my lord, the greatest of the great, thou richest of the rich, whose greatness is true greatness, whose riches are true riches, thou rudder of heaven, thou pole of the earth, thou measuring rope for heavy weights (?) ! O rudder, slip not, O pole, topple not, O measuring rope, make no mistake in measuring ! The great lord taketh away from her that hath no master (or owner), and stealeth from him that is alone [in the world]. Thy rations are in thy house—a pot of beer and three bread-cakes. What dost thou spend in satisfying those who depend upon thee ? Shall he who must die die with his people ? Wilt thou be a man of eternity (*i.e.* wilt thou live for ever ?) Behold, are not these things evils, namely, the balance that leaneth sideways, the pointer of the balance that doth not show the correct weight, and an upright and just man who departeth from his path of integrity ? Observe ! the truth goeth badly with thee, being driven out of her proper place, and the officials commit acts of injustice. He who ought to estimate a case correctly giveth a wrong decision. He who ought to keep himself from stealing committeth an act of robbery. He who should be strenuous to arrest the man who breaketh the word (*i.e.* Law) in its smallest point, is himself guilty of departing therefrom. He who should give breath stifleth him that could breathe. The land that ought to give repose driveth repose away. He who should divide in fairness hath become a robber. He who should blot out the oppressor giveth him the command to turn the town into a waste of water. He who should drive away evil himself committeth acts of injustice."

Then Rensi, the son of Meru, the steward, said [to the peasant], " Doth thy case appear in thy heart so serious that I must have my servant [Tehutinekht] seized on thy account ? " This peasant said, " He who measureth the heaps of corn filcheth from them for himself, and he who filleth [the measure] for others robbeth his neighbours. Since he who should carry out the behests of the Law giveth the order to rob, who is to repress crime ? He who should do away with offences against the Law himself committeth them. He who should act with integrity behaveth crookedly. He who doeth acts of injustice is applauded. When wilt thou find thyself able to resist and to put down acts of injustice ? [When] the . . . cometh to his place of yesterday the command cometh : ' Do a [good] deed in order that one may do a [good] deed [to thee],' that is to say, ' Give thanks unto everyone for what he doeth.' This is to drive back the bolt before it is shot, and to give a command to the man who is already overburdened with orders. Would that a moment of destruction might come, wherein thy vines should be laid low, and thy geese diminished, and thy water-fowl be made few in number ! [Thus] it cometh that the man who ought to see clearly hath become blind, and he who ought to hear distinctly hath become deaf, and he who ought to be a just guide hath become one who leadeth into error. Observe ! thou art strong and powerful. Thine arm is able to do deeds of might, and [yet] thy heart is avaricious. Compassion hath removed itself from thee. The wretched man whom thou hast destroyed crieth aloud in his anguish. Thou art like unto the messenger of the god Henti (the Crocodile-god). Set not out [to do evil] for the Lady of the Plague (*i.e.* Sekhmet). . . . As there is nothing between thee and her for a certain purpose, so there is nothing against thee and her. If thou wilt not do it [then] she will not show compassion. The beggar hath the powerful owner of possessions (or revenues) robbed, and the man who hath nothing hath the man who hath secreted [much] stolen goods. To steal anything at all from the beggar is an absolute crime on the part of the man who is not in want, and [if he doth this] shall his action not be inquired into ? Thou art filled full with thy bread, and art drunken with thy beer, and thou art rich [beyond count]. When the face of the steersman is directed to what is in front of him, the boat falleth out of its course, and saileth whithersoever it pleaseth. When the King [remaineth] in his house, and when thou workest the rudder, acts of injustice take place round about thee, complaints are widespread, and the loss (?) is very serious. And one saith, ' What is taking place ? ' Thou shouldst make thyself a place of refuge [for the needy]. Thy quay should be safe. But observe ! Thy town is in commotion. Thy tongue is righteous, make no mistake [in judgment]. The abominable behaviour of a man is, as it were, [one of] his members. Speak no lies thyself, and take good heed that thy high officials do not do so. Those who assess the dues on the crops are like unto a . . ., and to tell lies is very dear to their hearts. Thou who hast knowledge of the affairs of all the people, dost thou not understand my circumstances? Observe, thou who relievest the wants of all who have suffered by water, I am on the path of him that hath no boat. O thou who bringest every drowning man to land, and who savest the man whose boat hath foundered, art thou going to let me perish?"

And this peasant came a third time to lay his complaint [before Rensi], and he said, "O my Lord Rensi, the steward! Thou art Rā, the lord of heaven with thy great chiefs. The affairs of all men [are ruled by thee]. Thou art like the water-flood. Thou art Hep (the Nile-god) who maketh green the fields, and who maketh the islands that are deserts to become productive. Exterminate the robber, be thou the advocate of those who are in misery, and be not towards the petitioner like the water-flood that sweepeth him away. Take heed to thyself likewise, for eternity cometh, and behave in such a way that the proverb, 'Righteousness (or truth) is the breath of the nostrils,' may be applicable unto thee. Punish those who are deserving of punishment, and then these shall be like unto thee in dispensing justice. Do not the small scales weigh incorrectly? Doth not the large balance incline to one side? In such cases is not Thoth merciful? When thou doest acts of injustice thou becomest the second of these three, and if these be merciful thou also mayest be merciful. Answer not good with evil, and do not set one thing in the place of another. Speech flourisheth more than the *senmit* plants, and groweth stronger than the smell of the same. Make no answer to it whilst thou pourest out acts of injustice, to make to grow apparel, which three . . . will cause him to make. [If] thou workest the steering pole against the sail (?), the flood shall gather strength against the doing of what is right. Take good heed to thyself and set thyself on the mat (?) on the look-out place. The equilibrium of the earth is maintained by the doing of what is right. Tell not lies, for thou art a great man. Act

not in a light manner, for thou art a man of solid worth.
Tell not lies, for thou art a pair of scales.   Make no mistake
[in thy weighing], for thou art a correct reckoner (?).   Observe !   Thou art all of a piece with the pair of scales.   If
they weigh incorrectly, thou also shalt act falsely.   Let not
the boat run aground when thou art working the steering
pole . . . the look-out place.   When thou hast to proceed
against one who hath carried off something, take thou
nothing, for behold, the great man ceaseth to be a great man
when he is avaricious.   Thy tongue is the pointer of the
scales ; thy heart is the weight ; thy lips are the two arms
of the scales.   If thou coverest thy face so as not to see the
doer of violent deeds, who is there [left] to repress lawless
deeds ?   Observe !   Thou art like a poor man for the man
who washeth clothes, who is avaricious and destroyeth kindly
feeling (?).   He who forsaketh the friend who endoweth him
for the sake of his client is his brother, who hath come and
brought him a gift.   Observe !   Thou art a ferryman who
ferriest over the stream only the man who possesseth the
proper fare, whose integrity is well attested (?).   Observe !
Thou art like the overseer of a granary who doth not at once
permit to pass him that cometh empty.   Observe !   Thou
art among men like a bird of prey that liveth upon weak
little birds.   Observe !   Thou art like the cook whose sole
joy is to kill, whom no creature escapeth.   Observe !   Thou
art like a shepherd who is careless about the loss of his sheep
through the rapacious crocodile ; thou never countest [thy
sheep].   Would that thou wouldst make evil and rapacious
men to be fewer !   Safety hath departed from [every] town
throughout the land.   Thou shouldst hear, but most assuredly thou hearest not !   Why hast thou not heard that I
have this day driven back the rapacious man ?   When the
crocodile pursueth. . . .   How long is this condition of thine
to last ?   Truth which is concealed shall be found, and falsehood shall perish.   Do not imagine that thou art master of
to-morrow, which hath not yet come, for the evils which it
may bring with it are unknown."
    And behold, when this peasant had said these things to

Rensi, the son of Meru, the steward, at the entrance to the hall of the palace, Rensi caused two men with leather whips to seize him, and they beat him in every member of his body. Then this peasant said : " The son of Meru hath made a mistake. His face is blind in respect of what he seeth, he is deaf in respect of what he heareth, and he is forgetting that which he ought to remember. Observe ! Thou art like unto a town that hath no governor, and a community that hath no chief, and a ship that hath no captain, and a body of men who have no guide. Observe ! Thou art like a high official who is a thief, a governor of a town who taketh [bribes], and the overseer of a province who hath been appointed to suppress robbery, but who hath become the captain of those who practise it."

And this peasant came a fourth time to lay his complaint before Rensi, and he met him as he was coming out from the door of the temple of the god Herushefit, and said, " O thou who art praised, the god Herushefit, from whose house thou comest forth, praiseth thee. When well-doing perisheth, and there is none who seeketh to prevent its destruction, falsehood maketh itself seen boldly in the land. If it happen that the ferry-boat is not brought for thee to cross the stream in, how wilt thou be able to cross the stream ? If thou hast to cross the stream in thy sandals, is thy crossing pleasant ? Assuredly it is not ! What man is there who continueth to sleep until it is broad daylight ? [This habit] destroyeth the marching by night, and the travelling by day, and the possibility of a man profiting by his good luck, in very truth. Observe ! One cannot tell thee sufficiently often that ' Compassion hath departed from thee.' And behold, how the oppressed man whom thou hast destroyed complaineth ! Observe ! Thou art like unto a man of the chase who would satisfy his craving for bold deeds, who determineth to do what he wisheth, to spear the hippopotamus, to shoot the wild bull, to catch fish, and to catch birds in his nets. He who is without hastiness will not speak without due thought. He whose habit is to ponder deeply will not be light-minded. Apply thy heart earnestly and thou shalt know the truth.

Pursue diligently the course which thou hast chosen, and let him that heareth the plaintiff act rightly. He who followeth a right course of action will not treat a plaintiff wrongly. When the arm is brought, and when the two eyes see, and when the heart is of good courage, boast not loudly in proportion to thy strength, in order that calamity may not come unto thee. He who passeth by [his] fate halteth between two opinions. The man who eateth tasteth [his food], the man who is spoken to answereth, the man who sleepeth seeth visions, but nothing can resist the presiding judge when he is the pilot of the doer [of evil]. Observe, O stupid man, thou art apprehended. Observe, O ignorant man, thou art freely discussed. Observe, too, that men intrude upon thy most private moments. Steersman, let not thy boat run aground. Nourisher [of men], let not men die. Destroyer [of men], let not men perish. Shadow, let not men perish through the burning heat. Place of refuge, let not the crocodile commit ravages. It is now four times that I have laid my complaint before thee. How much more time shall I spend in doing this ? "

This peasant came a fifth time to make his complaint, and said, " O my lord steward, the fisherman with a *khut* instrument . . ., the fisherman with a . . . killeth *i*-fish, the fisherman with a harpoon speareth the *āubbu* fish, the fisherman with a *tchabhu* instrument catcheth the *paqru* fish, and the common fishermen are always drawing fish from the river. Observe ! Thou art even as they. Wrest not the goods of the poor man from him. The helpless man thou knowest him. The goods of the poor man are the breath of his life ; to seize them and carry them off from him is to block up his nostrils. Thou art committed to the hearing of a case and to the judging between two parties at law, so that thou mayest suppress the robber ; but, verily, what thou doest is to support the thief. The people love thee, and yet thou art a law-breaker. Thou hast been set as a dam before the man of misery, take heed that he is not drowned. Verily, thou art like a lake to him, O thou who flowest quickly."

This peasant came the sixth time to lay his complaint [before Rensi], and said, " O my lord steward . . . who makest truth to be, who makest happiness (or, what is good) to be, who destroyest [all evil] ; thou art like unto the satiety that cometh to put an end to hunger, thou art like unto the raiment that cometh to do away nakedness ; thou art like unto the heavens that become calm after a violent storm and refresh with warmth those who are cold ; thou art like unto the fire that cooketh that which is raw, and thou art like unto the water that quencheth the thirst. Yet look round about thee ! He who ought to make a division fairly is a robber. He who ought to make everyone to be satisfied hath been the cause of the trouble. He who ought to be the source of healing is one of those who cause sicknesses. The transgressor diminisheth the truth. He who filleth well the right measure acteth rightly, provided that he giveth neither too little nor too much. If an offering be brought unto thee, do thou share it with thy brother (or neighbour), for that which is given in charity is free from after-thought (?). The man who is dissatisfied induceth separation, and the man who hath been condemned bringeth on schisms, even before one can know what is in his mind. When thou hast arrived at a decision delay not in declaring it. Who keepeth within him that which he can eject ? . . . When a boat cometh into port it is unloaded, and the freight thereof is landed everywhere on the quay. It is [well] known that thou hast been educated, and trained, and experienced, but behold, it is not that thou mayest rob [the people]. Nevertheless thou dost [rob them] just as other people do, and those who are found about thee are thieves (?). Thou who shouldst be the most upright man of all the people art the greatest transgressor in the whole country. [Thou art] the wicked gardener who watereth his plot of ground with evil deeds in order to make his plot to tell lies, so that he may flood the town (or estate) with evil deeds (or calamities)."

This peasant came the seventh time in order to lay his complaint [before Rensi], and said, " O my lord steward, thou art the steering pole of the whole land, and the land saileth according to thy command. Thou art the second (or counterpart) of Thoth, who judgeth impartially. My lord, permit thou a man to appeal to thee in respect of his cause which is righteous. Let not thy heart fight against it, for it is unseemly for thee to do so ; [if thou doest this] thou of the broad face wilt become evil-hearted. Curse not the thing that hath not yet taken place, and rejoice not over that which hath not yet come to pass. The tolerant judge rejoiceth in showing kindness, and he withholdeth all action concerning a decision that hath been given, when he knoweth not what plan was in the heart. In the case of the judge who breaketh the Law, and overthroweth uprightness, the poor man cannot live [before him], for the judge plundereth him, and the truth saluteth him not. But my body is full, and my heart is overloaded, and the expression thereof cometh forth from my body by reason of the condition of the same. [When] there is a breach in the dam the water poureth out through it : even so is my mouth opened and it uttereth speech. I have now emptied myself, I have poured out what I had to pour out, I have unburdened my body, I have finished washing my linen. What I had to say before thee is said, my misery hath been fully set out before thee ; now what hast thou to say in excuse (or apology) ? Thy lazy cowardice hath been the cause of thy sin, thine avarice hath rendered thee stupid, and thy gluttony hath been thine enemy. Thinkest thou that thou wilt never find another peasant like unto me ? If he hath a complaint to make thinkest thou that he will not stand, if he is a lazy man, at the door of his house ? He whom thou forcest to speak will not remain silent. He whom thou forcest to wake up will not remain asleep. The faces which thou makest keen will not remain stupid. The mouth which thou openest will not remain closed. He whom thou makest intelligent will not remain ignorant. He whom thou instructest will not remain a fool. These are they who destroy evils. These are the officials, the lords of what is good. These are the craftsfolk who make what existeth. These are they who put on their bodies again the heads that have been cut off.''

This peasant came the eighth time to lay his complaint [before Rensi], and said, " O my lord steward, a man falleth because of covetousness. The avaricious man hath no aim, for his aim is frustrated. Thy heart is avaricious, which befitteth thee not. Thou plunderest, and thy plunder is no use to thee. And yet formerly thou didst permit a man to enjoy that to which he had good right ! Thy daily bread is in thy house, thy belly is filled, grain overfloweth [in thy granaries], and the overflow perisheth and is wasted. The officials who have been appointed to suppress acts of injustice have been rapacious robbers, and the officials who have been appointed to stamp out falsehood have become hiding-places for those who work iniquity. It is not fear of thee that hath driven me to make my complaint to thee, for thou dost not understand my mind (or heart). The man who is silent and who turneth back in order to bring his miserable state [before thee] is not afraid to place it before thee, and his brother doth not bring [gifts] from the interior of [his quarter]. Thy estates are in the fields, thy food is on [thy] territory, and thy bread is in the storehouse, yet the officials make gifts to thee and thou seizest them. Art thou not then a robber ? Will not the men who plunder hasten with thee to the divisions of the fields ? Perform the truth for the Lord of Truth, who possesseth the real truth. Thou writing reed, thou roll of papyrus, thou palette, thou Thoth, thou art remote from acts of justice. O Good One, thou art still goodness. O Good One, thou art truly good. Truth endureth for ever. It goeth down to the grave with those who perform truth, it is laid in the coffin and is buried in the earth ; its name is never removed from the earth, and its name is remembered on earth for good (or blessing). That is the ordinance of the word of God. If it be a matter of a hand-balance it never goeth askew ; if it be a matter of a large pair of scales, the standard thereof never inclineth to one side. Whether it be I who come, or another, verily thou must make speech, but do not answer whether thou speakest to one who ought to hold his peace, or whether thou seizest one who cannot seize thee. Thou art not merciful, thou art not considerate. Thou hast not withdrawn thyself, thou hast not gone afar off. But thou hast not in any way given in respect of me any judgment in accordance with the command, which came forth from the mouth of Rā himself, saying, 'Speak the truth, perform the truth, for truth is great, mighty, and everlasting. When thou performest the truth thou wilt find its virtues (?), and it will lead thee to the state of being blessed (?). If the hand-balance is askew, the pans of the balance, which perform the weighing, hang crookedly, and a correct weighing cannot be carried out, and the result is a false one ; even so the result of wickedness is wickedness.'"

This peasant came the ninth time to lay his complaint [before Rensi], and said, " The great balance of men is their tongues, and all the rest is put to the test by the hand balance. When thou punishest the man who ought to be punished, the act telleth in thy favour. [When he doeth not this] falsehood becometh his possession, truth turneth away from before him, his goods are falsehood, truth forsaketh him, and supporteth him not. If falsehood advanceth, she maketh a mistake, and goeth not over with the ferry-boat [to the Island of Osiris]. The man with whom falsehood prevaileth hath no children and no heirs upon the earth. The man in whose boat falsehood saileth never reacheth land, and his boat never cometh into port. Be not heavy, but at the same time do not be too light. Be not slow, but at the same time be not too quick. Rage not at the man who is listening to thee. Cover not over thy face before the man with whom thou art acquainted. Make not blind thy face towards the man who is looking at thee. Thrust not aside the suppliant as thou goest down. Be not indolent in making known thy decision. Do [good] unto him that will do [good] unto thee. Hearken not unto the cry of the mob, who say, 'A man will assuredly cry out when his case is really righteous.' There is no yesterday for the indolent man, there is no friend for the man who is deaf to [the words of] truth, and there is no day of rejoicing for the avaricious man. The informer becometh a poor man, and the poor man becometh a beggar, and the unfriendly man becometh a dead person. Observe now, I have laid my complaint before thee, but thou wilt not hearken unto it ; I shall now depart, and make my complaint against thee to Anubis."

Then Rensi, the son of Meru, the steward, caused two of his servants to go and bring back the peasant. Now this peasant was afraid, for he believed that he would be beaten severely because of the words which he had spoken to him. And this peasant said, " This is [like] the coming of the thirsty man to salt tears, and the taking of the mouth of the suckling child to the breast of the woman that is dry. That the sight of which is longed for cometh not, and only death approacheth."

Then Rensi, the son of Meru, the steward, said, " Be not afraid, O peasant, for behold, thou shalt dwell with me." Then this peasant swore an oath, saying, " Assuredly I will eat of thy bread, and drink of thy beer for ever." Then Rensi, the son of Meru, the steward, said, " Come hither, however, so that thou mayest hear thy petitions " ; and he caused to be [written] on a roll of new papyrus all the complaints which this peasant had made, each complaint according to its day. And Rensi, the son of Meru, the steward, sent the papyrus to the King of the South, the King of the North, Nebkaurā, whose word is truth, and it pleased the heart of His Majesty more than anything else in the whole land. And His Majesty said, " Pass judgment on thyself, O son of Meru." And Rensi, the son of Meru, the steward, despatched two men to bring him back. And he was brought back, and an embassy was despatched to Sekhet Hemat. . . . Six persons, besides . . . his grain, and his millet, and his asses, and his dogs. . . . [The remaining lines are mutilated, but the words which are visible make it certain that Tehutinekht the thief was punished, and that he was made to restore to the peasant everything which he had stolen from him.]

THE JOURNEY OF THE PRIEST UNU-AMEN INTO SYRIA TO
BUY CEDAR WOOD TO MAKE A NEW BOAT FOR AMEN-RĀ

The text of this narrative is written in the hieratic character upon a papyrus preserved in St. Petersburg ; it gives
an excellent description of the troubles that befell the priest
Unu-Amen during his journey into Syria in the second half
of the eleventh century before Christ. The text reads :

On the eighteenth day of the third month of the season of
the Inundation, of the fifth year, Unu-Amen, the senior
priest of the Hait chamber of the house of Amen, the Lord
of the thrones of the Two Lands, set out on his journey to
bring back wood for the great and holy Boat of Amen-Rā,
the King of the Gods, which is called " User-hat," and
floateth on the canal of Amen. On the day wherein I arrived
at Tchān (Tanis or Zoan), the territory of Nessubanebtet
(*i.e.* King Smendes) and Thent-Amen, I delivered unto
them the credentials which I had received from Amen-Rā,
the King of the Gods, and when they had had my letters
read before them, they said, " We will certainly do whatsoever Amen-Rā, the King of the Gods, our Lord, commandeth." And I lived in that place until the fourth month of
the season of the Inundation, and I abode in the palace at
Zoan. Then Nessubanebtet and Thent-Amen despatched
me with the captain of the large ship called Menkabuta, and
I set sail on the sea of Kharu (Syria) on the first day of the
fourth month of the Season of the Inundation. I arrived at
Dhir, a city of Tchakaru, and Badhilu, its prince, made his
servants bring me bread-cakes by the ten thousand, and a
large jar of wine, and a leg of beef. And a man who belonged
to the crew of my boat ran away, having stolen vessels of
gold that weighed five *teben*, and four vessels of silver that
weighed twenty *teben*, and silver in a leather bag that weighed
eleven *teben ;* thus he stole five *teben* of gold and thirty-one
teben of silver.

On the following morning I rose up, and I went to the place
where the prince of the country was, and I said unto him,

" I have been robbed in thy port. Since thou art the prince of this land, and the leader thereof, thou must make search and find out what hath become of my money. I swear unto thee that the money [once] belonged to Amen-Rā, King of the Gods, the Lord of the Two Lands; it belonged to Nessubanebtet, it belonged to my lord Her-Heru, and to the other great kings of Egypt, but it now belongeth to Uartha, and to Makamāru, and to Tchakar-Bāl, Prince of Kepuna (Byblos)." And he said unto me, " Be angry or be pleased, [as thou likest], but, behold, I know absolutely nothing about the matter of which thou speakest unto me. Had the thief been a man who was a subject of mine, who had gone down into thy ship and stolen thy money, I would in that case have made good thy loss from the moneys in my own treasury, until such time as it had been found out who it was that robbed thee, and what his name was, but the thief who hath robbed thee belongeth to thine own ship. Yet tarry here for a few days, and stay with me, so that I may seek him out." So I tarried there for nine days, and my ship lay at anchor in his port. And I went to him and I said unto him, " Verily thou hast not found my money, [but I must depart] with the captain of the ship and with those who are travelling with him." . . . [The text here is mutilated, but from the fragments of the lines that remain it seems clear that Unu-Amen left the port of Dhir, and proceeded in his ship to Tyre. After a short stay there he left Tyre very early one morning and sailed to Kepuna (Byblos), so that he might have an interview with the governor of that town, who was called Tchakar-Bāl. During his interview with Tchakar-Bāl the governor of Tyre produced a bag containing thirty *teben* of silver, and Unu-Amen promptly seized it, and declared that he intended to keep it until his own money which had been stolen was returned to him. Whilst Unu-Amen was at Byblos he buried in some secret place the image of the god Amen and the amulets belonging to it, which he had brought with him to protect him and to guide him on his way. The name of this image was " Amen-ta-mat." The text then proceeds in a connected form thus :]

And I passed nineteen days in the port of Byblos, and the governor passed his days in sending messages to me each day, saying, " Get thee gone out of my harbour." Now on one occasion when he was making an offering to his gods, the god took possession of a certain young chief of his chiefs, and he caused him to fall into a fit of frenzy, and the young man said, " Bring up the god.[1] Bring the messenger who hath possession of him. Make him to set out on his way. Make him to depart immediately." Now the man who had been seized with the fit of divine frenzy continued to be moved by the same during the night. And I found a certain ship, which was bound for Egypt, and when I had transferred to it all my property, I cast a glance at the darkness, saying, " If the darkness increaseth I will transfer the god to the ship also, and not permit any other eye whatsoever to look upon him." Then the superintendent of the harbour came unto me, saying, " Tarry thou here until to-morrow morning, according to the orders of the governor." And I said unto him, " Art not thou thyself he who hath passed his days in coming to me daily and saying, ' Get thee gone out of my harbour ? ' Dost thou not say, ' Tarry here,' so that I may let the ship which I have found [bound for Egypt] depart, when thou wilt again come and say, ' Haste thee to be gone ' ? "

And the superintendent of the harbour turned away and departed, and told the governor what I had said. And the governor sent a message to the captain of the ship bound for Egypt, saying, " Tarry till the morning ; these are the orders of the governor." And when the morning had come, the governor sent a messenger, who took me to the place where offerings were being made to the god in the fortress wherein the governor lived on the sea coast. And I found him seated in his upper chamber, and he was reclining with his back towards an opening in the wall, and the waves of the great Syrian sea were rolling in from seawards and breaking on the shore behind him. And I said unto him, " The grace of Amen [be with thee] ! " And he said unto me,

---

[1] *i.e.* the figure of Amen-ta-mat.

" Including this day, how long is it since thou camest from
the place where Amen is ? "   And I said unto him, " Five
months and one day, including to-day."   And he said unto
me, " Verily if that which thou sayest is true, where are the
letters of Amen which ought to be in thy hand ?   Where
are the letters of the high priest of Amen which ought to be
in thy hand ? "

And I said unto him, " I gave them to Nessubanebtet
and Thent-Amen."   Then was he very angry indeed, and he
said unto me, " Verily, there are neither letters nor writings
in thy hands for us !   Where is the ship made of acacia wood
which Nessubanebtet gave unto thee ?   Where are his Syrian
sailors ?   Did he not hand thee over to the captain of the
ship so that after thou hadst started on thy journey they
might kill thee and cast thee into the sea ?   Whose permission did they seek to attack the god ?   And indeed
whose permission were they seeking before they attacked
thee ? "   This is what he said unto me.

And I said unto him, " The ship [wherein I sailed] was in
very truth an Egyptian ship, and it had a crew of Egyptian
sailors who sailed it on behalf of Nessubanebtet.   There
were no Syrian sailors placed on board of it by him."   He
said unto me, " I swear that there are twenty ships lying in
my harbour, the captains of which are in partnership with
Nessubanebtet.   And as for the city of Sidon, whereto thou
wishest to travel, I swear that there are there ten thousand
other ships, the captains of which are in partnership with
Uarkathar, and they are sailed for the benefit of his house."
At this grave moment I held my peace.   And he answered
and said unto me, " On what matter of business hast thou
come hither ? "   And I said unto him, " The matter concerning which I have come is wood for the great and holy
Boat of Amen-Rā, the King of the Gods.   What thy father
did [for the god], and what thy father's father did for him,
do thou also."   That was what I said unto him.   And he
said unto me, " They certainly did do work for it (*i.e.* the
boat).   Give me a gift for my work for the boat, and then
I also will work for it.   Assuredly my father and my grand-

father did do the work that was demanded of them, and Pharaoh, life, strength, and health be to him! caused six ships laden with the products of Egypt to come hither, and the contents thereof were unloaded into their storehouses. Now, thou must most certainly cause some goods to be brought and given to me for myself."

Then he caused to be brought the books which his father had kept day by day, and he had them read out before me, and it was found that one thousand *teben* of silver of all kinds were [entered] in his books. And he said unto me, " If the Ruler of Egypt had been the lord of my possessions, and if I had indeed been his servant, he would never have had silver and gold brought [to pay my father and my father's father] when he told them to carry out the commands of Amen. The instructions which they (*i.e.* Pharaoh) gave to my father were by no means the command of one who was their king. As for me, I am assuredly not thy servant, and indeed I am not the servant of him that made thee to set out on thy way. If I were to cry out now, and to shout to the cedars of Lebanon, the heavens would open, and the trees would be lying spread out on the sea-shore. I ask thee now to show me the sails which thou hast brought to carry thy ships which shall be loaded with thy timber to Egypt. And show me also the tackle with which thou wilt transfer to thy ships the trees which I shall cut down for thee for. . . . [Unless I make for thee the tackle] and the sails of thy ships, the tops will be too heavy, and they will snap off, and thou wilt perish in the midst of the sea, [especially if] Amen uttereth his voice in the sky,[1] and he unfettereth Sutekh[2] at the moment when he rageth. Now Amen hath assumed the overlordship of all lands, and he hath made himself their master, but first and foremost he is the overlord of Egypt, whence thou hast come. Excellent things have come forth from Egypt, and have reached even unto this place wherein I am ; and moreover, knowledge (or learning) hath come forth therefrom, and hath reached even unto this place

---

[1] *i.e.* if there is thunder.
[2] Here the Storm-god.

wherein I am. But of what use is this beggarly journey of thine which thou hast been made to take ? "

And I said unto him, " What a shameful thing [to say] ! It is not a beggarly journey whereon I have been despatched by those among whom I live. And besides, assuredly there is not a single boat that floateth that doth not belong to Amen. To him belong the sea and the cedars of Lebanon, concerning which thou sayest, ' They are my property.' In Lebanon groweth [the wood] for the Boat Amen-userhat, the lord of boats. Amen-Rā, the King of the Gods, spake and told Her-Heru, my lord, to send me forth ; and therefore he caused me to set out on my journey together with this great god.[1] Now behold, thou hast caused this great god to pass nine and twenty days here in a boat that is lying at anchor in thy harbour, for most assuredly thou didst know that he was resting here. Amen is now what he hath always been, and yet thou wouldst dare to stand up and haggle about the [cedars of] Lebanon with the god who is their lord ! And as concerning what thou hast spoken, saying, ' The kings of Egypt in former times caused silver and gold to be brought [to my father and father's father, thou art mistaken].' Since they had bestowed upon them life and health, they would never have caused gold and silver to be brought to them ; but they might have caused gold and silver to be brought to thy fathers instead of life and health. And Amen-Rā, the King of the Gods, is the Lord of life and health. He was the god of thy fathers, and they served him all their lives, and made offerings unto him, and indeed thou thyself art a servant of Amen. If now thou wilt say unto Amen, ' I will perform thy commands, I will perform thy commands,' and wilt bring this business to a prosperous ending, thou shalt live, thou shalt be strong, thou shalt be healthy, and thou shalt rule thy country to its uttermost limits wisely and well, and thou shalt do good to thy people. But take good heed that thou lovest not the possessions of Amen-Rā, the King of the Gods, for the lion loveth the things that belong unto him. And now, I pray thee to allow my scribe

---

[1] *i.e.* the figure of Amen already referred to.

to be summoned to me, and I will send him to Nessubanebtet
and Thent-Amen, the local governors whom Amen hath
appointed to rule the northern portion of his land, and they
will send to me everything which I shall tell them to send to
me, saying, ' Let such and such a thing be brought,' until
such time as I can make the journey to the South (*i.e.* to
Egypt), when I will have thy miserable dross brought to thee,
even to the uttermost portion thereof, in very truth." That
was what I said unto him.

And he gave my letter into the hand of his ambassador.
And he loaded up on a ship wood for the fore part and wood
for the hind part [of the Boat of Amen], and four other trunks
of cedar trees which had been cut down, in all seven trunks,
and he despatched them to Egypt. And his ambassador
departed to Egypt, and he returned to me in Syria in the
first month of the winter season (November–December).
And Nessubanebtet and Thent-Amen sent to me five vessels
of gold, five vessels of silver, ten pieces of byssus, each sufficiently large to make a suit of raiment, five hundred rolls of
fine papyrus, five hundred hides of oxen, five hundred ropes,
twenty sacks of lentils, and thirty vessels full of dried fish.
And for my personal use they sent to me five pieces of byssus,
each sufficiently large to make a suit of raiment, a sack of
lentils, and five vessels full of dried fish. Then the Governor
was exceedingly glad and rejoiced greatly, and he sent three
hundred men and three hundred oxen [to Lebanon] to cut
down the cedar trees, and he appointed overseers to direct
them. And they cut down the trees, the trunks of which
lay there during the whole of the winter season. And
when the third month of the summer season had come,
they dragged the tree trunks down to the sea-shore.
And the Governor came out of his palace, and took up
his stand before the trunks, and he sent a message to
me, saying, "Come." Now as I was passing close by
him, the shadow of his umbrella fell upon me, whereupon
Pen-Amen, an officer of his bodyguard, placed himself
between him and me, saying, "The shadow of Pharaoh,
life, strength, and health, be to him! thy Lord, falleth

upon thee." [1] And the Governor was wroth with Pen-
Amen, and he said, " Let him alone." Therefore I walked
close to him.

And the Governor answered and said unto me, " Behold,
the orders [of Pharaoh] which my fathers carried out in times
of old, I also have carried out, notwithstanding the fact that
thou hast not done for me what thy fathers were wont to do
for me. However, look for thyself, and take note that the
last of the cedar trunks hath arrived, and here it lieth. Do
now whatsoever thou pleaseth with them, and take steps to
load them into ships, for assuredly they are given to thee as
a gift. I beg thee to pay no heed to the terror of the sea
voyage, but if thou persistest in contemplating [with fear]
the sea voyage, thou must also contemplate [with fear] the
terror of me [if thou tarriest here]. Certainly I have not
treated thee as the envoys of Khā-em-Uast [2] were treated
here, for they were made to pass seventeen (or fifteen) years
in this country, and they died here." [3]

Then the Governor spake to the officer of his bodyguard,
saying, " Lay hands on him, and take him to see the tombs
wherein they lie." And I said unto him, " Far be it from me
to look upon such [ill-omened] things ! As concerning the
messengers of Khā-em-Uast, the men whom he sent unto
thee as ambassadors were merely [officials] of his, and there
was no god with his ambassadors, and so thou sayest, ' Make
haste to look upon thy colleagues.' Behold, wouldst thou
not have greater pleasure, and shouldst thou not [instead of
saying such things] cause to be made a stele whereon should
be said by thee :

" Amen-Rā, the King of the Gods, sent to me Amen-
ta-mat, his divine ambassador, together with Unu-Amen,
his human ambassador, in quest of trunks of cedar wood

---

[1] Pen-Amen means to say that as the shadow of the Governor had fallen
upon the Egyptian, Unu-Amen was henceforth his servant. The shadow
of a man was supposed to carry with it some of the vital power and authority of the man.

[2] Otherwise known as Rameses IX, a king of the twentieth dynasty.

[3] *i.e.* they were kept prisoners in Syria until their death.

for the Great and Holy Boat of Amen-Rā, the King of the Gods. And I cut down cedar trees, and I loaded them into ships. I provided the ships myself, and I manned them with my own sailors, and I made them to arrive in Egypt that they might bespeak [from the god for me] ten thousand years of life, in addition to the span of life which was decreed for me. And this petition hath been granted.

" [And wouldst thou not rather] that, after the lapse of time, when another ambassador came from the land of Egypt who understood this writing, he should utter thy name which should be on the stele, and pray that thou shouldst receive water in Amentet, even like the gods who subsist ? "

And he said unto me, " These words which thou hast spoken unto me are of a certainty a great testimony." And I said unto him, " Now, as concerning the multitude of words which thou hast spoken unto me : As soon as I arrive at the place where the First Prophet (*i.e.* Her-Heru) of Amen dwelleth, and he knoweth [how thou hast] performed the commands of the God [Amen], he will cause to be conveyed to thee [a gift of] certain things." Then I walked down to the beach, to the place where the trunks of cedar had been lying, and I saw eleven ships [ready] to put out to sea ; and they belonged to Tchakar-Bāl. [And the governor sent out an order] saying, " Stop him, and do not let any ship with him on board [depart] to the land of Egypt." Then I sat myself down and wept. And the scribe of the Governor came out to me, and said unto me, " What aileth thee ? " And I said unto him, " Consider the *kashu* birds that fly to Egypt again and again ! And consider how they flock to the cool water brooks ! Until the coming of whom must I remain cast aside hither ? Assuredly thou seest those who have come to prevent my departure a second time."

Then [the scribe] went away and told the Governor what I had said ; and the Governor shed tears because of the words that had been repeated to him, for they were full of pain. And he caused the scribe to come out to me again, and he brought with him two skins [full] of wine and a goat.

And he caused to be brought out to me Thentmut, an Egyptian singing woman who lived in his house, and he said to her, " Sing to him, and let not the cares of his business lay hold upon his heart." And to me he sent a message, saying, " Eat and drink, and let not business lay hold upon thy heart. Thou shalt hear everything which I have to say unto thee to-morrow morning."

And when the morning had come, he caused [the inhabitants of the town] to be assembled on the quay, and having stood up in their midst, he said to the Tchakaru, " For what purpose have ye come hither ? " And they said unto him, " We have come hither seeking for the ships which have been broken and dashed to pieces, that is to say, the ships which thou didst despatch to Egypt, with our unfortunate fellow-sailors in them." And he said unto them, " I know not how to detain the ambassador of Amen in my country any longer. I beg of you to let me send him away, and then do ye pursue him, and prevent him [from escaping]." And he made me embark in a ship, and sent me forth from the sea-coast, and the winds drove me ashore to the land of Alasu (Cyprus ?). And the people of the city came forth to slay me, and I was dragged along in their midst to the place where their queen Hathaba lived ; and I met her when she was coming forth from one house to go into another. Then I cried out in entreaty to her, and I said unto the people who were standing about her, " Surely there must be among you someone who understandeth the language of Egypt." And one of them said, " I understand the speech [of Egypt]." Then I said unto him, " Tell my Lady these words : I have heard it said far from here, even in the city of [Thebes], the place where Amen dwelleth, that wrong is done in every city, and that only in the land of Alasu (Cyprus ?) is right done. And yet wrong is done here every day ! " And she said, " What is it that thou really wishest to say ? " I said unto her, " Now that the angry sea and the winds have cast me up on the land wherein thou dwellest, thou wilt surely not permit these men who have received me to slay me ! Moreover, I am an ambassador of Amen. And consider carefully, for I am a

man who will be searched for every day. And as for the
sailors of Byblos whom they wish to kill, if their lord findeth
ten of thy sailors he will assuredly slay them." Then she
caused her people to be called off me, and they were made to
stand still, and she said unto me, " Lie down and sleep. . . ."
[The rest of the narrative is wanting].

CHAPTER XI

FAIRY TALES

ONE of the most interesting tales that have come down to us in Egyptian dress is the tale commonly called the " Tale of the Two Brothers." It is found written in the hieratic character upon a papyrus preserved in the British Museum (D'Orbiney, No. 10,183), and the form which the story has there is that which was current under the nineteenth dynasty, about 1300 B.C. The two principal male characters in the story, Anpu and Bata, were originally gods, but in the hands of the Egyptian story-teller they became men, and their deeds were treated in such a way as to form an interesting fairy story. It is beyond the scope of this little book to treat of the mythological ideas that underlie certain parts of the narrative, and we therefore proceed to give a rendering of this very curious and important " fairy tale."

It is said that there were two brothers, [the children] of one mother and of one father ; the name of the elder was Anpu, and Bata was the name of the younger. Anpu had a house and a wife, and Bata lived with him like a younger brother. It was Bata who made the clothes ; he tended and herded his cattle in the fields, he ploughed the land, he did the hard work during the time of harvest, and he kept the account of everything that related to the fields. And Bata was a most excellent farmer, and his like there was not in the whole country-side ; and behold, the power of the God was in him. And very many days passed during which Anpu's young brother tended his flocks and herds daily, and he returned to his house each evening loaded with field pro-duce of every kind. And when he had returned from the

A Page of the Hieratic Text of the Tale of the Two Brothers.

fields, he set [food] before his elder brother, who sat with his wife drinking and eating, and then Bata went out to the byre and [slept] with the cattle. On the following morning as soon as it was day, Bata took bread-cakes newly baked, and set them before Anpu, who gave him food to take with him to the fields. Then Bata drove out his cattle into the fields to feed, and [as] he walked behind them they said unto him, " The pasturage is good in such and such a place," and he listened to their voices, and took them where they wished to go. Thus the cattle in Bata's charge became exceedingly fine, and their calves doubled in number, and they multiplied exceedingly. And when it was the season for ploughing Anpu said unto Bata, " Come, let us get our teams ready for plough-ing the fields, and our implements, for the ground hath appeared,[1] and it is in the proper condition for the plough. Go to the fields and take the seed-corn with thee to-day, and at daybreak to-morrow we will do the ploughing " ; this is what he said to him. And Bata did everything which Anpu had told him to do. The next morning, as soon as it was daylight, the two brothers went into the fields with their teams and their ploughs, and they ploughed the land, and they were exceedingly happy as they ploughed, from the begin-ning of their work to the very end thereof.

Now when the two brothers had been living in this way for a considerable time, they were in the fields one day [ploughing], and Anpu said to Bata, " Run back to the farm and fetch some [more] seed corn." And Bata did so, and when he arrived there he found his brother's wife seated dressing her hair. And he said to her, " Get up and give me some seed corn that I may hurry back to the fields, for Anpu ordered me not to loiter on the way." Anpu's wife said to him, " Go thyself to the grain shed, and open the bin, and take out from it as much corn as thou wishest ; I could fetch it for thee myself, only I am afraid that my hair would fall down on the way." Then the young man went to the bin, and filled a very large jar full of grain, for it was his desire

---

[1] *i.e.* the waters of the Inundation had subsided, leaving the ground visible.

to carry off a large quantity of seed corn, and he lifted up on his shoulders the pot, which was filled full of wheat and barley, and came out of the shed with it. And Anpu's wife said to him, " How much grain hast thou on thy shoulders ? " And Bata said to her, " Three measures of barley and two measures of wheat, in all five measures of grain ; that is what I have on my shoulders." These were the words which he spake to her. And she said to him, " How strong thou art ! I have been observing thy vigorousness day by day." And her heart inclined to him, and she entreated him to stay with her, promising to give him beautiful apparel if he would do so. Then the young man became filled with fury like a panther of the south because of her words, and when she saw how angry he was she became terribly afraid. And he said to her, " Verily thou art to me as my mother, and thy husband is as my father, and being my elder brother he hath provided me with the means of living. Thou hast said unto me what ought not to have been said, and I pray thee not to repeat it. On my part I shall tell no man of it, and on thine thou must never declare the matter to man or woman." Then Bata took up his load on his shoulders, and departed to the fields. And when he arrived at the place where his elder brother was they continued their ploughing and laboured diligently at their work.

And when the evening was come the elder brother returned to his house. And having loaded himself with the products of the fields, Bata drove his flocks and herds back to the farm and put them in their enclosures.

And behold, Anpu's wife was smitten with fear, because of the words which she had spoken to Bata, and she took some grease and a piece of linen, and she made herself to appear like a woman who had been assaulted, and who had been violently beaten by her assailant, for she wished to say to her husband, " Thy young brother hath beaten me sorely." And when Anpu returned in the evening according to his daily custom, and arrived at his house, he found his wife lying on the ground in the condition of one who had been assaulted with violence. She did not [appear to] pour water over his hands according to custom, she did not light a light before him ; his house was in darkness, and she was lying prostrate and sick. And her husband said unto her, " Who hath been talking to thee ? " And she said unto him, " No one hath been talking to me except thy young brother. When he came to fetch the seed corn he found me sitting alone, and he spake words of love to me, and he told me to tie up my hair. But I would not listen to him, and I said to him, ' Am I not like thy mother ? Is not thy elder brother like thy father ? ' Then he was greatly afraid, and he beat me to prevent me from telling thee about this matter. Now, if thou dost not kill him I shall kill myself, for since I have complained to thee about his words, when he cometh back in the evening what he will do [to me] is manifest."

Then the elder brother became like a panther of the southern desert with wrath. And he seized his dagger, and sharpened it, and went and stood behind the stable door, so that he might slay Bata when he returned in the evening and came to the byre to bring in his cattle. And when the sun was about to set Bata loaded himself with products of the field of every kind, according to his custom, [and returned to the farm]. And as he was coming back the cow that led the herd said to Bata as she was entering the byre, " Verily thy elder brother is waiting with his dagger to slay thee ; flee thou from before him " ; and Bata hearkened to the words of the leading cow. And when the second cow as she was about to enter into the byre spake unto him even as did the first cow, Bata looked under the door of the byre, and saw the feet of his elder brother as he stood behind the door with his dagger in his hand. Then he set down his load upon the ground, and he ran away as fast as he could run, and Anpu followed him grasping his dagger. And Bata cried out to Rā-Harmakhis (the Sun-god) and said, " O my fair Lord, thou art he who judgeth between the wrong and the right." And the god Rā hearkened unto all his words, and he caused a great stream to come into being, and to separate the two brothers, and the water was filled with crocodiles. Now Anpu was on one side of the stream and Bata on the other, and Anpu wrung his hands together in bitter wrath because he could not kill his brother. Then Bata cried out to Anpu on the other bank, saying, " Stay where thou art until daylight, and until the Disk (*i.e.* the Sun-god) riseth. I will enter into judgment with thee in his presence, for it is he who setteth right what is wrong. I shall never more live with thee, and I shall never again dwell in the place where thou art. I am going to the Valley of the Acacia."

And when the day dawned, and there was light on the earth, and Rā-Harmakhis was shining, the two brothers looked at each other. And Bata spake unto Anpu, saying, " Why hast thou pursued me in this treacherous way, wishing to slay me without first hearing what I had to say ? I am thy brother, younger than thou art, and thou art as a father and thy wife is as a mother to me. Is it not so ? When thou didst send me to fetch seed corn for our work, it was thy wife who said, ' I pray thee to stay with me,' but behold, the facts have been misrepresented to thee, and the reverse of what happened hath been put before thee." Then Bata explained everything to Anpu, and made him to understand exactly what had taken place between him and his brother's wife. And Bata swore an oath by Rā-Harmakhis, saying, " By Rā-Harmakhis, to lie in wait for me and to pursue me, with thy knife in thy hand ready to slay me, was a wicked and abominable thing to do." And Bata took [from his side] the knife which he used in cutting reeds, and drove it into his body, and he sank down fainting upon the ground. Then Anpu cursed himself with bitter curses, and he lifted up his voice and wept ; and he did not know how to cross over the stream to the bank where Bata was because of the crocodiles. And Bata cried out to him, saying, " Behold, thou art ready to remember against me one bad deed of mine, but thou dost not remember my good deeds, or even one of the many things that have been done for thee by me. Shame on thee ! Get thee back to thy house and tend thine own cattle, for I will no longer stay with thee. I will depart to the Valley of the Acacia. But thou shalt come to minister to me, therefore take heed to what I say. Now know that certain things are about to happen to me. I am going to cast a spell on my heart, so that I may be able to place it on a flower of the Acacia tree. When this Acacia is cut down my heart shall fall to the ground, and thou shalt come to seek for it. Thou shalt pass seven years in seeking for it, but let not thy heart be sick with disappointment, for thou shalt find it. When thou findest it, place it in a vessel of cold water, and verily my heart shall live again, and shall make answer to him that attacketh me. And thou shalt know what hath happened to me [by the following sign]. A vessel of beer shall be placed in thy hand, and it shall froth and run over; and another vessel with wine in it shall be placed [in thy hand], and it shall become sour. Then make no tarrying, for indeed these things shall happen to thee." So the younger brother departed to the Valley of the Acacia, and the elder brother departed to his house. And Anpu's hand was laid upon his head, and he cast dust upon himself [in grief for Bata], and when he arrived at his house he slew his wife, and threw her to the dogs, and he sat down and mourned for his young brother.

And when many days had passed, Bata was living alone in the Valley of the Acacia, and he spent his days in hunting the wild animals of the desert; and at night he slept under the Acacia, on the top of the flowers of which rested his heart. And after many days he built himself, with his own hand, a large house in the Valley of the Acacia, and it was filled with beautiful things of every kind, for he delighted in the possession of a house. And as he came forth [one day] from his house, he met the Company of the Gods, and they were on their way to work out their plans in their realm. And one of them said unto him, " Hail, Bata, thou Bull of the gods, hast thou not been living here alone since the time when thou didst forsake thy town through the wife of thy elder brother Anpu? Behold, his wife hath been slain [by him], and moreover thou hast made an adequate answer to the attack which he made upon thee "; and their hearts were very sore indeed for Bata. Then Rā-Harmakhis said unto Khnemu,[1] " Fashion a wife for Bata, so that thou, O Bata,

---

[1] The god who fashioned the bodies of men.

mayest not dwell alone." And Khnemu made a wife to live
with Bata, and her body was more beautiful than the body
of any other woman in the whole country, and the essence
of every god was in her ; and the Seven Hathor Goddesses
came to her, and they said, " She shall die by the sword."
And Bata loved her most dearly, and she lived in his house,
and he passed all his days in hunting the wild animals of the
desert so that he might bring them and lay them before her.
And he said to her, " Go not out of the house lest the River
carry thee off, for I know not how to deliver thee from it.
My heart is set upon the flower of the Acacia, and if any man
find it I must do battle with him for it " ; and he told her
everything that had happened concerning his heart.

And many days afterwards, when Bata had gone out
hunting as usual, the young woman went out of the house
and walked under the Acacia tree, which was close by, and
the River saw her, and sent its waters rolling after her ; and
she fled before them and ran away into her house. And the
River said, " I love her," and the Acacia took to the River a
lock of her hair, and the River carried it to Egypt, and cast
it up on the bank at the place where the washermen washed
the clothes of Pharaoh, life, strength, health [be to him] !
And the odour of the lock of hair passed into the clothing of
Pharaoh. Then the washermen of Pharaoh quarrelled among
themselves, saying, " There is an odour [as of] perfumed oil
in the clothes of Pharaoh." And quarrels among them went
on daily, and at length they did not know what they were
doing. And the overseer of the washermen of Pharaoh
walked to the river bank, being exceedingly angry because
of the quarrels that came before him daily, and he stood still
on the spot that was exactly opposite to the lock of hair as
it lay in the water. Then he sent a certain man into the
water to fetch it, and when he brought it back, the overseer,
finding that it had an exceedingly sweet odour, took it to
Pharaoh. And the scribes and the magicians were summoned
into the presence of Pharaoh, and they said to him, " This
lock of hair belongeth to a maiden of Rā-Harmakhis, and
the essence of every god is in her. It cometh to thee from a

strange land as a salutation of praise to thee. We therefore
pray thee send ambassadors into every land to seek her out.
And as concerning the ambassador to the Valley of the Acacia,
we beg thee to send a strong escort with him to fetch her."
And His Majesty said unto them, " What we have decided
is very good," and he despatched the ambassadors.

And when many days had passed by, the ambassadors
who had been despatched to foreign lands returned to make
a report to His Majesty, but those who had gone to the Valley
of the Acacia did not come back, for Bata had slain them,
with the exception of one who returned to tell the matter to
His Majesty. Then His Majesty despatched foot-soldiers
and horsemen and charioteers to bring back the young woman,
and there was also with them a woman who had in her hands
beautiful trinkets of all kinds, such as are suitable for maidens,
to give to the young woman. And this woman returned to
Egypt with the young woman, and everyone in all parts of
the country rejoiced at her arrival. And His Majesty loved
her exceedingly, and he paid her homage as the Great August
One, the Chief Wife. And he spake to her and made her tell
him what had become of her husband, and she said to His
Majesty, " I pray thee to cut down the Acacia Tree and then
to destroy it." Then the King caused men and bowmen to
set out with axes to cut down the Acacia, and when they
arrived in the Valley of the Acacia, they cut down the flower
on which was the heart of Bata, and he fell down dead at
that very moment of evil.

And on the following morning when the light had come
upon the earth, and the Acacia had been cut down, Anpu,
Bata's elder brother, went into his house and sat down, and
he washed his hands ; and one gave him a vessel of beer, and
it frothed up, and the froth ran over, and one gave him
another vessel containing wine, and it was sour. Then he
grasped his staff, and [taking] his sandals, and his apparel,
and his weapons which he used in fighting and hunting, he
set out to march to the Valley of the Acacia. And when he
arrived there he went into Bata's house, and he found his
young brother there lying dead on his bed ; and when he

looked upon his young brother he wept on seeing that he was dead. Then he set out to seek for the heart of Bata, under the Acacia where he was wont to sleep at night, and he passed three years in seeking for it but found it not. And when the fourth year of his search had begun, his heart craved to return to Egypt, and he said, " I will depart thither to-morrow morning " ; that was what he said to himself. And on the following day he walked about under the Acacia all day long looking for Bata's heart, and as he was returning [to the house] in the evening, and was looking about him still searching for it, he found a seed, which he took back with him, and behold, it was Bata's heart. Then he fetched a vessel of cold water, and having placed the seed in it, he sat down according to his custom. And when the night came, the heart had absorbed all the water ; and Bata [on his bed] trembled in all his members, and he looked at Anpu, whilst his heart remained in the vessel of water. And Anpu took up the vessel wherein was his brother's heart, which had absorbed the water. And Bata's heart ascended its throne [in his body], and Bata became as he had been aforetime, and the two brothers embraced each other, and each spake to the other.

And Bata said to Anpu, " Behold, I am about to take the form of a great bull, with beautiful hair, and a disposition (?) which is unknown. When the sun riseth, do thou mount on my back, and we will go to the place where my wife is, and I will make answer [for myself]. Then shalt thou take me to the place where the King is, for he will bestow great favours upon thee, and he will heap gold and silver upon thee because thou wilt have brought me to him. For I am going to become a great and wonderful thing, and men and women shall rejoice because of me throughout the country." And on the following day Bata changed himself into the form of which he had spoken to his brother. Then Anpu seated himself on his back early in the morning, and when he had come to the place where the King was, and His Majesty had been informed concerning him, he looked at him, and he had very great joy in him. And he made a great festival, saying,

" This is a very great wonder which hath happened " ; and the people rejoiced everywhere throughout the whole country. And Pharaoh loaded Anpu with silver and gold, and he dwelt in his native town, and the King gave him large numbers of slaves, and very many possessions, for Pharaoh loved him very much, far more than any other person in the whole land.

And when many days had passed by the bull went into the house of purification, and he stood up in the place where the August Lady was, and said unto her, " Look upon me, I am alive in very truth." And she said unto him, " Who art thou ? " And he said unto her, " I am Bata. When thou didst cause the Acacia which held my heart to be destroyed by Pharaoh, well didst thou know that thou wouldst kill me. Nevertheless, I am alive indeed, in the form of a bull. Look at me ! " And the August Lady was greatly afraid because of what she had said concerning her husband [to the King] ; and the bull departed from the place of purification. And His Majesty went to tarry in her house and to rejoice with her, and she ate and drank with him ; and the King was exceedingly happy. And the August Lady said to His Majesty, " Say these words : ' Whatsoever she saith I will hearken unto for her sake,' and swear an oath by God that thou wilt do them." And the King hearkened unto everything which she spake, saying, " I beseech thee to give me the liver of this bull to eat, for he is wholly useless for any kind of work." And the King cursed many, many times the request which she had uttered, and Pharaoh's heart was exceedingly sore thereat.

On the following morning, when it was day, the King proclaimed a great feast, and he ordered the bull to be offered up as an offering, and one of the chief royal slaughterers of His Majesty was brought to slay the bull. And after the knife had been driven into him, and whilst he was still on the shoulders of the men, the bull shook his neck, and two drops of blood from it fell by the jambs of the doorway of His Majesty, one by one jamb of Pharaoh's door, and the other by the other, and they became immediately two mighty acacia trees, and each was of the greatest magnificence.

Then one went and reported to His Majesty, saying, " Two mighty acacia trees, whereat His Majesty will marvel exceedingly, have sprung up during the night by the Great Door of His Majesty." And men and women rejoiced in them everywhere in the country, and the King made offerings unto them. And many days after this His Majesty put on his tiara of lapis-lazuli, and hung a wreath of flowers of every kind about his neck, and he mounted his chariot of silvergold, and went forth from the Palace to see the two acacia trees. And the August Lady came following after Pharaoh [in a chariot drawn by] horses, and His Majesty sat down under one acacia, and the August Lady sat under the other. And when she had seated herself the Acacia spake unto his wife, saying, " O woman, who art full of guile, I am Bata, and I am alive even though thou hast entreated me evilly. Well didst thou know when thou didst make Pharaoh to cut down the Acacia that held my heart that thou wouldst kill me, and when I transformed myself into a bull thou didst cause me to be slain."

And several days after this the August Lady was eating and drinking at the table of His Majesty, and the King was enjoying her society greatly, and she said unto His Majesty, " Swear to me an oath by God, saying, I will hearken unto whatsoever the August Lady shall say unto me for her sake ; let her say on." And he hearkened unto everything which she said, and she said, " I entreat thee to cut down these two acacia trees, and to let them be made into great beams " ; and the King hearkened unto everything which she said. And several days after this His Majesty made cunning woodmen to go and cut down the acacia trees of Pharaoh, and whilst the August Lady was standing and watching their being cut down, a splinter flew from one of them into her mouth, and she knew that she had conceived, and the King did for her everything which her heart desired. And many days after this happened she brought forth a man child, and one said to His Majesty, " A man child hath been born unto thee " ; and a nurse was found for him and women to watch over him and tend him, and the people rejoiced throughout the whole land. And the King sat down to enjoy a feast, and he began to call the child by his name, and he loved him very dearly, and at that same time the King gave him the title of " Royal son of Kash." [1] Some time after this His Majesty appointed him " Erpā " [2] of the whole country. And when he had served the office of Erpā for many years, His Majesty flew up to heaven (*i.e.* he died). And the King (*i.e.* Bata) said, " Let all the chief princes be summoned before me, so that I may inform them about everything which hath happened unto me." And they brought his wife, and he entered into judgment with her, and the sentence which he passed upon her was carried out. And Anpu, the brother of the King, was brought unto His Majesty, and the King made him Erpā of the whole country. When His Majesty had reigned over Egypt for twenty years, he departed to life (*i.e.* he died), and his brother Anpu took his place on the day in which he was buried.

Here endeth the book happily [in] peace.[3]

Under the heading of this chapter may well be included the Story of the Shipwrecked Traveller. The text of this remarkable story is written in the hieratic character upon a roll of papyrus, which is preserved in the Imperial Library at St. Petersburg. It is probable that a layer of facts underlies the story, but the form in which we have it justifies us in assigning to it a place among the fairy stories of Ancient Egypt. Prefixed to the narrative of the shipwrecked traveller is the following :

" A certain servant of wise understanding hath said, Let thy heart be of good cheer, O prince. Verily we have arrived at [our] homes. The mallet hath been grasped, and the anchor-post hath been driven into the ground, and the bow of the boat hath grounded on the bank. Thanksgivings have been offered up to God, and every man hath embraced

---

[1] *i.e.* Prince of Kash, or Viceroy of the Sūdān.

[2] *i.e.* hereditary chief, or heir.

[3] According to the colophon, the papyrus was written for an officer of Pharaoh's treasury, called Qakabu, and the scribes Herua and Meremaptu by Annana, the scribe, the lord of books. The man who shall speak [against] this book shall have Thoth for a foe !

his neighbour. Our sailors have returned in peace and safety, and our fighting men have lost none of their comrades, even though we travelled to the uttermost parts of Uauat (Nubia), and through the country of Senmut (Northern Nubia). Verily we have arrived in peace, and we have reached our own land [again]. Hearken, O prince, unto me, even though I be a poor man. Wash thyself, and let water run over thy fingers. I would that thou shouldst be ready to return an answer to the man who addresseth thee, and to speak to the King [from] thy heart, and assuredly thou must give thine answer promptly and without hesitation. The mouth of a man delivereth him, and his words provide a covering for [his] face. Act thou according to the promptings of thine heart, and when thou hast spoken [thou wilt have made him] to be at rest." The shipwrecked traveller then narrates his experiences in the following words : I will now speak and give thee a description of the things that [once] happened to me myself [when] I was journeying to the copper mines of the king. I went down into the sea ¹ in a ship that was one hundred and fifty cubits (225 feet) in length, and forty cubits (60 feet) in breadth, and it was manned by one hundred and fifty sailors who were chosen from among the best sailors of Egypt. They had looked upon the sky, they had looked upon the land, and their hearts were more understanding than the hearts of lions. Now although they were able to say beforehand when a tempest was coming, and could tell when a squall was going to rise before it broke upon them, a storm actually overtook us when we were still on the sea. Before we could make the land the wind blew with redoubled violence, and it drove before it upon us a wave that was eight cubits (12 feet) [high]. A plank was driven towards me by it, and I seized it ; and as for the ship, those who were therein perished, and not one of them escaped.

Then a wave of the sea bore me along and cast me up upon an island, and I passed three days there by myself, with none but mine own heart for a companion ; I laid me down and

¹ The sea was the Red Sea, and the narrator must have been on his way to Wādī Maghārah or Sarābīt al-Khādim in the Peninsula of Sinai.

slept in a hollow in a thicket, and I hugged the shade.   And
I lifted up my legs (*i.e.* I walked about), so that I might find
out what to put in my mouth, and I found there figs and
grapes, and all kinds of fine large berries ; and there were
there gourds, and melons, and pumpkins as large as barrels (?),
and there were also there fish and water-fowl.   There was no
[food] of any sort or kind that did not grow in this island.
And when I had eaten all I could eat, I laid the remainder
of the food upon the ground, for it was too much for me [to
carry] in my arms.   I then dug a hole in the ground and made
a fire, and I prepared pieces of wood and a burnt-offering
for the gods.

And I heard a sound [as of] thunder, which I thought to
be [caused by] a wave of the sea, and the trees rocked and the
earth quaked, and I covered my face.   And I found [that the
sound was caused by] a serpent that was coming towards me.
It was thirty cubits (45 feet) in length, and its beard was more
than two cubits in length, and its body was covered with
[scales of] gold, and the two ridges over its eyes were of
pure lapis-lazuli (*i.e.* they were blue) ; and it coiled its whole
length up before me.   And it opened its mouth to me, now
I was lying flat on my stomach in front of it, and it said unto
me, " Who hath brought thee hither ?   Who hath brought
thee hither, O miserable one ?   Who hath brought thee
hither ?   If thou dost not immediately declare unto me who
hath brought thee to this island, I will make thee to know
what it is to be burnt with fire, and thou wilt become a thing
that is invisible.   Thou speakest to me, but I cannot hear
what thou sayest ; I am before thee, dost thou not know
me ? "   Then the serpent took me in its mouth, and carried
me off to the place where it was wont to rest, and it set me
down there, having done me no harm whatsoever ; I was
sound and whole, and it had not carried away any portion
of my body.   And it opened its mouth to me whilst I was
lying flat on my stomach, and it said unto me, " Who hath
brought thee thither ?   Who hath brought thee hither, O
miserable one ?   Who hath brought thee to this island of
the sea, the two sides of which are in the waves ? "

Then I made answer to the serpent, my two hands being

folded humbly before it, and I said unto it, " I am one who
was travelling to the mines on a mission of the king in a
ship that was one hundred and fifty cubits long, and fifty
cubits in breadth, and it was manned by a crew of one hundred and fifty men, who were chosen from among the best
sailors of Egypt.　They had looked upon the sky, they had
looked upon the earth, and their hearts were more understanding than the hearts of lions.　They were able to say
beforehand when a tempest was coming, and to tell when a
squall was about to rise before it broke.　The heart of every
man among them was wiser than that of his neighbour, and
the arm of each was stronger than that of his neighbour ;
there was not one weak man among them.　Nevertheless it
blew a gale of wind whilst we were still on the sea and before
we could make the land.　A gale rose, which continued to
increase in violence, and with it there came upon [us] a wave
eight cubits [high].　A plank of wood was driven towards
me by this wave, and I seized it ; and as for the ship, those
who were therein perished and not one of them escaped alive
[except] myself.　And now behold me by thy side ! It was
a wave of the sea that brought me to this island."

And the serpent said unto me, " Have no fear, have no
fear, O little one, and let not thy face be sad, now that thou
hast arrived at the place where I am.　Verily, God hath
spared thy life, and thou hast been brought to this island
where there is food.　There is no kind of food that is not
here, and it is filled with good things of every kind.　Verily,
thou shalt pass month after month on this island, until thou
hast come to the end of four months, and then a ship shall
come, and there shall be therein sailors who are acquaintances
of thine, and thou shalt go with them to thy country, and
thou shalt die in thy native town."　[And the serpent continued,] " What a joyful thing it is for the man who hath
experienced evil fortunes, and hath passed safely through
them, to declare them ! I will now describe unto thee some
of the things that have happened unto me on this island.
I used to live here with my brethren, and with my children
who dwelt among them ; now my children and my brethren

together numbered seventy-five. I do not make mention of a little maiden who had been brought to me by fate. And a star fell [from heaven], and these (*i.e.* his children, and his brethren, and the maiden) came into the fire which fell with it. I myself was not with those who were burnt in the fire, and I was not in their midst, but I [well-nigh] died [of grief] for them. And I found a place wherein I buried them all together. Now, if thou art strong, and thy heart flourisheth, thou shalt fill both thy arms (*i.e.* embrace) with thy children, and thou shalt kiss thy wife, and thou shalt see thine own house, which is the most beautiful thing of all, and thou shalt reach thy country, and thou shalt live therein again together with thy brethren, and dwell therein."

Then I cast myself down flat upon my stomach, and I pressed the ground before the serpent with my forehead, saying, " I will describe thy power to the King, and I will make him to understand thy greatness. I will cause to be brought unto thee the unguent and spices called *aba*, and *hekenu*, and *inteneb*, and *khasait*, and the incense that is offered up in the temples, whereby every god is propitiated. I will relate [unto him] the things that have happened unto me, and declare the things that have been seen by me through thy power, and praise and thanksgiving shall be made unto thee in my city in the presence of all the nobles of the country. I will slaughter bulls for thee, and will offer them up as burnt-offerings, and I will pluck feathered fowl in thine [honour]. And I will cause to come to thee boats laden with all the most costly products of the land of Egypt, even according to what is done for a god who is beloved by men and women in a land far away, whom they know not." Then the serpent smiled at me, and the things which I had said to it were regarded by it in its heart as nonsense, for it said unto me, " Thou hast not a very great store of myrrh [in Egypt], and all that thou hast is incense. Behold, I am the Prince of Punt, and the myrrh which is therein belongeth to me. And as for the *heken* which thou hast said thou wilt cause to be brought to me, is it not one of the chief [products] of this island ? And behold, it shall come to pass that when thou hast once departed from this place, thou shalt never more see this island, for it shall disappear into the waves."

And in due course, even as the serpent had predicted, a ship arrived, and I climbed up to the top of a high tree, and I recognised those who were in it. Then I went to announce the matter to the serpent, but I found that it had knowledge thereof already. And the serpent said unto me, " A safe [journey], a safe [journey], O little one, to thy house. Thou shalt see thy children [again]. I beseech thee that my name may be held in fair repute in thy city, for verily this is the thing which I desire of thee." Then I threw myself flat upon my stomach, and my two hands were folded humbly before the serpent. And the serpent gave me a [ship-] load of things, namely, myrrh, *heken*, *inteneb*, *khasait*, *thsheps* and *shaas* spices, eye-paint (antimony), skins of panthers, great balls of incense, tusks of elephants, greyhounds, apes, monkeys, and beautiful and costly products of all sorts and kinds. And when I had loaded these things into the ship, and had thrown myself flat upon my stomach in order to give thanks unto it for the same, it spake unto me, saying, " Verily thou shalt travel to [thy] country in two months, and thou shalt fill both thy arms with thy children, and thou shalt renew thy youth in thy coffin." Then I went down to the place on the sea-shore where the ship was, and I hailed the bowmen who were in the ship, and I spake words of thanksgiving to the lord of this island, and those who were in the ship did the same. Then we set sail, and we journeyed on and returned to the country of the King, and we arrived there at the end of two months, according to all that the serpent had said. And I entered into the presence of the King, and I took with me for him the offerings which I had brought out of the island. And the King praised me and thanked me in the presence of the nobles of all his country, and he appointed me to be one of his bodyguard, and I received my wages along with those who were his [regular] servants.

Cast thou thy glance then upon me [O Prince], now that I have set my feet on my native land once more, having seen and experienced what I have seen and experienced. Hearken thou unto me, for verily it is a good thing to hearken unto men. And the Prince said unto me, " Make not thyself out to be perfect, my friend ! Doth a man give water to a fowl at daybreak which he is going to kill during the day ? "

Here endeth [The Story of the Shipwrecked Traveller], which hath been written from the beginning to the end thereof according to the text that hath been found written in an [ancient] book. It hath been written (*i.e.* copied) by Ameni-Amen-āa, a scribe with skilful fingers. Life, strength, and health be to him !

CHAPTER XII

In this chapter are given translations of Hymns that were sung in the temples in honour of the great gods of Egypt between 1600 B.C. and 900 B.C., and of Hymns that were used by kings and private individuals. The following Hymn to Amen-Rā is found in a papyrus preserved in the Egyptian Museum in Cairo; the asterisk marks groups of words which are equivalent to our lines in poetical compositions.

I. A Hymn to Amen-Rā,* the Bull, dweller in Anu, chief of all the gods,* the beneficent god, beloved one,* giving the warmth of life to all * beautiful cattle.*

II. Homage to thee, Amen-Rā, Lord of the throne of Egypt.* Master of the Apts (Karnak).* Kamutef at the head of his fields.* The long-strider, Master of the Land of the South.* Lord of the Matchau (Nubians), Governor of Punt,* King of heaven, first-born son of earth,* Lord of things that are, stablisher of things (*i.e.* the universe), stablisher of all things.*

III. One in his actions, as with the gods,* Beneficent Bull of the Company of the Gods (or of the Nine Gods),* Chief of all the gods,* Lord of Truth, father of the gods,* maker of men, creator of all animals,* Lord of things that are, creator of the staff of life,* Maker of the herbage that sustaineth the life of cattle.*

IV. Power made by Ptah,* Beautiful child of love.* The gods ascribe praises to him.* Maker of things celestial [and] of things terrestrial, he illumineth Egypt,* Traverser of the celestial heights in peace.* King of the South, King of the North, Rā, whose word is truth, Chief of Egypt.* Mighty

in power, lord of awe-inspiring terror,* Chief, creator of everything on earth,* Whose dispensations are greater than those
of every other god.*

V. The gods rejoice in his beautiful acts.* They acclaim
him in the Great House (*i.e.* the sky).* They crown him
with crowns in the House of Fire.* They love the odour of
him,* when he cometh from Punt.* ¹ Prince of the dew,
he traverseth the lands of the Nubians.* Beautiful of face,
[he] cometh from the Land of the God.* ²

VI. The gods fall down awestruck at his feet,* when they
recognise His Majesty their Lord.* Lord of terror, great
one of victory,* Great one of Souls, mighty one of crowns.*
He maketh offerings abundant, [and] createth food.* Praise
be unto thee, creator of the gods.* Suspender of the sky,
who hammered out the earth.*

VII. Strong Watcher, Menu-Amen,* Lord of eternity,
creator of everlastingness,* Lord of praises, chief of the Apts
(Karnak and Luxor), firm of horns, beautiful of faces.*

VIII. Lord of the Urrt Crown, with lofty plumes,* Whose
diadem is beautiful, whose White Crown is high.* Mehen and
the Uatchti serpents belong to his face.* His apparel (?)
is in the Great House,* the double crown, the *nemes* bandlet,
and the helmet.* Beautiful of face, he receiveth the Atef
crown.* Beloved of the South and North.* Master of the
double crown he receiveth the *ames* sceptre.* He is the
Lord of the Mekes sceptre and the whip.*

IX. Beautiful Governor, crowned with the White Crown,*
Lord of light, creator of splendour,* The gods ascribe to him
praises.* He giveth his hand to him that loveth him.*
The flame destroyeth his enemies.* His eye overthroweth
the Seba devil.* It casteth forth its spear, which pierceth
the sky, and maketh Nak to vomit (?) what it hath swallowed.*

X. Homage to thee, Rā, Lord of Truth.* Hidden is the
shrine of the Lord of the gods.* Khepera in his boat * giveth
the order, and the gods come into being.* [He is] Tem,

¹ The Southern and Eastern Sūdān.
² Somaliland and Southern Arabia.

maker of the Rekhit beings,* however many be their forms
he maketh them to live,* distinguishing one kind from
another.*

XI. He heareth the cry of him that is oppressed.* He
is gracious of heart to him that appealeth to him.* He
delivereth the timid man from the man of violence.* He
regardeth the poor man and considereth [his] misery.*

XII. He is the lord Sa (*i.e.* Taste) ; abundance is his
utterance.* The Nile cometh at his will.* He is the lord
of graciousness, who is greatly beloved.* He cometh and
sustaineth mankind.* He setteth in motion everything
that is made.* He worketh in the Celestial Water,* making
to be the pleasantness of the light.* The gods rejoice in
[his] beauties,* and their hearts live when they see him.*

XIII. He is Rā who is worshipped in the Apts.* He is the
one of many crowns in the House of the Benben ¹ Stone.* He
is the god Ani, the lord of the ninth-day festival.* The
festival of the sixth day and the Tenat festival are kept for
him.* He is KING, life, strength, and health be to him !
and the Lord of all the gods.* He maketh himself to be seen
in the horizon,* Chief of the beings of the Other World.*
His name is hidden from the gods who are his children,* in
his name of " Amen." * ²

XIV. Homage to thee, dweller in peace. Lord of joy of
heart, mighty one of crowns,* lord of the Urrt Crown with
the lofty plumes,* with a beautiful tiara and a lofty White
Crown.* The gods love to behold thee.* The double crown
is stablished on thy head.* Thy love passeth throughout
Egypt.* Thou sendest out light, thou risest with [thy] two
beautiful eyes.* The Pāt beings [faint] when thou appearest
in the sky,* animals become helpless under thy rays.* Thy
loveliness is in the southern sky,* thy graciousness is in the
northern sky.* Thy beauties seize upon hearts,* thy loveliness maketh the arms weak,* thy beautiful operations
make the hands idle,* hearts become weak at the sight of
thee.*

¹ The Benben was the abode of the Spirit of Rā at times.
² *Amen* means " hidden."

XV. [He is] the Form One, the creator of everything that is.* The One only, the creator of things that shall be.* Men and women proceeded from his two eyes. His utterance became the gods.* He is the creator of the pasturage wherein herds and flocks live,* [and] the staff of life for mankind.* He maketh to live the fish in the river,* and the geese and the feathered fowl of the sky.* He giveth air to the creature that is in the egg. He nourisheth the geese in their pens.* He maketh to live the water-fowl,* and the reptiles and every insect that flieth.* He provideth food for the mice in their holes,* he nourisheth the flying creatures on every bough.*

XVI. Homage to thee, O creator of every one of these creatures,* the One only whose hands are many.* He watcheth over all those who lie down to sleep,* he seeketh the well-being of his animal creation,* Amen, establisher of every thing,* Temu-Herukhuti.* They all praise thee with their words,* adorations be to thee because thou restest among us,* we smell the earth before thee because thou hast fashioned us.*

XVII. All the animals cry out, "Homage to thee."* Every country adoreth thee,* to the height of heaven, to the breadth of the earth,* to the depths of the Great Green Sea.* The gods bend their backs in homage to thy Majesty,* to exalt the Souls of their Creator,* they rejoice when they meet their begetter.* They say unto thee, "Welcome, O father of the fathers of all the gods,* suspender of the sky, beater out of the earth,* maker of things that are, creator of things that shall be,* KING, life, strength, and health be to thee ! Chief of the gods, we praise thy Souls,* inasmuch as thou hast created us. Thou workest for us thy children,* we adore thee because thou restest among us."*

XVIII. Homage to thee, O maker of everything that is.* Lord of Truth, father of the gods,* maker of men, creator of animals,* lord of the divine grain, making to live the wild animals of the mountains.* Amen, Bull, Beautiful Face,* Beloved one in the Apts,* great one of diadems in the House of the Benben Stone,* binding on the tiara in Anu (On),*

judge of the Two Men (*i.e.* Horus and Set) in the Great
Hall.*

XIX. Chief of the Great Company of the gods,* One only,
who hath no second,* President of the Apts,* Ani, President
of his Company of the gods,* living by Truth every day,*
Khuti, Horus of the East.* He hath created the mountains,
the gold * [and] the real lapis-lazuli by his will,* the incense
and the natron that are mixed by the Nubians,* and fresh
myrrh for thy nostrils.* Beautiful Face, coming from the
Nubians,* Amen-Rā, lord of the throne of Egypt,* President
of the Apts,* Ani, President of his palace.*

XX. King, One among the gods.* [His] names are so
many, how many cannot be known.* He riseth in the eastern horizon, he setteth in the western horizon.*

XXI. He overthroweth his enemies at dawn, when he is
born each day.* Thoth exalteth his two eyes.* When he
setteth in his splendour the gods rejoice in his beauties,* and
the Apes (*i.e.* dawn spirits) exalt him.* Lord of the Sektet
Boat and of the Āntet Boat,* they transport thee [over] Nu
in peace.* Thy sailors rejoice * when they see thee overthrowing the Seba fiend,* [and] stabbing his limbs with the
knife.* The flame devoureth him, his soul is torn out of
his body,* the feet (?) of this serpent Nak are carried off.*

XXII. The gods rejoice, the sailors of Rā are satisfied.*
Anu rejoiceth,* the enemies of Temu are overthrown.* The
Apts are in peace.* The heart of the goddess Nebt-ānkh is
happy,* [for] the enemies of her Lord are overthrown.* The
gods of Kher-āha make adorations [to him].* Those who
are in their hidden shrines smell the earth before him,* when
they see him mighty in his power.*

XXIII. [O] Power of the gods,* [lord of] Truth, lord of
the Apts,* in thy name of " Maker of Truth." * Lord of
food, bull of offerings,* in thy name of " Amen-Ka-mutef," *
Maker of human beings,* maker to be of . . . , creator of
everything that is * in thy name of " Temu Khepera." *

XXIV. Great Hawk, making the body festal.* Beautiful
Face, making the breast festal,* Image . . . with the lofty
Mehen crown.* The two serpent-goddesses fly before him.*

The hearts of the Pāt beings leap towards him.*   The
Hememet beings turn to him.*   Egypt rejoiceth at his appear-
ances.*   Homage to thee, Amen-Rā, Lord of the throne of
Egypt.*   His town [Thebes] loveth him when he riseth.*
HERE ENDETH * [THE HYMN] IN PEACE,* ACCORDING
TO AN ANCIENT COPY.*

The following extract is taken from a work in which the
power and glory of Amen are described in a long series of
Chapters ; the papyrus in which it is written is in Leyden.
" [He, i.e. Amen], driveth away evils and scattereth
diseases.   He is the physician who healeth the eye without
[the use of] medicaments.   He openeth the eyes, he driveth
away inflammation (?) . . . He delivereth whom he pleaseth,
even from the Tuat (the Other World).   He saveth a man
from what is ordained for him at the dictates of his heart.
To him belong both eyes and ears, [he is] on every path of
him whom he loveth.   He heareth the petitions of him that
appealeth to him.   He cometh from afar to him that calleth
[before] a moment hath passed.   He maketh high (i.e. long)
the life [of a man], he cutteth it short.   To him whom he
loveth he giveth more than hath been fated for him.   [When]
Amen casteth a spell on the water, and his name is on the
waters, if this name of his be uttered the crocodile (?) hath no
power.   The winds are driven back, the hurricane is repulsed.
At the remembrance of him the wrath of the angry man dieth
down.   He speaketh the gentle word at the moment of
strife.   He is a pleasant breeze to him that appealeth to him.
He delivereth the helpless one.   He is the wise (?) god whose
plans are beneficent. . . . He is more helpful than millions
to the man who hath set him in his heart.   One warrior
[who fighteth] under his name is better than hundreds of
thousands.   Indeed he is the beneficent strong one.   He is
perfect [and] seizeth his moment ; he is irresistible. . . .
All the gods are three, Amen, Rā and Ptah, and there are none
like unto them.   He whose name is hidden is Amen.   Rā
belongeth to him as his face, and his body is Ptah.   Their
cities are established upon the earth for ever, [namely,]

Thebes, Anu (Heliopolis), and Hetkaptah (Memphis). When
a message is sent from heaven it is heard in Anu, and is repeated in Memphis to the Beautiful Face (*i.e.* Ptah). It is
done into writing, in the letters of Thoth (*i.e.* hieroglyphs),
and despatched to the City of Amen (*i.e.* Thebes), with their
things. The matters are answered in Thebes. . . . His
heart is Understanding, his lips are Taste, his Ka is all the
things that are in his mouth. He entereth, the two caverns
are beneath his feet. The Nile appeareth from the hollow
beneath his sandals. His soul is Shu, his heart is Tefnut.
He is Heru-Khuti in the upper heaven. His right eye is
day. His left eye is night. He is the leader of faces on
every path. His body is Nu. The dweller in it is the Nile,
producing everything that is, nourishing all that is. He
breatheth breath into all nostrils. The Luck and the Destiny
of every man are with him. His wife is the earth, he uniteth
with her, his seed is the tree of life, his emanations are the
grain."

Hymns to the Sun-god

The following extracts from Hymns to the Sun-god and
Osiris are written in the hieratic character upon slices of limestone now preserved in the Egyptian Museum in Cairo.

"Well dost thou watch, O Horus, who sailest over the
sky, thou child who proceedest from the divine father, thou
child of fire, who shinest like crystal, who destroyest the
darkness and the night. Thou child who growest rapidly,
with gracious form, who restest in thine eye. Thou wakest
up men who are asleep on their beds, and the reptiles in their
nests. Thy boat saileth on the fiery Lake Neserser, and thou
traversest the upper sky by means of the winds thereof.
The two daughters of the Nile-god crush for thee the fiend
Neka, Nubti (*i.e.* Set) pierceth him with his arrows. Keb
seizeth (?) him by the joint of his back, Serqet grippeth him
at his throat. The flame of this serpent that is over the door
of thy house burneth him up. The Great Company of the
Gods are wroth with him, and they rejoice because he is cut
to pieces. The Children of Horus grasp their knives, and

inflict very many gashes in him. Hail ! Thine enemy hath fallen, and Truth standeth firm before thee. When thou again transformest thyself into Tem, thou givest thy hand to the Lords of Akert (*i.e.* the dead), those who lie in death give thanks for thy beauties when thy light falleth upon them. They declare unto thee what is their hearts' wish, which is that they may see thee again. When thou hast passed them by, the darkness covereth them, each one in his coffin. Thou art the lord of those who cry out (?) to thee, the god who is beneficent for ever. Thou art the Judge of words and deeds, the Chief of chief judges, who stablishest truth, and doest away sin. May he who attacketh me be judged rightly, behold, he is stronger than I am ; he hath seized upon my office, and hath carried it off with falsehood. May it be restored to me."

HYMN TO OSIRIS

" [Praise be] unto thee, O thou who extendest thine arms, who liest asleep on thy side, who liest on the sand, the Lord of the earth, the divine mummy. . . . Thou art the Child of the Earth Serpent, of great age. Thy head . . . and goeth round over thy feet. Rā-Khepera shineth upon thy body, when thou liest on thy bed in the form of Seker, so that he may drive away the darkness that shroudeth thee, and may infuse light in thy two eyes. He passeth a long period of time shining upon thee, and sheddeth tears over thee. The earth resteth upon thy shoulders, and its corners rest upon thee as far as the four pillars of heaven. If thou movest thyself, the earth quaketh, for thou art greater than. . . . [The Nile] appeareth out of the sweat of thy two hands. Thou breathest forth the air that is in thy throat into the nostrils of men ; divine is that thing whereon they live. Through thy nostrils (?) subsist the flowers, the herbage, the reeds, the flags (?), the barley, the wheat, and the plants whereon men live. If canals are dug . . . and houses and temples are built, and great statues are dragged along, and lands are ploughed up, and tombs and funerary monuments are made, they [all] rest upon thee. It is thou who makest them. They are upon thy back. They are more than can be done into writing (*i.e.* described). There is no vacant space on thy back, they all lie on thy back, and yet [thou sayest] not, "I am [over] weighted therewith. Thou art the father and mother of men and women, they live by thy breath, they eat the flesh of thy members. 'Pautti' (*i.e.* Primeval God) is thy name." The writer of this hymn says in the four broken lines that remain that he is unable to understand the nature (?) of Osiris, which is hidden (?), and his attributes, which are sublime.

HYMN TO SHU

The following Hymn is found in the Magical Papyrus (Harris, No. 501), which is preserved in the British Museum. The text is written in the hieratic character, and reads :

"Homage to thee, O flesh and bone of Rā, thou first-born son who didst proceed from his members, who wast chosen to be the chief of those who were brought forth, thou mighty one, thou divine form, who art endowed with strength as the lord of transformations. Thou overthrowest the Seba fiends each day. The divine boat hath the wind [behind it], thy heart is glad. Those who are in the Āntti Boat utter loud cries of joy when they see Shu, the son of Rā, triumphant, [and] driving his spear into the serpent fiend Nekau. Rā setteth out to sail over the heavens at dawn daily. The goddess Tefnut is seated on thy head, she hurleth her flames of fire against thy enemies, and maketh them to be destroyed utterly. Thou art equipped by Rā, thou art mighty through his words of power, thou art the heir of thy father upon his throne, and thy Doubles rest in the Doubles of Rā, even as the taste of what hath been in the mouth remaineth therein. A will hath been done into writing by the lord of Khemenu (Thoth), the scribe of the library of Rā-Harmakhis, in the hall of the divine house (or temple) of Anu (Heliopolis), stablished, perfected, and made permanent in hieroglyphs under the feet of Rā-Harmakhis, and he shall transmit it to the son of his son for ever and ever.   Homage to thee, O son of Rā, who wast begotten by Temu himself.   Thou didst create thyself, and thou hadst no mother.   Thou art Truth, the lord of Truth, thou art the Power, the ruling power of the gods.   Thou dost conduct the Eye of thy father Rā.   They give gifts unto thee into thine own hands.   Thou makest to be at peace the Great Goddess, when storms are passing over her.   Thou dost stretch out the heavens on high, and dost establish them with thine own hands.   Every god boweth in homage before thee, the King of the South, the King of the North, Shu, the son of Rā, life, strength and health be to thee !   Thou, O great god Pautti, art furnished with the brilliance of the Eye [of Rā] in Heliopolis, to overthrow the Seba fiends on behalf of thy father.   Thou makest the divine Boat to sail onwards in peace.   The mariners who are therein exult, and all the gods shout for joy when they hear thy divine name.   Greater, yea greater (*i.e.* twice great) art thou than the gods in thy name of Shu, son of Rā."

CHAPTER XIII

MORAL AND PHILOSOPHICAL LITERATURE

SIDE by side with the great mass of literature of a magical and religious character that flourished in Egypt under the Ancient Empire, we find that there existed also a class of writings that are remarkably like those contained in the Book of Proverbs, which is attributed to Solomon, the King of Israel, and in "Ecclesiasticus," and the "Book of Wisdom." The priests of Egypt took the greatest trouble to compose Books of the Dead and Guides to the Other World in order to help the souls of the dead to traverse in safety the region that lay between this world and the next, or Dead Land, and the high officials who flourished under the Pharaohs of the early dynasties drew up works, the object of which was to enable the living man to conduct himself in such a way as to satisfy his social superiors, to please his equals, and to content his inferiors, and at the same time to advance to honours and wealth himself. These works represent the experience, and shrewdness, and knowledge which their writers had gained at the Court of the Pharaohs, and are full of sound worldly wisdom and high moral excellence. They were written to teach young men of the royal and aristocratic classes to fear God, to honour the king, to do their duty efficiently, to lead strictly moral, if not exactly religious, lives, to treat every man with the respect due to his position in life, to cultivate home life, and to do their duty to their neighbours, both to those who were rich and those who were poor. The oldest Egyptian book of Moral Precepts, or Maxims, or Admonitions, is that of Ptah-hetep, governor of the town of Memphis, and high confidential adviser of the king ; he flourished in the reign of Assa, a king of the fifth dynasty, about 3500 B.C. His work is found, more or less complete, in several papyri, which are preserved in the British Museum and in the National Library in Paris, and extracts from it, which were used by Egyptian pupils in the schools attached to the temples, and which are written upon slices of limestone, are to be seen in the Egyptian Museum in Cairo and elsewhere. The oldest copy of the work contains many mistakes, and in some places the text is unintelligible, but many parts of it can be translated, and the following extracts will illustrate the piety and moral worth, and the sagacity and experience of the shrewd but kindly " man of the world " who undertook to guide the young prince of his day. The sage begins his work with a lament about the evil effects that follow old age in a man— " Depression seizeth upon him every day, his eyesight faileth, his ears become deaf, his strength declineth, his heart hath no rest, the mouth becometh silent and speaketh not, the intelligence diminisheth, and it is impossible to remember to-day what happened yesterday. The bones are full of pain, the pursuit that was formerly attended with pleasure is now fraught with pain, and the sense of taste departeth. Old age is the worst of all the miseries that can befall a man. The nose becometh stopped up and one cannot smell at all." At this point Ptah-hetep asks, rhetorically, " Who will give me authority to speak ? Who is it that will authorise me to repeat to the prince the Precepts of those who had know- ledge of the wise counsels of the learned men of old ? " In answer to these questions the king replies to Ptah-hetep, " Instruct thou my son in the words of wisdom of olden time. It is instruction of this kind alone that formeth the character of the sons of noblemen, and the youth who hearkeneth to such instruction will acquire a right understanding and the faculty of judging justly, and he will not feel weary of his duties." Immediately following these words come the " Precepts of beautiful speech " of Ptah-hetep, whose full titles are given, viz. the Erpā, the Duke, the father of the god (i.e. the king), the friend of God, the son of the king, Governor of Memphis, confidential servant of the king.

These Precepts instruct the ignorant, and teach them to understand fine speech ; among them are the following :

" Be not haughty because of thy knowledge. Converse with the ignorant man as well as with him that is educated.

" Do not terrify the people, for if thou dost, God will punish thee. If any man saith that he is going to live by these means, God will make his mouth empty of food. If a man saith that he is going to make himself powerful (or rich) thereby, saying, ' I shall reap advantage, having knowledge,' and if he saith, ' I will beat down the other man,' he will arrive at the result of being able to do nothing. Let no man terrify the people, for the command of God is that they shall enjoy rest.

" If thou art one of a company seated to eat in the house of a man who is greater than thyself, take what he giveth thee [without remark]. Set it before thee. Look at what is before thee, but not too closely, and do not look at it too often. The man who rejecteth it is an ill-mannered person. Do not speak to interrupt when he is speaking, for one knoweth not when he may disapprove. Speak when he addresseth thee, and then thy words shall be acceptable. When a man hath wealth he ordereth his actions according to his own dictates. He doeth what he willeth. . . . The great man can effect by the mere lifting up of his hand what a [poor] man cannot. Since the eating of bread is according to the dispensation of God, a man cannot object thereto.

" If thou art a man whose duty it is to enter into the presence of a nobleman with a message from another nobleman, take care to say correctly and in the correct way what thou art sent to say ; give the message exactly as he said it. Take great care not to spoil it in delivery and so to set one nobleman against another. He who wresteth the truth in transmitting the message, and only repeateth it in words that give pleasure to all men, gentleman or common man, is an abominable person.

" If thou art a farmer, till the field which the great God hath given thee. Eat not too much when thou art near thy neighbours. . . . The children of the man who, being a man of substance, seizeth [prey] like the crocodile in the presence of the field labourers, are cursed because of his behaviour, his father suffereth poignant grief, and as for the mother who bore him, every other woman is happier than she. A man who is the leader of a clan (or tribe) that trusteth him and followeth him becometh a god.

" If thou dost humble thyself and dost obey a wise man, thy behaviour will be held to be good before God. Since thou knowest who are to serve, and who are to command, let not thy heart magnify itself against the latter. Since thou knowest who hath the power, hold in fear him that hath it. . . .

" Be diligent at all times. Do more than is commanded. Waste not the time wherein thou canst labour ; he is an abominable man who maketh a bad use of his time. Lose no chance day by day in adding to the riches of thy house. Work produceth wealth, and wealth endureth not when work is abandoned.

" If thou art a wise man, beget a son who shall be pleasing unto God.

" If thou art a wise man, be master of thy house. Love thy wife absolutely, give her food in abundance, and raiment for her back ; these are the medicines for her body. Anoint her with unguents, and make her happy as long as thou livest. She is thy field, and she reflecteth credit on her possessor. Be not harsh in thy house, for she will be more easily moved by persuasion than by violence. Satisfy her wish, observe what she expecteth, and take note of that whereon she hath fixed her gaze. This is the treatment that will keep her in her house ; if thou repel her advances, it is ruin for thee. Embrace her, call her by fond names, and treat her lovingly.

" Treat thy dependants as well as thou art able, for this is the duty of those whom God hath blessed.

" If thou art a wise man, and if thou hast a seat in the council chamber of thy lord, concentrate thy mind on the business [so as to arrive at] a wise decision. Keep silence, for this is better than to talk overmuch. When thou speakest thou must know what can be urged against thy words. To speak in the council chamber [needeth] skill and experience.

" If thou hast become a great man having once been a poor man, and hast attained to the headship of the city, study not to take the fullest advantage of thy situation. Be not harsh in respect of the grain, for thou art only an overseer of the food of God.

" Think much, but keep thy mouth closed ; if thou dost not how canst thou consult with the nobles ? Let thy opinion coincide with that of thy lord. Do what he saith, and then he shall say of thee to those who are listening, ' This is my son.' "

The above and all the other Precepts of Ptah-hetep were drawn up for the guidance of highly-placed young men, and have little to do with practical, every-day morality. But whilst the Egyptian scribes who lived under the Middle and New Empires were ready to pay all honour to the writings of an earlier age, they were not slow to perceive that the older Precepts did not supply advice on every important subject, and they therefore proceeded to write supplementary Precepts. A very interesting collection of such Precepts is found in a papyrus preserved in the Egyptian Museum, Cairo. They are generally known as the " Maxims of Ani," and the following examples will illustrate their scope and character :

" Celebrate thou the festival of thy God, and repeat the celebration thereof in its appointed season. God is wroth with the transgressor of this law. Bear testimony [to Him] after thy offering. . . .

" The opportunity having passed, one seeketh [in vain] to seize another.

" God will magnify the name of the man who exalteth His Souls, who singeth His praises, and boweth before Him, who offereth incense, and doeth homage [to Him] in his work.

" Enter not into the presence of the drunkard, even if his acquaintance be an honour to thee.

" Beware of the woman in the street who is not known in her native town. Follow her not, nor any woman who is

like her. Do not make her acquaintance. She is like a deep
stream the windings of which are unknown.

" Go not with common men, lest thy name be made to
stink.

" When an inquiry is held, and thou art present, multiply
not speech ; thou wilt do better if thou holdest thy peace.
Act not the part of the chatterer.

" The sanctuary of God abhorreth noisy demonstrations.
Pray thou with a loving heart, and let thy words be hidden
(or secret). Do this, and He will do thy business for thee. He
will hearken unto thy words, and He will receive thy offering.

" Place water before thy father and thy mother who rest
in their tombs. . . . Forget not to do this when thou art
outside thy house, and as thou doest for them so shall thy son
do for thee.

" Frequent not the house where men drink beer, for the
words that fall from thy mouth will be repeated, and it is a
bad thing for thee not to know what thou didst really say.
Thou wilt fall down, thy bones may be broken, and there will
be no one to give thee a hand [to help thee]. Thy boon
companions who are drinking with thee will say, ' Throw this
drunken man out of the door.' When thy friends come to
look for thee, they will find thee lying on the ground as helpless as a babe.

" When the messenger of [death] cometh to carry thee
away, let him find thee prepared. Alas, thou wilt have no
opportunity for speech, for verily his terror will be before
thee. Say not, ' Thou art carrying me off in my youth.'
Thou knowest not when thy death will take place. Death
cometh, and he seizeth the babe at the breast of his mother,
as well as the man who hath arrived at a ripe old age. Observe this, for I speak unto thee good advice which thou
shalt meditate upon in thy heart. Do these things, and
thou wilt be a good man, and evils of all kinds shall remove
themselves from thee.

" Remain not seated whilst another is standing, especially
if he be an old man, even though thy social position (or rank)
be higher than his.

" The man who uttereth ill-natured words must not expect
to receive good-natured deeds.

" If thou journeyest on a road [made by] thy hands each
day, thou wilt arrive at the place where thou wouldst be.

" What ought people to talk about every day ?   Adminis-
trators of high rank should discuss the laws, women should
talk about their husbands, and every man should speak about
his own affairs.

" Never speak an ill-natured word to any visitor ; a word
dropped some day when thou art gossiping may overturn
thy house.

" If thou art well-versed in books, and hast gone into them,
set them in thy heart ; whatsoever thou then utterest will
be good.   If the scribe be appointed to any position, he will
converse about his documents.   The director of the treasury
hath no son, and the overseer of the seal hath no heir.   High
officials esteem the scribe, whose hand is his position of
honour, which they do not give to children. . . .

" The ruin of a man resteth on his tongue ; take heed that
thou harmest not thyself.

" The heart of a man is [like] the store-chamber of a granary
that is full of answers of every kind; choose thou those
that are good, and utter them, and keep those that are bad
closely confined within thee.   To answer roughly is like the
brandishing of weapons, but if thou wilt speak kindly and
quietly thou wilt always [be loved].

" When thou offerest up offerings to thy God, beware lest
thou offer the things that are an abomination [to Him].
Chatter not [during] his journeyings (or processions), seek
not to prolong (?) his appearance, disturb not those who carry
him, chant not his offices too loudly, and beware lest thou. . . .
Let thine eye observe his dispensations. Devote thyself
to the adoration of his name.   It is he who giveth souls to
millions of forms, and he magnifieth the man who magnifieth
him. . . .

" I gave thee thy mother who bore thee, and in bearing
thee she took upon herself a great burden, which she bore
without help from me.   When after some months thou wast

born, she placed herself under a yoke, for three years she suckled thee. . . . When thou wast sent to school to be educated, she brought bread and beer for thee from her house to thy master regularly each day. Thou art now grown up, and thou hast a wife and a house of thy own. Keep thine eye on thy child, and bring him up as thy mother brought thee up. Do nothing whatsoever that will cause her (*i.e.* thy mother) to suffer, lest she lift up her hands to God, and He hear her complaint, [and punish thee].

" Eat not bread, whilst another standeth by, without pointing out to him the bread with thy hand. . . .

" Devote thyself to God, take heed to thyself daily for the sake of God, and let to-morrow be as to-day. Work thou [for him]. God seeth him that worketh for Him, and He esteemeth lightly the man who esteemeth Him lightly.

" Follow not after a woman, and let her not take possession of thy heart.

" Answer not a man when he is wroth, but remove thyself from him. Speak gently to him that hath spoken in anger, for soft words are the medicine for his heart.

" Seek silence for thyself."

For the study of the moral character of the ancient Egyptian, a document, of which a mutilated copy is found on a papyrus preserved in the Royal Library in Berlin, is of peculiar importance. As the opening lines are wanting it is impossible to know what the title of the work was, but because the text records a conversation that took place between a man who had suffered grievous misfortunes, and was weary of the world and of all in it, and wished to kill himself, it is generally called the " TALK OF A MAN WHO WAS TIRED OF LIFE WITH HIS SOUL." The general meaning of the document is clear. The man weary of life discusses with his soul, as if it were a being wholly distinct from himself, whether he shall kill himself or not. He is willing to do so, but is only kept from his purpose by his soul's observation that if he does there will be no one to bury him properly, and to see that the funerary ceremonies are duly performed.

This shows that the man who was tired of life was alone in the world, and that all his relations and friends had either forsaken him, or had been driven away by him. His soul then advised him to destroy himself by means of fire, probably, as has been suggested, because the ashes of a burnt body would need no further care. The man accepted the advice of his soul, and was about to follow it literally, when the soul itself drew back, being afraid to undergo the sufferings inherent in such a death for the body. The man then asked his soul to perform for him the last rites, but it absolutely refused to do so, and told him that it objected to death in any form, and that it had no desire at all to depart to the kingdom of the dead. The soul supports its objection to suffer by telling the man who is tired of life that the mere remembrance of burial is fraught with mourning, and tears, and sorrow. It means that a man is torn away from his house and thrown out upon a hill, and that he will never go up again to see the sun. And after all, what is the good of burial ? Take the case of those who have had granite tombs, and funerary monuments in the form of pyramids made for them, and who lie in them in great state and dignity. If we look at the slabs in their tombs, which have been placed there on purpose to receive offerings from the kinsfolk and friends of the deceased, we shall find that they are just as bare as are the tablets for offerings of the wretched people who belong to the Corvée, of whom some die on the banks of the canals, leaving one part of their bodies on the land and the other in the water, and some fall into the water altogether and are eaten by the fish, and others under the burning heat of the sun become bloated and loathsome objects. Because men receive fine burials it does not follow that offerings of food, which will enable them to continue their existence, will be made by their kinsfolk. Finally the soul ends its speech with the advice that represented the view of the average Egyptian in all ages, " Follow after the day of happiness, and banish care," that is to say, spare no pains in making thyself happy at all times, and let nothing that concerns the present or the future trouble thee.

This advice, which is well expressed by the words which the rich man spake to his soul, " Take thine ease, eat, drink, and be merry " (St. Luke xii. 19), was not acceptable to the man who was tired of life, and he at once addressed to his soul a series of remarks, couched in rhythmical language, in which he made it clear that, so far as he was concerned, death would be preferable to life.   He begins by saying that his name is more detested than the smell of birds on a summer's day when the heavens are hot, and the smell of a handler of fish newly caught when the heavens are hot, and the smell of water-fowl in a bed of willows wherein geese collect, and the smell of fishermen in the marshes where fishing hath been carried on, and the stench of crocodiles, and the place where crocodiles do congregate.   In a second group of rhythmical passages the man who was tired of life goes on to describe the unsatisfactory and corrupt condition of society, and his wholesale condemnation of it includes his own kinsfolk. Each passage begins with the words, " Unto whom do I speak this day ? " and he says, " Brothers are bad, and the friends of to-day lack love.   Hearts are shameless, and every man seizeth the goods of his neighbour.   The meek man goeth to ground (i.e. is destroyed), and the audacious man maketh his way into all places.   The man of gracious countenance is wretched, and the good are everywhere treated as con-temptible.   When a man stirreth thee up to wrath by his wickedness, his evil acts make all people laugh.   One robbeth, and everyone stealeth the possessions of his neighbour. Disease is continual, and the brother who is with it becometh an enemy.   One remembereth not yesterday, and one doeth nothing . . . in this hour.   Brothers are bad. . . . Faces disappear, and each hath a worse aspect than that of his brother.   Hearts are shameless, and the man upon whom one leaneth hath no heart.   There are no righteous men left, the earth is an example of those who do evil.   There is no true man left, and each is ignorant of what he hath learnt.   No man is content with what he hath ; go with the man [you believe to be contented], and he is not [to be found].   I am heavily laden with misery, and I have no true friend. Evil hath smitten the land, and there is no end to it."

The state of the world being thus, the man who was tired of life is driven to think that there is nothing left for him but death ; it is hopeless to expect the whole state of society to change for the better, therefore death must be his deliverer. To his soul he says, " Death standeth before me this day, [and is to me as] the restoration to health of a man who hath been sick, and as the coming out into the fresh air after sickness. Death standeth before me this day like the smell of myrrh, and the sitting under the sail of a boat on a day with a fresh breeze. Death standeth before me this day like the smell of lotus flowers, and like one who is sitting on the bank of drunkenness.[1] Death standeth before me this day like a brook filled with rain water, and like the return of a man to his own house from the ship of war. Death standeth before me this day like the brightening of the sky after a storm, and like one. . . . Death standeth before me this day as a man who wisheth to see his home once again, having passed many years as a prisoner." The three rhythmical passages that follow show that the man who was tired of life looked beyond death to a happier state of existence, in which wrong would be righted, and he who had suffered on this earth would be abundantly rewarded. The place where justice reigned supreme was ruled over by Rā, and the man does not call it " heaven," but merely " there." [2] He says, " He who is there shall indeed be like unto a loving god, and he shall punish him that doeth wickedness. He who is there shall certainly stand in the Boat of the Sun, and shall bestow upon the temples the best [offerings]. He who is there shall indeed become a man of understanding who cannot be resisted, and who prayeth to Rā when he speaketh." The arguments

---

[1] *i.e.* sitting on a seat in a tavern built on the river bank.
[2] Compare, " There the tears of earth are dried ;
      There its hidden things are clear ;
      There the work of life is tried
      By a juster judge than here."
           —*Hymns Ancient and Modern*, No. 401.

in favour of death of the man who was tired of life are superior
to those of the soul in favour of life, for he saw beyond death
the " there " which the soul apparently had not sufficiently
considered. The value of the discussion between the man
and his soul was great in the opinion of the ancient Egyptian
because it showed, with almost logical emphasis, that the
incomprehensible things of " here " would be made clear
" there."

The man who was tired of life did not stand alone in his
discontent with the surroundings in which he lived, and with
his fellow-man, for from a board inscribed in hieratic in the
British Museum (No. 5645) we find that a priest of Heliopolis
called Khakhepersenb, who was surnamed Ānkhu, shared
his discontent, and was filled with disgust at the widespread
corruption and decadence of all classes of society that were
everywhere in the land. In the introduction to this description of society as he saw it, he says that he wishes he possessed
new language in which to express himself, and that he could
find phrases that were not trite in which to utter his experience. He says that men of one generation are very much
like those of another, and have all done and said the same
kind of things. He wishes to unburden his mind, and to
remove his moral sickness by stating what he has to say in
words that have not before been used. He then goes on to
say, " I ponder on the things that have taken place, and the
events that have occurred throughout the land. Things
have happened, and they are different from those of last
year. Each year is more wearisome than the last. The
whole country is disturbed and is going to destruction.
Justice (or right) is thrust out, injustice (or sin) is in the
council hall, the plans of the gods are upset, and their behests
are set aside. The country is in a miserable state, grief is
in every place, and both towns and provinces lament. Every
one is suffering through wrong-doing. All respect of persons
is banished. The lords of quiet are set in commotion. When
daylight cometh each day [every] face turneth away from
the sight of what hath happened [during the night]. . . .
I ponder on the things that have taken place. Troubles

flow in to-day, and to-morrow [tribulations] will not cease.
Though all the country is full of unrest, none will speak about
it.   There is no innocent man [left], every one worketh
wickedness.   Hearts are bowed in grief.   He who giveth
orders is like unto the man to whom orders are given, and
their hearts are well pleased.   Men wake daily [and find it
so], yet they do not abate it.   The things of yesterday are
like those of to-day, and in many respects both days are alike.
Men's faces are stupid, and there is none capable of understanding, and none is driven to speak by his anger. . . .
My pain is keen and protracted.   The poor man hath not
the strength to protect himself against the man who is
stronger than he.   To hold the tongue about what one
heareth is agony, but to reply to the man who doth not
understand causeth suffering.   If one protesteth against
what is said, the result is hatred ; for the truth is not understood, and every protest is resented.   The only words which
any man will now listen to are his own.   Every one believes
in his own. . . . Truth hath forsaken speech altogether."

Whether the copy of the work from which the above extracts is taken be complete or not cannot be said, but in any
case there is no suggestion on the board in the British
Museum that the author of the work had any remedy in his
mind for the lamentable state of things which he describes.
Another Egyptian writer, called Apuur, who probably
flourished a little before the rule of the kings of the twelfth
dynasty, depicts the terrible state of misery and corruption
into which Egypt had fallen in his time, but his despair is
not so deep as that of the man who was tired of his life or
that of the priest Khakhepersenb.   On the contrary, he has
sufficient hope of his country to believe that the day will
come when society shall be reformed, and when wickedness
and corruption shall be done away, and when the land shall
be ruled by a just ruler.   It is difficult to say, but it seems
as if he thought this ruler would be a king who would govern
Egypt with righteousness, as did Rā in the remote ages,
and that his advent was not far off.   The Papyrus in which
the text on which these observations are based is preserved

in Leyden, No. 1344. It has been discussed carefully by several scholars, some of whom believe that its contents prove that the expectation of the coming of a Messiah was current in Egypt some forty-five centuries ago. The following extracts will give an idea of the character of the indictment which Apuur drew up against the Government and society of his day, and which he had the temerity to proclaim in the presence of the reigning king and his court. He says : " The guardians of houses say, ' Let us go and steal.' The snarers of birds have formed themselves into armed bands. The peasants of the Delta have provided themselves with bucklers. A man regardeth his son as his enemy. The righteous man grieveth because of what hath taken place in the country. A man goeth out with his shield to plough. The man with a bow is ready [to shoot], the wrongdoer is in every place. The inundation of the Nile cometh, yet no one goeth out to plough. Poor men have gotten costly goods, and the man who was unable to make his own sandals is a possessor of wealth. The hearts of slaves are sad, and the nobles no longer participate in the rejoicings of their people. Men's hearts are violent, there is plague everywhere, blood is in every place, death is common, and the mummy wrappings call to people before they are used. Multitudes are buried in the river, the stream is a tomb, and the place of mummification is a canal. The gentle folk weep, the simple folk are glad, and the people of every town say, ' Come, let us blot out these who have power and possessions among us.' Men resemble the mud-birds, filth is everywhere, and every one is clad in dirty garments. The land spinneth round like the wheel of the potter. The robber is a rich man, and [the rich man] is a robber. The poor man groaneth and saith, ' This is calamity indeed, but what can I do ? ' The river is blood, and men drink it ; they cease to be men who thirst for water. Gates and their buildings are consumed with fire, yet the palace is stable and flourishing. The boats of the peoples of the South have failed to arrive, the towns are destroyed, and Upper Egypt is desert. The crocodiles are sated with their prey, for men willingly go to them.

The desert hath covered the land, the Nomes are destroyed, and there are foreign troops in Egypt. People come hither [from everywhere], there are no Egyptians left in the land. On the necks of the women slaves [hang ornaments of] gold, lapis-lazuli, silver, turquoise, carnelian, bronze, and *abhet* stone. There is good food everywhere, and yet mistresses of houses say, ' Would that we had something to eat.' The skilled masons who build pyramids have become hinds on farms, and those who tended the Boat of the god are yoked together [in ploughing]. Men do not go on voyages to Kepuna (Byblos in Syria) to-day. What shall we do for cedar wood for our mummies, in coffins of which priests are buried, and with the oil of which men are embalmed ? They come no longer. There is no gold, the handicrafts languish. What is the good of a treasury if we have nothing to put in it ? Everything is in ruins. Laughter is dead, no one can laugh. Groaning and lamentation are everywhere in the land. Egyptians have turned into foreigners. The hair hath fallen out of the head of every man. A gentleman cannot be distinguished from a nobody. Every man saith, ' I would that I were dead,' and children say, ' [My father] ought not to have begotten me.' Children of princes are dashed against the walls, the children of desire are cast out into the desert, and Khnemu [1] groaneth in sheer exhaustion. The Asiatics have become workmen in the Delta. Noble ladies and slave girls suffer alike. The women who used to sing songs now sing dirges. Female slaves speak as they like, and when their mistress commandeth they are aggrieved. Princes go hungry and weep. The hasty man saith, ' If I only knew where God was I would make offerings to Him.' The hearts of the flocks weep, and the cattle groan because of the condition of the land. A man striketh his own brother. What is to be done ? The roads are watched by robbers, who hide in the bushes until a benighted traveller cometh, when they rob him. They seize his goods, and beat him to death with cudgels. Would that the human race might perish, and there be no more conceiving or bringing to the

[1] The god who fashioned the bodies of men.

birth ! If only the earth could be quiet, and revolts cease ! Men eat herbs and drink water, and there is no food for the birds, and even the swill is taken from the mouths of the swine. There is no grain anywhere, and people lack clothes, unguents, and oil. Every man saith, ' There is none.' The storehouse is destroyed, and its keeper lieth prone on the ground. The documents have been filched from their august chambers, and the shrine is desecrated. Words of power are unravelled, and spells made powerless. The public offices are broken open and their documents stolen, and serfs have become their own masters. The laws of the court-house are rejected, men trample on them in public, and the poor break them in the street. Things are now done that have never been done before, for a party of miserable men have removed the king. The secrets of the Kings of the South and of the North have been revealed. The man who could not make a coffin for himself hath a large tomb. The occupants of tombs have been cast out into the desert, and the man who could not make a coffin for himself hath now a treasury. He who could not build a hut for himself is now master of a habitation with walls. The rich man spendeth his night athirst, and he who begged for the leavings in the pots hath now brimming bowls. Men who had fine raiment are now in rags, and he who never wore a garment at all now dresseth in fine linen. The poor have become rich, and the rich poor. Noble ladies sell their children for beds. Those who once had beds now sleep on the ground. Noble ladies go hungry, whilst butchers are sated with what was once prepared for them. A man is slain by his brother's side, and that brother fleeth to save his own life."

Apuur next, in a series of five short exhortations, entreats his bearers to take action of some sort ; each exhortation begins with the words, "Destroy the enemies of the sacred palace (or Court)." These are followed by a series of sentences, each of which begins with the word " Remember," and contains one exhortation to his hearers to perform certain duties in connection with the service of the gods. Thus they are told to burn incense and to pour out libations each morning, to offer various kinds of geese to the gods, to eat natron, to make white bread, to set up poles on the temples and stelæ inside them, to make the priest to purify the temples, to remove from his office the priest who is unclean, &c. After many breaks in the text we come to the passage in which Apuur seems to foretell the coming of the king who is to restore order and prosperity to the land. He is to make cool that which is hot. He is to be the " shepherd of mankind," having no evil in his heart. When his herds are few [and scattered], he will devote his time to bringing them together, their hearts being inflamed. The passage continues, " Would that he had perceived their nature in the first generation (of men), then he would have repressed evils, he would have stretched forth (his) arm against it, he would have destroyed their seed (?) and their inheritance. . . . A fighter (?) goeth forth, that (he ?) may destroy the wrongs that (?) have been wrought. There is no pilot (?) in their moment. Where is he (?) to-day ? Is he sleeping ? Behold, his might is not seen." [1] Many of the passages in the indictment of Apuur resemble the descriptions of the state of the land of Israel and her people which are found in the writings of the Hebrew Prophets, and the " shepherd of mankind," *i.e.* of the Egyptians, forcibly reminds us of the appeal to the " Shepherd of Israel " in Psalm lxxx. 1.

[1] See A. H. Gardiner, *Admonitions of an Egyptian Sage*, Leipzic, 1909, p. 78.

CHAPTER XIV

EGYPTIAN POETICAL COMPOSITIONS

THE poetry of the Egyptians is wholly unlike that of western nations, but closely resembles the rhythmical compositions of the Hebrews, with their parallelism of members, with which we are all familiar in the Book of Psalms, the Song of Solomon, &c. The most important collection of Egyptian Songs known to us is contained in the famous papyrus in the British Museum, No. 10,060, more commonly known as "Harris 500." This papyrus was probably written in the thirteenth century B.C., but many of the songs belong to a far earlier date. Though dealing with a variety of subjects, there is no doubt that all of them must be classed under the heading of "Love Songs." In them the lover compares the lady of his choice to many beautiful flowers and plants, and describes at considerable length the pain and grief which her absence causes him. The lines of the strophes are short, and the construction is simple, and it seems certain that the words owed their effect chiefly to the voice of the singer, who then, as now, employed many semitones and thirds of tones, and to the skill with which he played the accompaniment on his harp. A papyrus at Leyden, which was written a little later than the "Love Songs," contains three very curious compositions. The first is a sort of lament of a pomegranate tree, which, in spite of the service which it has rendered to the "sister and her brother," is not included among trees of the first class. In the second a fig tree expresses its gratitude and its readiness to do the will of its mistress, and to allow its branches to be cut off to make a bed for her. In the third a sycamore tree invites the lady of the land on

which it stands to come under the shadow of its branches,
and to enjoy a happy time with her lover, and promises
her that it will never speak about what it sees.

More interesting than any of the above songs is the so-
called " Song of the Harper," of which two copies are known :
the first is found in the papyrus Harris 500, already mentioned, and the second in a papyrus at Leyden.   Extracts
of this poem are also found on the walls of the tomb of Nefer-
hetep at Thebes.   The copy in the papyrus reads :

THE POEM THAT IS IN THE HALL OF THE TOMB OF [THE KING
    OF THE SOUTH, THE KING OF THE NORTH], ANTUF,[1]
    WHOSE WORD IS TRUTH, [AND IS CUT] IN FRONT OF THE
    HARPER.

O good prince, it is a decree,
And what hath been ordained thereby is well,
That the bodies of men shall pass away and disappear,
Whilst others remain.

Since the time of the oldest ancestors,
The gods who lived in olden time,
Who lie at rest in their sepulchres,
The Masters and also the Shining Ones,
Who have been buried in their splendid tombs,
Who have built sacrificial halls in their tombs,
Their place is no more.
Consider what hath become of them !

I have heard the words of Imhetep [2] and Herutataf,[3]
Which are treasured above everything because they uttered
    them.
Consider what hath become of their tombs !
Their walls have been thrown down ;
Their places are no more ;
They are just as if they had never existed.

---

[1] He was one of the kings of the eleventh dynasty, about 2700 B.C.
[2] A high official of Tcheser, a king of the third dynasty.
[3] Son of Khufu, the builder of the Great Pyramid (fourth dynasty.)

Not one [of them] cometh from where they are.
Who can describe to us their form (or, condition),
Who can describe to us their surroundings,
Who can give comfort to our hearts,
And can act as our guide
To the place whereunto they have departed ?

Give comfort to thy heart,
And let thy heart forget these things ;
What is best for thee to do is
To follow thy heart's desire as long as thou livest.

Anoint thy head with scented unguents,
Let thine apparel be of byssus
Dipped in costly [perfumes],
In the veritable products (?) of the gods.

Enjoy thyself more than thou hast ever done before,
And let not thy heart pine for lack of pleasure.

Pursue thy heart's desire and thine own happiness.
Order thy surroundings on earth in such a way
That they may minister to the desire of thy heart ;
[For] at length that day of lamentation shall come,
Wherein he whose heart is still shall not hear the lamentation.
Never shall cries of grief cause
To beat [again] the heart of a man who is in the grave.

Therefore occupy thyself with thy pleasure daily,
And never cease to enjoy thyself.

Behold, a man is not permitted
To carry his possessions away with him.
Behold, there never was any one who, having departed,
Was able to come back again.

CHAPTER XV

In this chapter are given short notices of a series of works which the limits of this book make it impossible to describe at greater length.

I. The BOOK OF THE TWO WAYS.—This is a very ancient funerary work, which is found written in cursive hieroglyphs upon coffins of the eleventh and twelfth dynasties, of which many fine examples are to be seen in the British Museum. The object of the work is to provide the souls of the dead with a guide that will enable them, when they leave this world, to make a successful journey across the Tuat, *i.e.* the Other World or Dead Land, to the region where Osiris lived and ruled over the blessed dead. The work describes the roads that must be travelled over, and names the places where opposition is to be expected, and supplies the deceased with the words of power which he is to utter when in difficulties. The abode of the blessed dead could be reached either by water or by land, and the book affords the information necessary for journeying thither by either route. The sections of the book are often accompanied by coloured vignettes, which illustrate them, and serve as maps of the various regions of the Other World, and describe the exact positions of the streams and canals that have to be crossed, and the Islands of the Blest, and the awful country of blazing fire and boiling water in which the bodies, souls, and spirits of the wicked were destroyed.

II. The BOOK " AM TUAT," or Guide to him that is in the Tuat.—This Book has much in common with the Book of the Two Ways. According to it, the region that lay between this world and the realm of Osiris was divided into ten parts, which were traversed, once each night, by the Sun-god in the form which he took during the night. At the western end was a sort of vestibule, through which the god passed from the day sky into the Tuat, and at the eastern end was another vestibule, through which he passed on leaving the Tuat to re-enter the day sky. The two vestibules were places of gloom and semi-darkness, and the ten divisions of the Tuat were covered by black night. When the Sun-god set in the west in the evening he was obliged to travel through the Tuat to the eastern sky, in order to rise again on this earth on the following day. He entered the Tuat at or near Thebes, proceeded northwards, through the under-worlds of Thebes, Abydos, Herakleopolis, Memphis, and Saïs, then turned towards the east and crossed the Delta, and, having passed through the underworld of Heliopolis, appeared in the eastern sky to resume his daily course from east to west. His journey so far as Memphis he made in a boat, which sailed on the river of the Tuat. At Memphis he left the boat on the river, and entered a magical boat formed of a serpent's body, and so passed under the moun-tainous district round about Sakkārah. At or near Saïs he returned to his river boat, and sailing over the great marine lakes of the Delta reached Heliopolis. The sun-god was guided through each section of the Tuat by a goddess who belonged to the district, and for the sake of uniformity the journey through each section was supposed to occupy an hour ; the guiding goddess left the god's boat at the end of her hour, and the goddess of the next section took her place. The path of the god was lighted by fire, which the beings who lived in the various sections poured out of their mouths, and the attendant gods who were with them in his boat spake words of power, which overcame all opposition and removed every obstacle. As he passed through each section it was temporarily lighted up by the fire already mentioned, and he uttered words of power, the effect of which was to supply the inhabitants of the section with air, food, and drink, sufficient to last until the next night, when he would renew the supply. Many parts of the Tuat were filled with hideous monsters in human and animal forms, and with evil spirits of every kind, but they were all rendered powerless by the spells uttered by the gods who were in attendance on the Sun-god in his boat. At one time in the history of Egypt it became the earnest wish of every pious man to make the journey from this world to the next in the Boat of the Sun. Armed with words of power and amulets of all kinds, and relying on their lives of moral rectitude, and the effect of the offerings which they had made to the dead, their souls entered the Boat, and set out on their journey. When they reached Abydos their credentials were examined, and those who were found to be speakers of the truth and upright in their actions were allowed to continue their journey with the Sun-god, and to live with him ever after. Some souls preferred to remain at Abydos and to live with Osiris, and those who were found righteous in the Judgment were allowed to do so, and were granted estates in perpetuity in the kingdom of this god. The Book " AM TUAT " describes the sections of the Tuat and their inhabitants, and supplies all the information which the soul was supposed to require in passing from this world to the next. Many copies of certain sections of it are known, and some of these are in the British Museum ; [1] the most complete copy of it is in the tomb of Seti I at Thebes.

III. The BOOK OF GATES.—This book was also written to be a Guide to the Tuat, and has much in common with the Book of the Two Ways and with the Book Am Tuat. In it also the Tuat is divided into ten sections and has two vestibules, the Eastern and the Western, but at the entrance to each section is a strongly fortified Gate, guarded by a monster serpent-god and by the gods of the section. The Sun-god of night, as in the Book Am Tuat, makes his journey in a boat, and is attended by a number of gods, who remove all opposition from his path by the use of words of power. As he approaches each Gate, its doors are thrown open by the gods who guard them, and he passes into the section of

[1] See the massive stone sarcophagi of Nectonebus exhibited in the Southern Egyptian Gallery of the British Museum.

the Tuat behind it, carrying with him light, air, and food for its inhabitants. The Book of Gates embodies the teaching of the priests of the cult of Osiris, and the Book Am Tuat represents the modified form of it that was promulgated by the priests of Amen. From the Book of Gates we derive much information about the realm of Osiris, and the Great Judgment of souls, which took place in his Hall of Judgment once a day at midnight. Then all the souls that had collected during the past twenty-four hours from all parts of Egypt were weighed in the Balance ; the righteous were allotted estates in perpetuity in the " land of souls," and the wicked were destroyed by Shesmu, the executioner of the god, and by his assistants. The texts that describe the various " Gates " of the Book of Gates, explain who are the beings represented in the pictures, and state why they were there. And the Book proves conclusively that the Egyptians believed in the efficacy of sacrifices and offerings, and in the doctrine of righteous retribution ; liars and deceivers were condemned, and their bodies, souls, spirits, doubles, and names destroyed, and the righteous were rewarded for their upright lives and integrity upon earth by the gift of everlasting life and happiness. The most complete copy of this interesting work in England is cut on the alabaster sarcophagus of Seti I, about 1350 B.C. This unique sepulchral monument is exhibited gratis in Sir John Soane's Museum at 13 Lincoln's Inn Fields, and every student of the religion of the Egyptians should examine it.

IV. The RITUAL OF EMBALMMENT.—Two important fragments of a copy of this work are preserved in the Museum of the Louvre (No. 5158), and a part of another in the Egyptian Museum, Cairo (No. 3) ; the former copy was written for a priest of Amen called Heru, and the latter for a priest called Hetra. These fragments of the work describe minutely the process of mummifying certain parts of a human body, and state what materials were employed by the embalmer. Moreover, it gives the texts of the magical and religious spells that were ordered to be recited by the priest who superintended the embalmment, the effect of which was to " make divine" each member of the body, and to secure for it the protecting influence of the god or goddess who presided over it. The following extract refers to the embalming of the head : " Then anoint the head of the deceased and all his mouth with oil, both the head and the face, and wrap it in the bandages of Harmakhis in Hebit. The bandage of the goddess Nekhebet shall be put on the forehead, the bandage of Hathor in Heliopolis on the face, the bandage of Thoth on the ears, and the bandage of Nebt-hetepet on the back of the neck. All the coverings of the head and all the strips of linen used in fastening them shall be taken from sheets of linen that have been examined as to quality and texture in the presence of the inspector of the mysteries. On the head of the deceased shall be the bandage of Sekhmet, beloved of Ptah, in two pieces. On the two ears two bandages called the " Complete." On the nostrils two bandages called " Nehai " and " Smen." On the cheeks two bandages called " He shall live." On the forehead four pieces of linen called the " shining ones." On the skull two pieces called " The two Eyes of Rā in their fullness." On the two sides of the face and ears twenty-two pieces. As to the mouth two inside, and two out. On the chin two pieces. On the back of the neck four large pieces. Then tie the whole head firmly with a strip of linen two fingers wide, and anoint a second time, and then fill up all the crevices with the oil already mentioned. Then say, " O august goddess, Lady of the East, Mistress of the West, come and enter into the two ears of Osiris. O mighty goddess, who art ever young, O great one, Lady of the East, Mistress of the West, let there be breathing in the head of the deceased in the Tuat. Let him see with his eyes, hear with his ears, breathe with his nose, pronounce with his mouth, and speak with his tongue in the Tuat. Accept his voice in the Hall of Truth, and let him be proved to have been a speaker of the truth in the Hall of Keb, in the presence of the Great God, the Lord of Amenti."

V. The RITUAL OF THE DIVINE CULT.—This title is commonly given to a work consisting of sixty-six chapters, which were recited daily by the high priest of Amen-Rā, the King of the Gods, in his temple at Thebes, during the performance of a series of ceremonies of a highly important and symbolical character. The text of this Ritual is found cut in hieroglyphs on the walls of the temple of Seti I at Abydos, and written in hieratic upon papyri preserved in the Imperial Museum in Berlin. The work was originally intended to be recited by the king himself daily, but it was soon found that the Lord of Egypt could not spare the time necessary for its recital each day, and he therefore was personified by the high priest of each temple in which the Ritual was performed. The object of the Ritual was to place the king in direct contact with his god Amen-Rā once a day. The king was an incarnation of Amen-Rā, and ruled Egypt as the representative upon earth of the god. He drew his power and wisdom direct from the god, and it was believed that these required renewal daily. To bring about this renewal of the divine spirit in the god's vicegerent upon earth, the king entered the temple in the early morning, and performed ceremonies and recited formulæ that purified both the sactuary and himself. He then advanced to the shrine, which contained a small gilded wooden figure of the god, inlaid with precious stones and provided with a movable head, arms, and legs, and opened it and knelt down before the figure. He performed further ceremonies of purification, and finally took the figure of the god in his arms and embraced it. During this embrace the divine power of Amen-Rā, which was in the gilded figure at that moment, passed into the body of the king, and the divine power and wisdom, which were in the king as the god's representative, were renewed. The king then closed the doors of the shrine and left the sanctuary for a short time. When he returned he opened the shrine again, and made adoration to the god, and presented a series of offerings that symbolised Truth. After this the king dressed the figure of the god in sacred apparel, and decorated it. Then, having performed further acts of worship before it, he closed the doors of the shrine, sealed them with mud seals, and left the sanctuary.

VI. The BOOK "MAY MY NAME FLOURISH."—This was a very popular funerary work in the Roman Period. It is a development of a long prayer that is found in the Pyramid Texts, and was written by the priests and used as a spell to make the name of the deceased flourish eternally in heaven and on the earth. Many copies of it, written on narrow strips of papyrus, are preserved in the British Museum.

VII. The BOOK OF ĀAPEP, the great enemy of the Sun-god.—Āapep was the god of evil, who became incarnate in many forms, especially in wild and savage animals and in monster serpents and venomous reptiles of every kind. He was supposed to take the form of a huge serpent and to lie in wait near the portals of the dawn daily, so that he might swallow up the sun as he was about to rise in the eastern sky. He was accompanied by legions of devils and fiends, red and black, and by all the powers of storm, tempest, hurricane, whirlwind, thunder and lightning, and he was the deadly foe of all order, both physical and moral, and of all good in heaven and in earth. At certain times during the day and night the priests in the temple of Amen-Rā recited a series of chapters, and performed a number of magical ceremonies, which were intended to strengthen the arms of the Sun-god, and give him power to overcome the resistance of Āapep. These chapters acted on Āapep as spells, and they paralysed the monster just as he was about to attack the Sun-god. The god then approached and shot his fiery darts into him, and his attendant gods hacked the monster's body to pieces, which shrivelled up under the burning heat of the rays of the Sun-god, and all the devils and fiends of darkness fled shrieking in terror at their leader's fate. The sun then rose on this world, and all the stars and spirits of the morning and all the gods of heaven sang for joy. The complete text of this book is found in a long papyrus dated in the reign of Alexander II in the British Museum (No. 10,188).

VIII. The INSTRUCTIONS, OR PRECEPTS OF TUAUF to his son Pepi.—Two copies of this work, which has also been called a "Hymn in praise of learning," are contained in a papyri preserved in the British Museum (Sallier II and Anastasi VII). These " Instructions " in reality represent the advice of a father to his son, whom he was sending to school to be trained for the profession of the scribe. Whether the boy was merely sorry to leave his home, or whether he disliked the profession which his father had chosen for him, is not clear, but from first to last the father urges him to apply himself to the pursuit of learning, which, in his opinion, is the foundation of all great and lasting success. He says, " I have compared the people who are artisans and handicraftsmen [with the scribe], and indeed I am convinced that there is nothing superior to letters. Plunge into the study of Egyptian Learning, as thou wouldst plunge into the river, and thou wilt find that this is so. I would that thou wouldst love Learning as thou lovest thy mother. I wish I were able to make thee to see how beautiful Learning is. It is more important than any trade in the world. Learning is not a mere phrase, for the man who devoteth himself thereto from his youth is honoured, and he is despatched on missions. I have watched the blacksmith at the door of his furnace. His hands are like crocodiles' hide, and he stinketh worse than fishes' eggs. The metal worker hath no more rest than the peasant on the farm. The stone mason—at the end of the day his arms are powerless ; he sitteth huddled up together until the morning, and his knees and back are broken. The barber shaveth until far into the night, he only resteth when he eateth. He goeth from one street to another looking for work. He breaketh his arms to fill his belly, and, like the bees, he eateth his own labour. The builder of houses doeth his work with difficulty ; he is exposed to all weathers, and he must cling to the walls which he is building like a creeping plant. His clothes are in a horrible state, and he washeth his body only once a day. The farmer weareth always the same clothes. His voice is like the croak of a bird, his skin is cracked by the wind ; if he is healthy his health is that of the beasts. If he be ill he lieth down among them, and he sleepeth on the damp irrigated land. The envoy to foreign lands bequeatheth his property to his children before he setteth out, being afraid that he will be killed either by wild beasts of the desert or by the nomads therein. When he is in Egypt, what then ? No sooner hath he arrived at home than he is sent off on another mission. As for the dyer, his fingers stink like rotten fish, and his clothes are absolutely horrors. The shoemaker is a miserable wretch. He is always asking for work, and his health is that of a dying fish. The washerman is neighbour to the crocodile. His food is mixed up with his clothes, and every member of him is unclean. The catcher of water-fowl, even though he dive in the Nile, may catch nothing. The trade of the fisherman is the worst of all. He is in blind terror of the crocodile, and falleth among crocodiles." The text continues with a few further remarks on the honourable character of the profession of the scribe, and ends with a series of Precepts of the same character as those found in the works of Ptah-hetep and the scribe Ani, from which extracts have already been given.

IX. MEDICAL PAPYRI.—The Egyptians possessed a good practical knowledge of the anatomy of certain parts of the human body, but there is no evidence that they practised dissection before the arrival of the Greeks in Egypt. The medical papyri that have come down to us contain a large number of short, rough-and-ready descriptions of certain diseases, and prescriptions of very great interest. The most important medical papyrus known is that which was bought at Luxor by the late Professor Ebers in 1872-3, and which is now preserved in Leipzig. This papyrus is about 65 feet long, and the text is written in the hieratic character. It was written in the ninth year of the reign of a king who is not yet satisfactorily identified, but who probably lived before the period of the rule of the eighteenth dynasty, perhaps about 1800 B.C. A short papyrus in the British Museum contains extracts from it, and other papyri with somewhat similar contents are preserved in the Museums of Paris, Leyden, Berlin, and California.

X. MAGICAL PAPYRI.—The widespread use of magic in Egypt in all ages suggests that the magical literature of Egypt must have been very large. Much of it was incorporated at a very early period into the Religious Literature of the country, and was used for legitimate purposes, in fact for the working of what we call " white magic." The Egyptian saw no wrong in the working of magic, and it was only condemned by him when the magician wished to produce evil results. The gods themselves were supposed to use spells and incantations, and every traveller by land or water carried with him magical formulæ which he recited when he was in danger from the wild beasts of the desert or the crocodile of the river and its canals. Specimens of these will be found in the famous magical papyri in the British Museum, *e.g.* the Salt Papyrus, the Rhind Papyrus, and the Harris Papyrus. Under this heading may be mentioned Papyrus Sallier IV in the British Museum, which contains a list of lucky and unlucky days. Here is a specimen of its contents :

1st day of Hathor. The whole day is lucky. There is festival in heaven with Rā and Hathor.

2nd day of Hathor. The whole day is lucky. The gods go out. The goddess Uatchet comes from Tep to the gods who are in the shrine of the bull, in order to protect the divine members.

3rd day of Hathor. The whole day is lucky.

4th day of Hathor. The whole day is unlucky. The house of the man who goes on a voyage on that day comes to ruin.

6th day of Hathor. The whole day is unlucky. Do not light a fire in thy house on this day, and do not look at one.

18th day of Pharmuthi. The whole day is unlucky. Do not bathe on this day.

20th day of Pharmuthi. The whole day is unlucky. Do not work on this day.

22nd day of Pharmuthi. The whole day is unlucky. He who is born on this day will die on this day.

23rd day of Pharmuthi. The first two-thirds of the day are unlucky, and the last third lucky.

XI. LEGAL DOCUMENTS.—The first legal document written in Egypt was the will of Rā, in which he bequeathed all his property and the inheritance of the throne of Egypt to his first-born son Horus. Tradition asserted that this Will was preserved in the Library of the Sun-god in Heliopolis. The inscriptions contain many allusions to the Laws of Egypt, but no document containing any connected statement of them has come down to us. In the great inscription of Heruemheb, the last king of the eighteenth dynasty, a large number of good laws are given, but it must be confessed that as a whole the administration of the Law in many parts of Egypt must always have been very lax. Texts relating to bequests, endowments, grants of land, &c., are very difficult to translate, because it is well-nigh impossible to find equivalents for Egyptian legal terms. In the British Museum are two documents in hieratic that were drawn up in connection with prosecutions which the Government of Egypt undertook of certain thieves who had broken into some of the royal tombs at Thebes and robbed them, and of certain other thieves who had robbed the royal treasury and made away with a large amount of silver (Nos. 10,221, 10,052, 10,053, and 10,054). Equally interesting is the roll that describes the prosecution of certain highly placed officials and relations of Rameses III who had conspired against him and wanted to kill him. Several of the conspirators were compelled to commit suicide. The text is written in hieratic on papyrus, and is preserved in the Royal Museum, Leyden.

XII. HISTORICAL ROMANCES.—Examples of these are the narrative of the capture of the town of Joppa in Palestine by an officer of Thothmes III, and the history of the dispute that broke out between Seqenenrā, King of Upper Egypt, and Āapepi, King of Avaris in the Delta. These are written in hieratic and are preserved in the British Museum, in Harris Papyrus 500, and Sallier No. 1 (10,185).

XIII. MATHEMATICS.—The chief source of our knowledge of the Mathematics of the Egyptians is the Rhind Papyrus in the British Museum (No. 10,057), which was written before 1700 B.C., probably during the reign of one of the Hyksos kings. The papyrus contains a number of simple arithmetical examples and several geometrical problems. The

workings out of these prove that the Egyptian spared himself
no trouble in making his calculations, and that he worked
out both his arithmetical examples and problems in the most
cumbrous and laborious way possible.   He never studied
mathematics in order to make progress in his knowledge of
the science, but simply for purely practical everyday work ;
as long as his knowledge enabled him to obtain results which
he knew from experience were substantially correct he was
content.

EDITIONS OF EGYPTIAN TEXTS, TRANSLATIONS, &c.

AMÉLINEAU, E.—Morale Égyptien. Paris, 1892. 8vo.

BERGMANN, E.—Das Buch vom Durchwandeln der Ewigkeit. Vienna, 1877.

BIRCH, S.—Egyptian Texts from the Coffin of Amamu. London, 1886.
Egyptian Hieratic Papyrus of Rameses III. London, 1876.

BREASTED, J. H.—Ancient Records—Egypt. Chicago, 1906.

BRUGSCH, H.—Sieben Jahre der Hungersnoth. Leipzig, 1891.
Inscriptio Rosettana. Berlin, 1851.
Neue Weltordnung. Berlin, 1881.
Reise nach der grossen Oase. Leipzig, 1878.
Rhind's zwei Bilingue Papyri. Leipzig, 1865.
Shai an Sinsin. Berlin, 1851.

BUDGE, E. A. WALLIS.—Book of the Dead, Egyptian Texts, Translation and Vocabulary, 2nd ed. London, 1909.
Papyrus of Ani. London, 1913.
Papyri of Hunefer, Anhai, Netchemet, Kersher, and Nu. London, 1899.
Hieratic Papyri. Texts and translations. London, 1910.
Book of Opening the Mouth, Liturgy of Funerary Offerings, The Book of Am-Tuat, The Book of Gates. London, 1906–1909.
Legends of the Gods. London, 1912.
Annals of Nubian Kings. London, 1912.
Greenfield Papyrus. 1912.

DE HORRACK, P. J.—Les Lamentations d'Isis. Paris, 1866.

ERMAN, A.—Gespräch eines Lebensmüden. Berlin, 1896.
Die Märchen des Papyrus Westcar. Berlin, 1890.

GARDINER, A. H.—Egyptian Hieratic Texts, Part I. Leipzig, 1911.
The Admonitions of an Egyptian Sage. Leipzig, 1909.
Die Erzählung des Sinuhe. Leipzig, 1904.
Die Klagen des Bauern. Leipzig, 1908.

GRÉBAUT, E.—Hymne à Ammon-Rā. Paris, 1874.

GRIFFITH, F. Ll.—Stories of the High Priests of Memphis. Oxford, 1900.

GOLENISCHEFF, W.—Die Metternichstele. Leipzig, 1877.
Le Conte du Naufragé. Cairo, 1912.
Les Papyrus Hiératiques. St. Petersburg, 1913.

JOACHIM, H.—Papyros Ebers. Berlin, 1890.

LEFÉBURE, E.—Le Mythe Osirien. Paris, 1874.
Traduction comparée des Hymnes. Paris, 1868.

LEGRAIN, G.—Livre des Transformations. Paris, 1890.

LIEBLEIN, J.—Le livre Égyptien, Que mon nom. Leipzig, 1895.

MASPERO, G.—Contes Populaires. Paris, 1912.
Une enquête judiciaire. Paris, 1872.
Études Égyptiennes. Tomm. I, II. Paris, 1883.
Du Genre Épistolaire. Paris, 1872.
Hymne au Nil. Paris, 1868, and Cairo, 1912.
Inscriptions des Pyramides de Saqqarah. Paris, 1894.
Mémoire sur quelques Papyrus. Paris, 1875.
Les Mémoires de Sinouhit. Cairo, 1908.

MÖLLER, G.—Die beiden Totenpapyrus Rhind. Leipzig, 1913.

MORET, A.—Le Rituel du Culte Divin. Paris, 1902.

MÜLLER, W. M.—Die Liebespoesie der alten Ägypter. Leipzig, 1899.

NAVILLE, E.—Das Aegyptische Todtenbuch. Berlin, 1886.
La Litanie du Soleil. Leipzig, 1875.
Papyrus Funéraires de la XXIe dynastie. Paris, 1912.
Textes relatifs au Mythe Horus. Geneva, 1870.

SCHACK-SCHACKENBURG, H.—Das Buch von den zwei Wegen. Leipzig, 1903.

SCHÄFER, H.—Die Aethiopische Königinschrift. Leipzig, 1901.
Ein Bruchstück altägyptischer Annalen. Berlin, 1902.

SCHIAPARELLI.—Libro dei Funerali. Turin, 1882.

SPIEGELBERG, W.—Der Sagenkreis des Königs Petubastis. Leipzig, 1910.

Das Demotische Totenbuch. Leipzig, 1910.

Der Papyrus Libbey. Strassburg, 1907.

Rechnungen aus der Zeit Setis I. Strassburg, 1896.

VIREY, PH.—Études sur le Papyrus Prisse. Paris, 1887.

VOGELSANG, F.—Die Klagen des Bauern. Leipzig, 1913.

WIEDEMANN, A.—Hieratische Texte aus den Museen zu Berlin und Paris. Leipzig, 1879.

Magie und Zauberei. Leipzig, 1905.

Die Unterhaltung's Litteratur der alten Aegypter. Leipzig, 1902.

INDEX

Aa, 159, 165
Āakheperenrā, 103, 144
Āakheperkarā, 142, 145
Āamu, 108, 128, 161, 163
Āapep, 48, 68
Āapepi, 254
Āataka, 114
Aat-Beqt, 151
Aatti, 141, 142
Abana, 140
Abhat, 136
Abtu Fish, 48
Abu, 73, 83, 86, 87, 128, 130, 132, 165
— products of, 85
Abydos, 44, 45, 47, 65, 99, 127, 138, 245, 246, 249 ; valley of, 200
Acacia, 46, 61, 201 ; and river, 202 ; cut down, 203, 206
Acacias, the two, 205
Africanus, 98
Aged God, 15, 48
Ahnas al-Madīnah, 170
Āina, 113
Air-god, 16 ; air supply, 43
Akert, 44, 46, 65, 115, 221
Akeru, 21
Akhet, 62, 64, 134, 151, 155
Aku, 156
Alasa, 194
Ale, 19
Alexander the Great, 71
— II, 250
Alexandria, 88 ; Library of, 98
Al-Kab, 140, 143
Altar stands, 147
Am, 90
Amam, 128, 132, 133, 134
Am-as, 13
Amasis I, 140, 143
— the naval officer, 140 ff.

Amasis Pen-Nekheb, 143 ff.
Amen, 60, 67, 70, 93, 95, 103, 104, 105, 111, 117, 146, 147, 185, 187, 188, 189, 193, 194, 216 217, 219, 220, 247
— Father, 119
— of Sīwah, 71
Amenemhat I, 155, 162
— II, 155
— III, 99
Amen-hetep I, 142, 144
Ameni Amen-āa, 213
— Amenemhat, 135 ff.
Amen-ka-mutef, 218
Amen-Rā, 68, 76, 106, 110, 115, 145, 148, 164, 185, 186, 189, 190, 192, 193, 218, 219, 249, 250 ; Hymn to, 214 ff.
Amen-shefit, 147
Amentamat, 186, 187, 192
Amentet, 46, 49, 50, 61, 149, 153 164
Amenti, 248
Amenuserhat, 190
Ames sceptre, 215
Amhet, 49
Am-khent, 13
Ammaau, 134
Ammon, 67, 71
Ammuiansha, 157, 161
Amsu, 151
Amtes, 128
Amulets, 41, 43, 246
Am-urtet, 153
An, 45, 46, 63, 65
An instrument, 15
Anatomy, 252
Ancestor-god, 70
Anebuheq, 156
Ani, 216, 218 ; Maxims of, 228 ; papyrus of, 44, 45

Ānkh Psemthek, 88
Ānkh-taui, 151, 152
Ānkhu, 238
Anmutef, 20
Annals of Thothmes III, 104
Annana, 207
Anointing, 13
Anpu, 15, 69, 196, 197 ff.
Anqet, 85
Anrekh, 64
Anrutef, 47, 81
Ant Fish, 48
Āntchmer, 155
Antef, 137, 138
Antes, 46
Āntet Boat, 218
Anti, 142, 143
Antiu, 106, 109, 141
Āntti Boat, 222
Antuf, 242
Anu (Heliopolis), 15, 20, 24, 36,
    37, 43, 45, 48, 61, 214, 217, 218,
    220, 222
Anubis, 15, 33, 50, 60, 69, 149
Ape-gods, 49
Apes, 212 ; spirits of dawn, 218
Apet, 29, 30, 32
Aphroditopolis, 128, 130
Apollinopolis, 78
Apts, 118, 143, 147, 148, 214, 215,
    216, 217, 218
Apuur, 236, 239, 240
Aqen, 101
Aqert, 64
Ara, 132
Arabia, 93, 215
Aram Naharayim, 109
Archers (stars), 21
Arm rings, 23
Arniau, 154
Aroeris, 164
Arsu, 110
Arthet, 128, 131, 133
Artheth, 133
Asbatau, 112
Asemt, 142
Ashtoreth, 78
Asi, 108
Asia, 108
Asiatics, 108, 238
Asri, 170
Ass, eater of, 48
Assa, 4, 134, 135, 224

Asten, 2
Astronomy, 1
Aswān, 83, 131
Atef Crown, 54, 111, 115, 215
Atem, 61, 67
Aten, 61, 62
Athettaui, 166
Athi-taui, 117
Aukehek, 144
Aukert, 54
Aunab, 90
Ausares, 68
Avaris, 140, 141, 256

BABA, 53
Badhilu, 185
Baiufrā, 27, 29
Balance, 23, 54 ; heaven weighed
    in, 47 ; keeper of, 50
— of Truth, 247
Bandlets, 16, 23
Baqanau, 112
Barber, 251
Barley, 34, 45
Bata, 196, 197, 204, 205
Baurtet, 134, 135
Beautiful Face, 218, 220
Beer, 203 ; drinking of, 229
— of Hathor, 73
Bees, 251
Beetle, sacred, 91
Befen, 88
Befent, 89
Behutet, 82
Bekhten, Princess of, 92 ff.
Benben Stone, 216, 217
Beni-hasan, 135
Bentresht, 93, 95
Benu bird, 43, 45, 91
Bequests, 254
Betti, 56
Betu incense, 28
Birds, sacred, 52
Black Fiends, 68
Blacks, 128, 129 ; character of,
    102 ; edict against, 101, 102 ;
    hand of, 110
Blacksmiths, 78, 81, 251
Blasphemy, 53, 72
Blood in beer, 73 ; of Isis, 56
Boat, magical, 43
— of Amen, 191
— of Amen-Rā, 185, 193

Boat of Millions of Years, 77, 91, 92
— of Rā, 43, 48, 49, 91 ; two
  Boats of Rā, 123
— of Rā-Harmakhis, 78
— of the Sun, 234, 246
Book, Am Tuat, 244
— boxes, 7
— " May my name," 250
— of Āapep, 250
— of Breathings, 40, 59 ff.
— of Gates, 246
— of knowing how Rā, 68
— of making splendid, 64 ff.
— of Opening the Mouth, 13, 38
— of overthrowing Āapepi, 67 ff.
— of Proverbs, 224
— of Psalms, 241
— of slaying the Hippopotamus,
  78
— of the Dead, 4, 6, 29, 37 ff., 41 ;
  the Recensions of, 39 ff. ; summary of Chapters of, 42 ff. ;
  Græco-Roman Books, 59 ff. ;
  hieratic, 4 ; hieroglyphic, 40
— of the Two Ways, 244
— of Traversing Eternity, 40, 61
— of Wisdom, 224
Books, 2 ; magical, 30
— of Thoth, 2 ; study of, 230
Bread cakes, 45
Bronze, 238
Brugsch, Dr. H., 9
Builder, 251
Bull, the ship, 140
— skin of, 14
Bulls, sacrifice of, 15
Burial, 232
Bushel, 52
Busiris, 39, 44, 46, 61
Buto, 92
Byblos, 186, 187, 195, 238
Byssus, 191, 243

Cairo, 4, 15, 169
Cake for journey, 17
Cakes, 19
Calf, sucking, 14
Canopus, 112
Caravans, 119
Carnelian, 238
Cataract, first, 73, 83, 116
Cedar, oil of, 18 ; wood of, 185
Champollion, J. F., 37, 92

Charcoal, 6
Charms, 41
Chattering, 229
Cheops, 25, 27
Children of Horus, 220
Christianity in Egypt, 38
Christians, Egyptian, 7, 68
Circuit of Great Circuit, 109
City of Amen, 220
— Eternity, 161
Cleopatra, 183
Coffins, inscribed, 4
Collar, 16 ; amulet of, 43
Coming forth by day, 43
Company of gods, the great, 218
Conspiracy, 254
Copper, 114 ; sulphate of, 6
Coptos, 113, 136
Copts, 7, 68
Cord for land measuring, 85
Cord-master, 22
Cow-goddess, 73, 74
Cow, the celestial, 74
Creation, story of, 67 ff.
Crocodile-god, 175
Crocodile of W.E.S. and N., 57
— waxen, 25–7 ; seizes a ser-
  vant, 35, 36 ; transformation
  into, 43 ; spells against, 42
Crocodilopolis, 124
Crown, the Double, 80 ; the Red,
  23 ; the White, 23, 215, 216
Crusher of bones, 53
Cush, 102, 142
Cymbals, 33
Cyprus, 108, 194

Dance, 134
Dancing women, 33
Darkness, 68
Daughters of Nile-god, 220
Day, 17 ; right eye of Rā, 220
Days, lucky and unlucky, 253
Dead hand, 224, 244
— the blessed, 244
Death, 234 ; god of, 14, 43, 154 ;
  messenger of, 229 ; the second,
  43, 44
Decapitation, 43
Deceit, 46, 47
Deeds, good, 230
Dekans, the Thirty-Six, 46, 62
Delta, 39, 44, 57, 77, 79, 81, 82,

92, 102, 105, 117, 128, 237, 245, 254
Demotic writing, 1
Dēr al-Baharī, 146
Destiny, 220
Dhir, 185, 186
Diligence, 227
Diocletian, 97
Disk, 165, 200
Dissection, 252
Documents, legal, 7
Dog-god, 15
Dog-star, 20, 24
D'Orbiney, 196
Double, the, 11, 16
Drafts, 7
Drunkard, 228, 229
Dwarf, 91 ; dancing, 133
Dyer, 252

EARTH-GOD, 22, 24, 44, 47, 69
Earth Serpent, 221
— the wife of Rā, 220
East, Souls of, 43
Ebers, Dr. G., 252
Ebony box, 26
— paddles, 28
Ecclesiasticus, 224
Edfū, 77, 78, 82
Egypt, invasion of, 116 ff. ; wisdom of, 2
Eight gods, 120
Eileithyiaspolis, 43, 47, 140
Elephantine, 83, 102, 128, 130, 132, 165
Elephants' tusks, 212
Elysian Fields, 40, 41, 42, 45
Embalmment, ritual of, 247
Endowments, 254
Enemies in Tuat, 42
Enemy, Serpent, 47
Envoy, 251
Erman, Prof. E., 25
Euphrates, 108
Eusebius, 98
Evening Boat, 48
Evil, god of, 2
Executioner of Osiris, 43
Eye of Horus, 14, 15, 17, 18, 19, 24 ; the two eyes, 17
— of Khepera, 70
— of Rā, 46, 55, 72, 223
— of Nebertcher, 69

Eye paint, 13, 212
Eyes of Rā, 248

FALCON, 21
Famine, the Seven Years', 83
Farāfrah, 169
Farmer, 226, 251
Father Rā, 123
Fayyūm, 121
Fenkhu, 102, 164
Ferryman, the celestial, 43
Festival Songs of Isis and Nephthys, 62
Festivals, duty of keeping, 228
Field of Offerings, 24, 60
— grasshoppers, 54, 60
Fields of Turquoise, 64
Fig tree, 241
Fire, 232, 245
— House of, 215
— Island of, 43
— Lake of, 22
Flint, box of, 32
Fog-fiend, 68
Followers of Horus, 48, 78
Food celestial, 47
Foods, 11
Fountain of the Sun, 123
Fowler, 252
Frog-goddess, 33
Funeral, Chapter of, 42
Funerary Ritual, 37

GARDINER, Mr. A. H., 240
Gates of Tuat, 60
Gazelle, 15
Gebel Barkal, 116, 119, 125
Geese, 15, 20
Gīzah, 126
Glue for papyrus, 6
Goatskin, 4
God, 238 ; devotion to, 231 ; origin of, 42
Gods, Great Company of, 15
— Legends of, 71 ff. ; of cardinal points, 21 ; origin of, 217 ; the Eighteen, 20 ; the Forty-two, 51 ; the Two Great, 24
God-house, 147, 148
Gold, 48 ; from Sūdān, 135 ; of valour, 140, 141
Goose, 89 ; a dead, restored, 31

Gourds, 209
Grain, an emanation of Rā, 220
Granite, 85, 131
Grants of land, 254
Great Bear, 20
— Circuit, 108
— Door, 188, 206
— Gate, 163
— God, 50
— Judgment, 50, 53, 247
— Green, 109, 113, 123, 217
— Hall, 60, 218
— Hawk, 218
— High Mouth, 111
— House, 15, 83, 161, 166, 215
— River, 112
— Scales, 50
— Throne, 147
Greyhounds, 212
Gum, 6

HAIR of Bata's wife, 202
Hait, 185
Hall of Keb, 60, 248
— of Judgment, 50, 247
— of Maāti, 51, 53
— of Shu, 60
— of Truth, 55, 60, 248
— of Tuat, 42
Hammāmāt, 113
Hap-Asar, 149
Happiness, 232
Harmakhis, 46, 248
Harper, Song of, 242
Harris Papyrus, No. 1, 110
— No. 500, 241, 242, 254
Hasau, 112
Hathaba, 194
Hathor, 21, 72, 73, 114, 134, 164,
 165, 248, 253
— month of, 253
— Sekhmet, 72
Hathors, the Seven, 202
Hatshepset, 145
Haughtiness, 226
Haunebu, 102
Hawk, golden, 43; divine, 43;
 the Great, 91
Hawks, 20
Head, lifting up of, 44
Headsman of Osiris, 43
Heart, 50; amulet of the, 42;
 of Bata, 201; of bull, 15;

Chapters of, 42; of a man,
 230; restoration of, 44
Heart-scarabs, 51
Heat in body, 44
Heaven, solar, 39
Heavens, the Two, 23
Heben, 79
Hebit, 248
Hebrews, 241
Heh, 101
Height, 19
Heliopolis, 15, 24, 32, 36, 39, 43,
 46, 48, 52, 61, 70, 72, 123, 220,
 222, 235, 245, 248
Heliopolitans, 67
Hememet, 219
Hensu, 47, 53, 73, 117, 121, 170,
 171, 175
Henu Boat, 46
Hep, 85, 86, 176
Heqet, 33, 34
Herakleopolis, 47, 73, 81, 117,
 121, 170, 245
Herānkh, 149, 150, 151
Herfhaf, 54
Her-Heru, 186, 190, 193
Herit, 156
Herkemmaāt, 56
Herkhuf, autobiography of, 131 ff.
Hermonthis, 123
Hermopolis, 39, 43, 50, 53, 60,
 84, 117, 119; Parva, 85
Hermopolitans, 67
Heron, 43
Hert, 19
Herua, 207
Heru-Behutet, Legend of, 78 ff.
Heru-uatu, 166
Heruemheb, 254
Heru-Hekenu, 77
Herukhentisemti, 114
Heru-Khuti, 45, 46, 111, 220
Herushefit, 178
Herutataf, 29, 30, 31, 33, 50, 242
Heru-ur, 164
Het Benben, 123
— Benu, 117–19
Hetkaptah, 45, 112, 149, 220
Het-neter-Sebek, 117
Het Nub, 130, 131, 146
Hetra, 247
Het Sekhmet, 34
— Suten, 117

Het Uārt, 140
Hieratic writing, 1
Hieroglyphic writing, 1
Hieroglyphs, 220
Hippopotami, 78
Holy Land, 45
— of Holies, 146
Honey, 159
Horizon, 30
Horus, 13, 14, 15, 17, 18, 19, 20, 21, 33, 44, 48, 53, 56, 65, 69, 77, 80, 85, 88, 91, 110, 111, 137, 149, 151, 162, 164, 165, 218, 220, 254; birth of, 90; children of, 221
— of Behutet, Legend of, 77 ff.
— of the East, 164, 218
— stung and restored to life, 90, 92
Horus-Set, 14
Horus the Slayer, 104
House, building of, 43
— of Amen, 113
— of Benben, 216
— of Books, 98
— of Fire, 215
— of Ka of Seker, 149
— of Life, 84
— of Seneferu, 100
— of Shent, 154
Humility, 227
Hunefer, Papyrus of, 45
Hyksos, 254
Hymn, funerary, 471; in praise of learning, 250
— to Nut, 18; to Rā, 18
Hymns to gods, 12, 214–21

Ibis-god, 84
Illahūn, 121
Imhetep, 84, 129, 242
Immortality, 38
Imouthis, 84
Incantations, 41
Incarnation, 11, 13, 249
Incense, 13, 218
Ink, 6; red and black, 4
Ink-pots, 7
Iron, 15; spear and chain, 78
Isis, 33, 34, 43, 46, 65, 69, 75, 80, 81, 85, 88, 89, 91, 92, 97, 109, 149
— and Rā, Legend of, 74 ff.

Isis, blood of, 56
— speech of, 63
— wanderings of, 87 ff.
Island of Elephantine, 83
— of Fire, 43
— of Osiris, 54
Islands of the Blest, 244
— — Mediterranean, 164
Israel, 224, 240
It, 151

Jackal-god, 15
Joppa, capture of, 254
Joseph, 83
Judge of the dead, 2
Judges, the Forty-two, 42, 52 ff.
Judgment Hall of Osiris, 42
— the Great, 2

Ka, 11, 16; of Osiris, 45
Kaau, 128
Kadesh, 104
Kaheni, 123
Kamur, 157
Kamutef, 76, 214
Karnak, 118, 147, 148, 214, 215
Kash, 102, 103, 114, 135, 142, 144, 207
Keb, 13, 16, 18, 19, 21, 22, 24, 33, 44, 60, 62, 72, 74, 85, 111, 151, 220
Keeper of the Balance, 50
Kefti, 108
Kenset, 146
Kepuna, 186, 238
Kerkut, 20
Kersher, 59
Ketu, 108
Khāemmennefer, 140
Khāemuast, 192
Khāfrā, 25, 36
Khāhap, 151, 154
Khākaurā, 101
Khākhepersenb, 235, 236
Khākhut, 146
Khānefer Merenrā, 130, 131
Khānēs, 170
Khartūm, 102
Kharu, 185
Khemenu, 22, 92, 95
Khensu-nefer-hetep, Legend of, 92 ff.
Khensu-paari-sekherenuast, 95 ff.

Khenthennefer, 141, 142
Khentiaaush, 164
Khent Keshu, 164
Khenti Amentiu, 65
Khepera, 47, 55, 68, 69, 70, 76, 121, 215
Kheperkarā, 135, 162
Khepra-Set, 111
Kheprer, 19
Kherāha, 46, 53, 218
Kher-Heb priest, 13, 25, 27, 63, 84, 131, 132, 151
Khert Nefer, 132, 148
Khet, 142
Khnemetast, 155
Khnemet-heru, 142
Khnemu, 33, 34, 39, 43, 50, 60, 137, 151, 201, 202, 222, 238 ; Legend of, 83 ff.
Khuenanpu, story of, 169 ff.
Khufu, 25, 27, 29, 30, 35, 36, 50, 242
Khuna, 133
Khut serpent, 108
Khuti, 218
Kīnā, 104
King an incarnation of God, 11
Kingdom of Osiris, 42, 45
Kummah, 101
Kutut, 112

LABU, 112
Ladder, 21
Lady of Plague, 175
— of the Stars, 167
Lake of Fire, 22
— of Kamur, 157
— of Neserser, 220
— of the North, 79
— of Seneferu, 156
— of Truth, 54
Lamentations, 238 ; of Isis and Nephthys, 62
Land of the Blacks, 100
— of everlasting Life, 41
— of Oxen, 169
— of Souls, 247
— of Spirits, 134
— of the God, 108, 113, 125
Lapis-lazuli, 50, 64, 218, 238 ; powdered, 6
Lasmersekni, 117
Laughter, 238

Law, the, 254
Law-goddess, 47
Lepsius, Dr. R., 28, 37
Letopolis, 91, 151
Letopolites, 32
Letters, business, 7
Leyden, 237, 242
Learning, value of, 250
Lebanon, 189, 190, 191
Library, 8 ; of Heliopolis, 254
Libyans, 109, 112, 156
Lies, 40
Life, everlasting, 44, 55
— fluid of, 16
Light-god, 43, 46
Light-soul, 74
Lightning, 250
Lime, white, 6
Limestone, slabs of, for writing upon, 7
Lion, 32
Lists, 7
Litany, 45 ; of Osiris, 42
Liturgy of Funerary Offerings, 16, 17, 38
— of Opening the Mouth, 13
Lord of Silence, 171
— of Truth, 183
— of Winds, 54
Lotus, 43
Louvre, 247
Love Songs, 241
Luck, 220
Luxor, 118, 148, 215, 252 ; temple of, 93

MAĀT, 44, 47, 48
Maātet, 88, 89
Maāti, the Two, 51
Maātka, 126
Maātkarā, 144, 145, 146
Magic, 26, 252, 253
Magical papyri, 252
Magicians, stories of, 25 ff.
Maka, 164
Makamāru, 186
Maker of Truth, 218
Malachite, 27
Mandrakes, 73
Manetho, 98
Mankind, destruction of, 71
Manu, Land of, 47, 48
Mariette, A., 10

Mashuashau, 112
Maspero, Prof. G., 10
Matcha, 128, 131
Matchau, 214
Mātet, 123
Mathematics, 254
Maxims of Ani, 228
Medicine, 252
Mediterranean, 79, 83, 109
Megiddo, Conquest of, 103
Mehen, 215, 218
Mehetch, 135, 136
Mehturit, 76
Mekes, 215
Mekher, 133
Melons, 209
Memory, 42
Memphis, 25, 45, 84, 112, 121, 122, 127, 133, 149, 151, 152, 153, 220, 224, 225, 245 ; capture of, 122 ; cakes of, 62
Men, creation of, 74, 217
Menats, 167
Menes, 38
Menkabuta, 185
Menkaurā, 4, 36, 38, 50, 126
Menkheperrā, 144, 145
Menth, 123
Menthu, 104, 161, 164, 165
Mentiu, 141
Menu, 151, 164
Menu-Amen, 215
Menus, 164
Mera, 86
Meremaptu, 207
Merenrā, 9, 130, 131, 132
Mernat, 170
Mer-Tem, 117
Mertet-Ament, 79
Meru, 170, 171, 172, 173, 174, 178, 184
Mesentiu, 13
Meskha, 23 ; instrument, 15
Meskhenet, 33, 34
Mesopotamia, 6, 92, 106, 144
Messiah, 237
Mest, 123
Mestet, 88, 89
Mestetef, 88, 89
Mesu Betshet, 48
Metal workers, 251
Meter, 83, 84 ff.
Methen, 109

Metternich Stele, 88
Mist, 68
Mitani, 109
Monkeys, 212
Monsters, 246
Moon, creation of, 69
Moon-god, 48
Moral character, 231
— rectitude, 246
Morning Boat, 47, 48
— Star, 24
Mother, duty to, 230
Mouth, Opening the, 11, 13, 42
Muhammad Ālī, 88
Muller, 7
Mummification, 247
Mummy, 55 ; chamber, 40, 42
Murder, 52
Mycerinus, 38
Myrrh, 168–211, 218

NAK serpent, 215
Name, a word of power, 69
— of Rā, 75
Napata, 119, 125
Natron, 14, 218 ; incense of, 38
Nāu, 57
Nebertcher, 44, 49, 53, 68, 69, 70, 121, 162, 167
Nebka, 25, 26, 27
Nebkaurā, 173, 184
Nebpehtirā, 140, 144
Nebt Amehet, 164
— Ānkh, 218
— hetepet, 248
Nebun, 88
Necklaces, 147
Nectanebus I, 88, 246
Neferbaiu, 164
Neferefrā, 127
Nefer-hetep, 242
Neferit, 155
Neferkarā, 134
Nefert, 169
Nefert-ari-karā, 127
Neferu Rā, 93–144
Nefrus, 117
Negative Confession, 61
Nehai, 248
Neharina, 143, 144
Nehern, 92, 106
Neith, 124
Neka, 220

Nekau, 156, 222
Nekheb, 127, 131, 140
Nekhebet, 60, 79, 82, 162, 248
Nekhen, 43, 47, 127, 128, 131
Nekhtnebtepnefer, 139
Nemart, 117, 119, 120
Nemes, 215
Nephthys, 33, 34, 69, 85, 90, 91, 109, 149 ; speech of, 63
Neserser, 220
Neshem Boat, 60
Nessubanebtet, 185, 186, 188, 191
Net to snare souls, 43
Netchemtchemānkh, 85
Night, 17 ; left eye of Rā, 220
Nile, 47, 65, 76, 82, 84, 85, 112, 122, 123, 165, 216, 220, 221, 237 ; the celestial, 23 ; floods of, 136, 137 ; god of, 86, 176, 220 ; heights of, 100 ; springs of, 83 ; water of, 5
Nine Bows, 106
— Gods, 111, 214
Nomes, 238 ; the Forty-two, 51
North Island, 129
Nose, 53
Nu, 24, 68, 69, 72, 86, 220
Nubia, 77, 78, 82, 83, 97, 102, 103, 106, 114, 116, 125, 135, 142, 144, 145, 146, 208
Nubians, 119, 155, 214, 215, 218
Nubt, 167
Nubti, 123, 220
Numbers, invention of, 1
Nut, 16, 18, 20, 33, 44, 46, 47, 69, 72, 74, 85, 164 ; as a cow, 73

Oasis of Farāfrah, 169
— of Sīwah, 71
Obedience, 227
Obelisks, 147
Ochre, 6
Offerings, efficacy of, 38, 247 ; to God, 230
Oils, 18
Ombos, 123
On (see Anu), 15, 217
One, 217
Onions, 17
Opening of the Mouth, 152
Opportunity, 228
Orion, 23
Osiris, 14, 15, 21, 22, 24, 33, 39,
40, 41, 42, 43, 45, 46, 50, 54, 55, 56, 57, 59, 60, 61, 62, 64, 67, 69, 85, 111, 151, 153, 163, 171, 244, 246 ; accused by Set, 2 ; death and resurrection of, 12 ; Hymn to, 42, 44, 45, 221 ; Island of, 54 ; Khenti Amenti, 61, 127 ; Litany to, 42 ; murder of, 87 ; mummy of, 91 ; tomb of, 81 ; Un-Nefer, 44
Other World, 10, 11, 16, 17, 42, 45, 216, 219, 244 ; guides to, 224
Oxyrrhynchus, 119

Paints, 6
Palermo Stone, 99
Palestine, 254
Palette, 2, 6
Panopolis, 151
Panther skins, 212
Paper, Egyptian, 4
Papyrus, 4, 191 ; how made into paper, 5 ; swamps, 88
Parchment, 4, 7
Pasherenptah, 152
Pa-Sui, 88
Pāt beings, 206, 218
Patchetku, 140
Pautti, 57, 68, 222, 223
Pectoral amulet, 147
Pellegrini, 100
Pe, 43
Pen, quill, or steel, 7
Pen-Amen, 191, 192
Pepi I, 9, 18, 19, 24, 127
— II, 9, 133
Perfefa, 170
Perfumer, 243
Per-Metchet, 117–19
Pernebtepahet, 117
Per-pek, 119
Per-Rehu, 79
Persea Tree, 54
Per Sekhem Kheper Rā, 117
Perseverance, 230
Pert, 32, 80, 101, 153
Pesh-Kef, 13
Pet, 19
Pe-Tep, 43, 92
Peta-Bast, 152, 153
Petamennebtnesttaui, 124
Peten, 157

Petet, 88, 89
Pharaoh, 93, 127, 189, 202
Pharaohs, 71
Pharmuthi, 253
Philae, 102
Phœnicia, 108
Phœnix, 45
Piānkhi invades Egypt, 116 ff.
Picture writing, 1
Pillow amulet, 43
Planets, 62
Pleasure, 243
Ploughing, 197
Poetical compositions, 241
Polisher, 6
Pomegranate, 241
Pool of the South, 54
Potsherds, 7
Power of Powers, 23
Prayers, 41 ; for the dead, 12
Priests, funerary, 9
Prisse d'Avennes, 92
Prophets, Hebrew, 200
Ptah, 25, 43, 60, 67, 70, 84, 111,
    121, 151, 152, 153, 214, 219, 220,
    248
Ptah-hetep, 225, 228 ; Precepts
    of, 224
Ptah-Seker-Osiris, 40
Ptah-Seker-Tem, 45
Ptah-Shepses, 126
Ptolemaïs, 151
Ptolemy II, 98
    — Philopator, 149
Puarma, 117, 124
Pumpkins, 209
Punt, 113, 134, 135, 147, 164, 211,
    214, 215
Purastau, 112
Pygmy, 133, 134
Pylons of Tuat, 42
Pyramid, the Great, 242
    — Texts, 9, 38
Pyramids, 36, 238 ; futility of, 232

Qaiqashau, 112
Qakabu, 207
Qanefer, 155
Qarabana, 112
Qebti, 136
Qebtit, 113
Qehequ, 112, 114
Qerti, 53, 85

Qetem, 157, 162
Qetma, 164
Qett, 113

Rā, 18, 20, 21, 24, 32, 34, 36, 39,
    43, 47, 48, 54, 55, 58, 60, 61,
    62, 64, 67, 69, 71, 73, 74, 75, 77,
    78, 86, 84, 85, 89, 91, 92, 103,
    111, 115, 116, 123, 146, 149,
    162, 164, 165, 167, 176, 199,
    214, 215, 216, 218, 219, 222,
    234, 236, 253 ; titles of, 75
Rā and Isis, Legend of, 74
    — three sons of, 33–6
    — Will of, 253
Raau, 127
Rā Harmakhis, 77, 199, 200, 201,
    202, 222
Rain clouds, 68
Rā-Khepera, 221
Ram, 91
Ram-god, 152
Rameses II, 92, 96, 99
    — III, 254 ; summary of reign
    of, 110 ff.
    — IV, 115, 116
    — IX, 192
Rāqet, 149, 153
Rāqetit, 149
Rastau, 43, 49, 53, 54, 153
Rāuser, 33, 34, 35
Reant, 140
Re-birth, 14
Receipts, 7
Recensions of Book of the Dead,
    39
Red Country, 138
    — Fiends, 68
    — Mountain, 156
    — Sea, 113, 208
    — water, 51
Reed for writing, 2, 7, 6
Register, 85 ; of heaven, 2
Reincarnation, 70
Rekhit, 216
Rekhti, 137
Rennet, 86
Rensi, 170–84
Respect for elders, 229
Resurrection, 59, 62, 88
Retenu, 108
Rethenu, 143
Rhind Papyrus, 253, 254

Ritual of Divine Cult, 248, 249
— of Embalmment, 247
River and Acacia, 202
Robbery of temples, 51
Romances, 254
Rubric, 56
Rut-tetet, 32–6

Sa, 216
Sacrifices, 247
Saah, 23
Sāara, 112
Sāhal, 83
Sāhu, 14
Sahurā, 126
Saïs, 122, 124, 245
Sakhabu, 32
Sakkārah, 4, 9, 10, 245
Salt Papyrus, 253
Salvation, 59
Sameref, 13
Sanctuary of God, 229
Sandals, town of, 88
Sanehat, travels of, 155 ff.
Sapti, 32
Sarābit al-Khādim, 208
Satet, 141
Satiu, 156, 157
Scarab, the heart, 50
Scents, 11
Sceptre, 14 ; amulet of, 43
School, 231 ; schools, 7
Scorpions, the Seven, 88
Scribe, 2, 230, 257
Scriptures, 7
Seal, clay, 7
Seasons, 1
Sea of Truth, 172
Seba, a devil, 48, 63, 215, 223
Sebek, 164
Sebur, 15
Sehetepabrā, 155, 157
Seker, 43, 44, 46, 49, 221
— Boat, 46
— Osiris, 149
Sekhem, 91, 151
Sekhet Aaru, 41, 45, 74
— Hemat, 169, 170, 184
— Hetep, 41, 74
Sekhmet, 157, 175, 248
Sektet, 123 ; Boat, 218
Sekti, 73
Sem, 13

Seman, 14
Semnah, 101
Semsuu, 164
Semt Ament, 44
Semti, 38
Seneferu, 27, 28, 29, 100, 156
Senmut, 208
Senut, 151
Sep, 13
Sept, 57, 85
Septet, 20
Seqenenrā, 140, 254
Serapis, 149
Serpent 30 cubits long, 209
Serpents, spells against, 43
Serqet, 57, 91, 220
Set, 13, 15, 18, 20, 21, 33, 48, 65,
    68, 69, 79, 80, 81, 87, 88, 90, 92,
    218, 220 ; vilifies Osiris, 2
Setcher, 128
Setem, 63
Seti I, 71, 99, 246, 247, 249
Set-nekht, 111
Setu, 133
Shadow, 192
Shaiqaemanu, 123
Shaiu, 112
Sharhana, 141
Shartanau, 110, 112, 114
Shasu, 112, 144
Sheepskin, 4
Shēkh of caravans, 131
Shemmu, 76, 151, 152
Shemit, 50
Shent, 154
Shepherd of Israel, 240
Shepseskaf, 126
Shert, 129
Shesmu, 22
Ship, 208 ; wreck of, 208
Shipwrecked traveller, story of,
    207 ff.
Shoemaker, 252
Shu, 16, 60, 61, 69, 72, 74, 85, 86,
    220
— Hymn to, 222
Sidon, 189
Silence, 227, 231
Silver-gold, 146
Sinai, 102, 114, 145, 208
Sistra, 33, 167
Sīwah, 71
Six Great Houses, 127

Skin for writing, 4, 7
Sky-goddess, 18, 20, 44, 47, 69
Slaughter, 43
Smait fiends, 81
Smamiu, 65
Smaur, 24
Smen, 21, 248
Smen Heru, 151
Smendes, 185
Smer, 13
Snakes, 43
Soane Museum, 247
Solomon, 224
Somaliland, 93, 215
Song of Solomon, 241
— the Harper, 242
Sothis, 20, 24, 85
Soul, 46 ; of God, 43 ; of Rā, 45 ;
    of Shu, 61 ; rejoining body, 43 ;
    talk with, 231
Souls of Anu, 20, 43 ; of East, 43 ;
    of Khemenu, 43 ; of Nekhen,
    43 ; of Pe, 43 ; of West, 43
Spells, 12, 41, 250 ; against croco-
    diles, 57 ; engraved, 43
Spirit-soul, 18, 44
Spirit-souls, 22 ; the Four, 21
Spirits, evil, 246 ; of heaven, 61
— of offerings, 11
Stanley, Sir H. M., 25
Star-gods, 21, 46
Stars, 62 ; imperishable, 24
Sti, 141
Stinking Face, 53, 80
Stone for writing upon, 4
Stonemason, 251
Stone of Abu, 85 ; of Truth, 60
Stone-splitter, 25
Storm, 208
Storm-god, 189
Stumbling in Tuat, 43
Sūdān, 4, 100, 133, 145, 165, 207,
    215
Sin, 49
Sui, 56
Sun-god, 15, 18, 19, 39, 57, 68, 70,
    199, 200, 245, 250 ; Hymn to,
    42, 220
Sutekh, 189
Suten ta hetep, 149
Swallow, 43
Sycamore, 89, 241
Syene, 165

Symbols, writing, 1
Syria, 102, 108, 114, 125, 129, 143,
    185, 192, 238

TABLE of Offerings, 18
Taboo, 51, 56, 57
Tafnekht, 117, 119, 121, 123, 124
Taha, 88
Taherstanef, 44
Tait, 113
Taiutchait, 117
Tale of Two Brothers, 196 ff.
Talismans, 147
Talk, subjects of, 230
Tamera, 53, 110, 111, 112, 164,
    167
Tambourines, 64 ; women, 152
Tanauna, 112
Tanis, 81, 185
Tashenatit, 59
Taskmasters, 50
Taste, 220
Ta-sti, 77, 106, 109
Ta-tchesert, 47, 48, 64
Ta-tehen, 119
Ta-Tenn, 115
Tatu (Busiris), 44, 45, 46, 61
Tatunen, 47
Tax gatherers, 7
Tchah, 108, 144
Tchakar-Bāl, 186, 193
Tchakaru, 185, 194
Tchal, 81
Tchān, 185
Tchār, 81
Tchatchamānkh, 27, 28, 29, 34, 36
Tchatchau, 50, 164
Tcheser, 242 ; and famine, 183
Tcheserkarā, 142, 144
Tcheser tcheseru, 146
Tcheser-tep, 22
Tefen, 88, 89
Tefnut, 18, 69, 72, 89, 220, 222
Tehnah, 119
Tehuti (god), 1
— autobiography of, 145 ff.
— em heb, 93
— Nekht, 170–4
Tem, Temu, 19, 22, 39, 56, 57, 60,
    67, 76, 77, 91, 111, 116, 121,
    123, 164, 215, 218, 221, 223
Temple of Aged One, 48
— of Millions of Years, 146

Temple of the Soul, 47
Temu-Heru-Khuti, 217
Temu Khepera, 218
Tenen, 154
Tep, 253
Terres, 133
Tet amulet of Isis, 43, 56
— pillar, 43, 151
Teta, 9, 127
— the magician, 29, 30, 31, 32, 33, 36
Tetaān, 142
Tet-Seneferu, 29, 30
Thaiemhetep, 149 ff.
Thakra, 112
Thebans, 67
Thebes, 68, 79, 92, 93, 104, 109, 118, 119, 161, 165, 194, 219, 220, 241, 242, 245, 249
Thehenu, 109, 156; oil of, 18
Thekansh, 117
Themeh, 128, 133, 157
Themehu, 156
Thenn, 165
Thennu, 159, 160, 162
Thent Amen, 185, 188, 191
— Mut, 194
Thenttaāmu, 141
Thes, 138
Thest, 129
Thetet, 88, 89
Thetha, Autobiography of, 137 ff.
Thieves, prosecution of, 254
This, 138
Thoth, 1–4, 13, 29, 30, 32, 37, 43, 45, 47, 48, 50, 55, 56, 60, 61, 67, 78, 82, 84, 87, 88, 91, 92, 120, 151, 176, 207, 218, 220, 222, 248; city of, 39
Thothmes I, 103, 144, 145
— II, 102, 103, 144
— III, 99, 103, 106, 144, 145, 154
Throne, crystal, 24
Thunders, 250
Thunderstorm, 18
Tomb, 42, 242
Tongue, 230
Transformations, 43
Transmutation of offerings, 17, 49
Tree of Life, 220
Triad, 69
Truth, 47, 48, 66, 218, 221, 236, 249

Truth, goddess of, 61
— Hall of, 60
— Lake of, 54
— Stone of, 60
Tuat, 11, 41, 43, 60, 61, 115, 219, 244, 245, 247; chamber, 17, 123, 151; described, 40, 56
Tuataua ships, 100
Tuauf, Precepts of, 250
Tuf, 20
Turin Papyri, 37, 99
Turquoise, 238
Two Brothers, the, 109, 196
— ears of king, 151
— eyes of king, 151
— Lands, 115
— Men, 218
— Sisters, 109
— Treasuries, 148
Tyre, 186

UAHĀNKH, 137, 138, 139
Uarkathar, 189
Uārt, 129
Uartha, 186
Uasheshu, 112
Uatchet, 60, 79, 82, 162
Uatch-merti, 57
Uatchti, 215
Uauat, 128, 131, 208
Uauatet, 77, 82, 84
Ubaaner, 25, 26, 27, 36
Uhat, 133
Un, 119
Una, Autobiography of, 127 ff.
Unas, 9, 18, 20, 21, 22
Understanding, 220
Unguents, the Seven, 13, 243
Un-Nefer, 44, 45, 46, 51, 63, 65, 67
Unti, 40
Unuamen, Travels of, 185 ff.
Upuatu, 21
Ur-kherp-hem, 152, 153
Urmau, 32
Urrit, 164
Urrt Crown, 15, 46, 215, 216
Userhat, 185
Userkaf, 36, 126
Userenrā, 127
Usert, 89
Usertsen I, 135, 155
— III, 99, 101, 152
Uthentiu, 109

VALLEY of Acacia, 200, 201, 203
Vegetation, 70
Venus, 24
Vignettes of Book of the Dead, 39
Vital power, 11
Vulture amulet, 43

WĀDĪ an-Natrūn, 169
Wādī Halfah, 101
— Maghārah, 208
Washerman, 252
Water, boiling, 43 ; celestial, 216 ;
  holy, 60, 66 ; offering, 229 ;
  supply, 43 ; fowl, 19
Wax figures, 68
Weighing of words, 22
West, souls of, 43
Westcar Papyrus, 25
Wheat, 45
Whip, 215

Whirlwind, 250
White Wall, 121, 151, 153
Wife, burning of a, 27 ; duties to,
  227
Wine, 17
Winged Disk, 77
Wisdom, 227
Wolf-god, 57
Woman, the strange, 228
Wood for writing upon, 4
Words, ill-natured, 230 ; of power,
  41, 42, 75, 246
Work, importance of, 227 ; to
  avoid, 42
Worms in tomb, 43
Writing, boards for, 7 ; exercises
  in, 7 ; three kinds of, 1 ff. ;
  sacred, 1 ; materials, 4

ZOAN, 81, 185

A CATALOG OF SELECTED
DOVER BOOKS
IN ALL FIELDS OF INTEREST

A CATALOG OF SELECTED DOVER
BOOKS IN ALL FIELDS OF INTEREST

CONCERNING THE SPIRITUAL IN ART, Wassily Kandinsky. Pioneering work by father of abstract art. Thoughts on color theory, nature of art. Analysis of earlier masters. 12 illustrations. 80pp. of text. 5⅜ × 8½.   23411-8 Pa. $3.95

ANIMALS: 1,419 Copyright-Free Illustrations of Mammals, Birds, Fish, Insects, etc., Jim Harter (ed.). Clear wood engravings present, in extremely lifelike poses, over 1,000 species of animals. One of the most extensive pictorial sourcebooks of its kind. Captions. Index. 284pp. 9 × 12.   23766-4 Pa. $12.95

CELTIC ART: The Methods of Construction, George Bain. Simple geometric techniques for making Celtic interlacements, spirals, Kells-type initials, animals, humans, etc. Over 500 illustrations. 160pp. 9 × 12. (USO)   22923-8 Pa. $9.95

AN ATLAS OF ANATOMY FOR ARTISTS, Fritz Schider. Most thorough reference work on art anatomy in the world. Hundreds of illustrations, including selections from works by Vesalius, Leonardo, Goya, Ingres, Michelangelo, others. 593 illustrations. 192pp. 7⅛ × 10¼.   20241-0 Pa. $9.95

CELTIC HAND STROKE-BY-STROKE (Irish Half-Uncial from "The Book of Kells"): An Arthur Baker Calligraphy Manual, Arthur Baker. Complete guide to creating each letter of the alphabet in distinctive Celtic manner. Covers hand position, strokes, pens, inks, paper, more. Illustrated. 48pp. 8¼ × 11.
24336-2 Pa. $3.95

EASY ORIGAMI, John Montroll. Charming collection of 32 projects (hat, cup, pelican, piano, swan, many more) specially designed for the novice origami hobbyist. Clearly illustrated easy-to-follow instructions insure that even beginning papercrafters will achieve successful results. 48pp. 8¼ × 11.   27298-2 Pa. $2.95

THE COMPLETE BOOK OF BIRDHOUSE CONSTRUCTION FOR WOODWORKERS, Scott D. Campbell. Detailed instructions, illustrations, tables. Also data on bird habitat and instinct patterns. Bibliography. 3 tables. 63 illustrations in 15 figures. 48pp. 5¼ × 8½.   24407-5 Pa. $1.95

BLOOMINGDALE'S ILLUSTRATED 1886 CATALOG: Fashions, Dry Goods and Housewares, Bloomingdale Brothers. Famed merchants' extremely rare catalog depicting about 1,700 products: clothing, housewares, firearms, dry goods, jewelry, more. Invaluable for dating, identifying vintage items. Also, copyright-free graphics for artists, designers. Co-published with Henry Ford Museum & Greenfield Village. 160pp. 8¼ × 11.   25780-0 Pa. $9.95

HISTORIC COSTUME IN PICTURES, Braun & Schneider. Over 1,450 costumed figures in clearly detailed engravings—from dawn of civilization to end of 19th century. Captions. Many folk costumes. 256pp. 8⅜ × 11¾.   23150-X Pa. $11.95

BRASS INSTRUMENTS: Their History and Development, Anthony Baines. Authoritative, updated survey of the evolution of trumpets, trombones, bugles, cornets, French horns, tubas and other brass wind instruments. Over 140 illustrations and 48 music examples. Corrected and updated by author. New preface. Bibliography. 320pp. 5⅜ × 8½. 27574-4 Pa. $9.95

HOLLYWOOD GLAMOR PORTRAITS, John Kobal (ed.). 145 photos from 1926–49. Harlow, Gable, Bogart, Bacall; 94 stars in all. Full background on photographers, technical aspects. 160pp. 8⅜ × 11¼. 23352-9 Pa. $11.95

MAX AND MORITZ, Wilhelm Busch. Great humor classic in both German and English. Also 10 other works: "Cat and Mouse," "Plisch and Plumm," etc. 216pp. 5⅜ × 8½. 20181-3 Pa. $5.95

THE RAVEN AND OTHER FAVORITE POEMS, Edgar Allan Poe. Over 40 of the author's most memorable poems: "The Bells," "Ulalume," "Israfel," "To Helen," "The Conqueror Worm," "Eldorado," "Annabel Lee," many more. Alphabetic lists of titles and first lines. 64pp. 5³⁄₁₆ × 8¼. 26685-0 Pa. $1.00

SEVEN SCIENCE FICTION NOVELS, H. G. Wells. The standard collection of the great novels. Complete, unabridged. First Men in the Moon, Island of Dr. Moreau, War of the Worlds, Food of the Gods, Invisible Man, Time Machine, In the Days of the Comet. Total of 1,015pp. 5⅜ × 8½. (USO) 20264-X Clothbd. $29.95

AMULETS AND SUPERSTITIONS, E. A. Wallis Budge. Comprehensive discourse on origin, powers of amulets in many ancient cultures: Arab, Persian, Babylonian, Assyrian, Egyptian, Gnostic, Hebrew, Phoenician, Syriac, etc. Covers cross, swastika, crucifix, seals, rings, stones, etc. 584pp. 5⅜ × 8½. 23573-4 Pa. $12.95

RUSSIAN STORIES/PYCCKNE PACCKA3bl: A Dual-Language Book, edited by Gleb Struve. Twelve tales by such masters as Chekhov, Tolstoy, Dostoevsky, Pushkin, others. Excellent word-for-word English translations on facing pages, plus teaching and study aids, Russian/English vocabulary, biographical/critical introductions, more. 416pp. 5⅜ × 8½. 26244-8 Pa. $8.95

PHILADELPHIA THEN AND NOW: 60 Sites Photographed in the Past and Present, Kenneth Finkel and Susan Oyama. Rare photographs of City Hall, Logan Square, Independence Hall, Betsy Ross House, other landmarks juxtaposed with contemporary views. Captures changing face of historic city. Introduction. Captions. 128pp. 8¼ × 11. 25790-8 Pa. $9.95

AIA ARCHITECTURAL GUIDE TO NASSAU AND SUFFOLK COUNTIES, LONG ISLAND, The American Institute of Architects, Long Island Chapter, and the Society for the Preservation of Long Island Antiquities. Comprehensive, well-researched and generously illustrated volume brings to life over three centuries of Long Island's great architectural heritage. More than 240 photographs with authoritative, extensively detailed captions. 176pp. 8¼ × 11. 26946-9 Pa. $14.95

NORTH AMERICAN INDIAN LIFE: Customs and Traditions of 23 Tribes, Elsie Clews Parsons (ed.). 27 fictionalized essays by noted anthropologists examine religion, customs, government, additional facets of life among the Winnebago, Crow, Zuni, Eskimo, other tribes. 480pp. 6⅛ × 9¼. 27377-6 Pa. $10.95

ANATOMY: A Complete Guide for Artists, Joseph Sheppard. A master of figure drawing shows artists how to render human anatomy convincingly. Over 460 illustrations. 224pp. 8⅜ × 11¼. 27279-6 Pa. $10.95

MEDIEVAL CALLIGRAPHY: Its History and Technique, Marc Drogin. Spirited history, comprehensive instruction manual covers 13 styles (ca. 4th century thru 15th). Excellent photographs; directions for duplicating medieval techniques with modern tools. 224pp. 8⅜ × 11¼. 26142-5 Pa. $11.95

DRIED FLOWERS: How to Prepare Them, Sarah Whitlock and Martha Rankin. Complete instructions on how to use silica gel, meal and borax, perlite aggregate, sand and borax, glycerine and water to create attractive permanent flower arrangements. 12 illustrations. 32pp. 5⅜ × 8½. 21802-3 Pa. $1.00

EASY-TO-MAKE BIRD FEEDERS FOR WOODWORKERS, Scott D. Campbell. Detailed, simple-to-use guide for designing, constructing, caring for and using feeders. Text, illustrations for 12 classic and contemporary designs. 96pp. 5⅜ × 8½. 25847-5 Pa. $2.95

OLD-TIME CRAFTS AND TRADES, Peter Stockham. An 1807 book created to teach children about crafts and trades open to them as future careers. It describes in detailed, nontechnical terms 24 different occupations, among them coachmaker, gardener, hairdresser, lacemaker, shoemaker, wheelwright, copper-plate printer, milliner, trunkmaker, merchant and brewer. Finely detailed engravings illustrate each occupation. 192pp. 4⅝ × 6. 27398-9 Pa. $4.95

THE HISTORY OF UNDERCLOTHES, C. Willett Cunnington and Phyllis Cunnington. Fascinating, well-documented survey covering six centuries of English undergarments, enhanced with over 100 illustrations: 12th-century laced-up bodice, footed long drawers (1795), 19th-century bustles, 19th-century corsets for men, Victorian "bust improvers," much more. 272pp. 5⅜ × 8¼. 27124-2 Pa. $9.95

ARTS AND CRAFTS FURNITURE: The Complete Brooks Catalog of 1912, Brooks Manufacturing Co. Photos and detailed descriptions of more than 150 now very collectible furniture designs from the Arts and Crafts movement depict davenports, settees, buffets, desks, tables, chairs, bedsteads, dressers and more, all built of solid, quarter-sawed oak. Invaluable for students and enthusiasts of antiques, Americana and the decorative arts. 80pp. 6½ × 9¼. 27471-3 Pa. $7.95

HOW WE INVENTED THE AIRPLANE: An Illustrated History, Orville Wright. Fascinating firsthand account covers early experiments, construction of planes and motors, first flights, much more. Introduction and commentary by Fred C. Kelly. 76 photographs. 96pp. 8¼ × 11. 25662-6 Pa. $8.95

THE ARTS OF THE SAILOR: Knotting, Splicing and Ropework, Hervey Garrett Smith. Indispensable shipboard reference covers tools, basic knots and useful hitches; handsewing and canvas work, more. Over 100 illustrations. Delightful reading for sea lovers. 256pp. 5⅜ × 8½. 26440-8 Pa. $7.95

FRANK LLOYD WRIGHT'S FALLINGWATER: The House and Its History, Second, Revised Edition, Donald Hoffmann. A total revision—both in text and illustrations—of the standard document on Fallingwater, the boldest, most personal architectural statement of Wright's mature years, updated with valuable new material from the recently opened Frank Lloyd Wright Archives. "Fascinating"—*The New York Times*. 116 illustrations. 128pp. 9¼ × 10¾. 27430-6 Pa. $10.95

CATALOG OF DOVER BOOKS

THE INFLUENCE OF SEA POWER UPON HISTORY, 1660-1783, A. T. Mahan. Influential classic of naval history and tactics still used as text in war colleges. First paperback edition. 4 maps. 24 battle plans. 640pp. 5⅜ × 8½.
25509-3 Pa. $12.95

THE STORY OF THE TITANIC AS TOLD BY ITS SURVIVORS, Jack Winocour (ed.). What it was really like. Panic, despair, shocking inefficiency, and a little heroism. More thrilling than any fictional account. 26 illustrations. 320pp. 5⅜ × 8½.
20610-6 Pa. $8.95

FAIRY AND FOLK TALES OF THE IRISH PEASANTRY, William Butler Yeats (ed.). Treasury of 64 tales from the twilight world of Celtic myth and legend: "The Soul Cages," "The Kildare Pooka," "King O'Toole and his Goose," many more. Introduction and Notes by W. B. Yeats. 352pp. 5⅜ × 8½.
26941-8 Pa. $8.95

BUDDHIST MAHAYANA TEXTS, E. B. Cowell and Others (eds.). Superb, accurate translations of basic documents in Mahayana Buddhism, highly important in history of religions. The Buddha-karita of Asvaghosha, Larger Sukhavativyuha, more. 448pp. 5⅜ × 8½. ,
25552-2 Pa. $9.95

ONE TWO THREE . . . INFINITY: Facts and Speculations of Science, George Gamow. Great physicist's fascinating, readable overview of contemporary science: number theory, relativity, fourth dimension, entropy, genes, atomic structure, much more. 128 illustrations. Index. 352pp. 5⅜ × 8½.
25664-2 Pa. $8.95

ENGINEERING IN HISTORY, Richard Shelton Kirby, et al. Broad, nontechnical survey of history's major technological advances: birth of Greek science, industrial revolution, electricity and applied science, 20th-century automation, much more. 181 illustrations. ". . . excellent . . ."—Isis. Bibliography. vii + 530pp. 5⅜ × 8¼.
26412-2 Pa. $14.95